Writing Our Lives

——

D1157938

Writing Our Lives

Rhoda J. Maxwell

University of Wisconsin–Eau Claire

ALLYN AND BACON
Boston   London   Toronto   Sydney   Tokyo   Singapore

Vice President: Eben W. Ludlow
Editorial Assistant: Tania Sanchez
Senior Marketing Manager: Lisa Kimball
Production Administrator: Donna Simons
Editorial-Production Service: Omegatype Typography, Inc.
Composition and Prepress Buyer: Linda Cox
Manufacturing Buyer: Suzanne Lareau
Cover Administrator: Jennifer Hart
Electronic Composition: Omegatype Typography, Inc.

Copyright © 1999 by Allyn & Bacon
A Viacom Company
160 Gould Street
Needham Heights, MA 02494

Internet: www.abacon.com

Library of Congress Cataloging-in-Publication Data

Maxwell, Rhoda J.
    Writing our lives / Rhoda J. Maxwell.
       p.   cm.
    Includes index.
    ISBN 0-205-27380-7
      1. Autobiography—Authorship—Problems, exercises, etc.
    2. English language—Rhetoric—Problems, exercises, etc.
    3. Readers—Autobiography. 4. College readers. I. Title.
PE1479.A88M39   1999
808'.0427—dc21   98-41799
                                      CIP

Permissions acknowledgments appear on pages 303–306, which
constitute an extension to the copyright page.

Printed in the United States of America

10 9 8 7 6 5 4 3 2 1   03 02 01 00 99 98

To my English 110 students,
who with good humor diligently read,
responded, discussed, analyzed, and wrote.
You were my inspiration for this book.

Contents

Part Two. Writing about Ourselves 33

3. Childhood Memories 35

4. Creating Believable Stories 49

Part Three. Friendships 71

5. What Does "Friend" Mean? 73

6. Friends across Generations and Time 94

9.   Relationships with Family Members   **168**

10.   Family Perspectives   **181**

Part Five.   Knowing Oneself   223

14. Writing Research Papers   288

Preface

For several years I searched for a textbook for a first-year college writing course that would meet the needs of my students and the course objectives. I could not find a balance of readings that were of interest to the mix of students in my classes: foreign students, returning students, English as a second language students, students who came from small towns and from metropolitan areas, transfer students who already had one to two years of college. Even within each of these groups, my students demonstrated a wide range of abilities and experiences. I was especially troubled by textbooks that focused on young people leaving home for the first time, when in my classes were mothers in their thirties coming back to work on a degree. I finally chose not to use any textbook but instead compiled readings from a variety of sources.

My own students read, discussed, and critiqued the selections over several semesters. With the help of their comments, I culled from the readings those that generated a high level of discussion and involvement. The result is *Writing Our Lives*, a text and reader that reflects the interests of students of diverse ages, backgrounds, and experiences.

Good writing requires making choices. The assignments in *Writing Our Lives* are designed to help students realize that they have control over their writing and must take responsibility for writing with clarity, meaning, and style. Assignments are constructed so that students must make their meaning clear, to reflect not only on what they have read but also on what new knowledge they have gained.

In many texts on writing, assignments are disjointed, with little continuity from one to another. The sequence of assignments usually begins with descriptive writing and moves through classification, process, definition, cause and effect, comparison and contrast, and argument. Understanding the patterns of writing is important for college writers, but my concern is that when the patterns are taught with little connection to one another, students do not learn how to make choices about when and how to use them. We want to help students develop into independent writers and thinkers. If they write in a particular pattern only because the assignment requires it, they are not understanding the importance of considering audience and purpose. Often a writer needs to employ more than one pattern in a writing task in order to achieve the intended outcome.

In *Writing Our Lives,* after an introduction to the patterns of writing, students select the approach, style, and voice best suited to what they want to accomplish. Doing so helps them develop a stronger sense of ownership in their writing. Their purpose moves from what they think the teacher wants to what they want to achieve in their writing. This independent decision making previews the kind of thinking students will do as they engage in writing in their future careers.

At the same time, even at the college level, students need opportunities to practice and to receive feedback on early drafts. Therefore, exercises that encourage sharing are an integral part of the text. During revising and editing, as throughout the entire writing process, students help each other clarify what approach to use for their topic, what to include, and how to make the paper effective. When students listen and help one another, their own writing abilities improve as they learn about different viewpoints and styles.

To facilitate revision, many writing activities throughout the text showcase drafts that are not intended as final papers. These activities provide a springboard for students to analyze the effectiveness of their own and others' writing. The writing process is integrated throughout all the assignments, encouraging students to recognize revision as an ongoing process rather than as a quick fix just before one turns in an assignment for evaluation.

Writing Our Lives is organized to immerse students in the writing process. The process is explained in stages with examples and activities. Chapter 1 explains the many reasons we write, the variety of purposes writing fulfills, and the choice of forms available to writers. Writing is necessary not only for college classes but also to get the business of the world done, both in our personal lives and at the workplace. Chapter 2 details the processes of close reading through responding, taking notes, summarizing, and paraphrasing.

Chapters 3 through 13 follow a progression from students' pasts to their futures. The advantage of such a sequence is that, regardless of age and experiences, everyone has a knowledge base and a compelling interest in a subject. Beginning with childhood memories gives everyone a common starting point; it has the added benefit of helping students to know each other better, an important prerequisite for a willingness to share in small groups.

These chapters focus on themes that encourage students to examine issues that affect their lives: relationships, gender and sexuality, values, and decision making. The chapters are structured to encourage students to engage in critical thinking about each theme. Questions requiring critical thinking and close examination of the readings help them move beyond simple answers. Readings are integrated into the discussions, promoting a wider view and also serving as models through which students can examine strategies writers use to achieve their purpose. Readings also serve as connections to students' lives and to society as a whole.

Chapter 14 focuses on the research process, explaining how to integrate information from a variety of sources with the writer's own commentary, drawn from experience and critical thinking.

The organization of the book is adaptable for use in both quarter or semester systems. For a one-quarter course, Chapters 1 through 8 are appropriate; for the second quarter, Chapters 9 through 14 can be used. Assignment options and additional reading suggestions in the Instructor's Manual make the book useful for teaching assistants as well as for instructors with many years of teaching experience.

Acknowledgments

The author's appreciation goes to the following reviewers for their comments on the manuscript: Laura Arzola, Houston Community College–Southeast; Kitty Chen Dean, Nassau Community College; Tim Pingelton, Maple Woods Community College; Julia Ruengert, Ozarks Technical Community College; Shirley Sawdon, South Puget Sound Community College; and Chris Saxild, Mount Senario College.

Writing Our Lives

PART

One

━━━

Purposes of Writing

━━━

Understanding the many purposes of writing allows writers to achieve effective, well-written results for a variety of audiences. College writing focuses on writing to explain and inform—on showing your audience, the professors, how much you know and remember. When writing papers for a class, you demonstrate your ability to organize and connect information from a variety of sources. This textbook is designed to improve your skills in these areas.

In addition to meeting class requirements, writing has a multitude of other purposes. We write to remember (lists, study notes), to persuade (letters to family), to entertain (letters to friends from home), to inform (explanations to someone using your car), to create (stories, poems, memoirs). We look at what types of writing best fit the reasons for the writing. How do we persuade someone to help us out, whether we are asking for money, borrowing a car, or seeking a baby-sitter? Examining style and audience helps us achieve the desired results; to put it another way, a writer needs to write with the intended audience and desired outcome firmly in mind.

Part One covers the ways a writing process helps a writer achieve his or her best work. From the beginning of a writing task to the end, opportunities occur to improve the writing. In Part One you will be introduced to the organizational patterns of writing, and throughout the course, as you work on the various writing assignments, you will select the pattern that best fits your intended audience and purpose. Part One sets the stage for involvement in writing effective, interesting papers.

Chapters 1 and 2 cover the fundamentals you need for the assignments in the entire book. Chapter 1 introduces methods that increase your confidence in composing and help you create interesting and cogent papers. Chapter 2 focuses on how to get the most out of reading. When we read with purposeful intent, we not only retain the information longer but have more interest in it. Relating reading to our present and past knowledge and experience increases our ability to understand the material from others' viewpoints and heightens our own wisdom.

Reading and writing with purpose will help you in all your classes as well as in your everyday life. By knowing what you want to achieve in your writing, you can write with authority. By reading with purpose, you can choose a pace for reading that best suits that purpose. Purposes for reading and writing change for every reading and writing you engage in. Part One assists you in knowing the possibilities and in assessing the appropriateness of choices.

1

Writing as a Process

Do you enjoy writing? Many of you may have ambivalent feelings about writing, while others may enjoy personal writing but not required writing. Not uncommonly, people come to dislike writing or feel inadequate to the task; however, young children like to write and often, even before they learn how to form letters, "write" stories. Some of you have probably observed your own children or young relatives writing stories and letters. In early elementary grades, children write with enthusiasm and enjoyment. But through the school years that may gradually change, and writing may become a dreaded task.

A fearful awareness of how others expect you to write or of how they may criticize your word choice, punctuation, and sentence construction can destroy your self-confidence and pleasure in writing. Being afraid of making mistakes interferes with your ability to write well. For those for whom English is a second language, writing creates additional difficulties. In all cases, writers need opportunities to practice writing and should not expect to produce error-free papers without multiple drafts. We all need practice when improving skills in any area. Writing is no exception. Throughout this textbook, there are opportunities for you to practice and to receive help as you compose.

The Writing Process

Looking at writing as a process that includes several steps or stages, rather than only considering a finished product, allows you to improve while actually composing. The result will be a composition that is more developed because you have included examples, details, and description and have refined your sense of purpose.

Writing as a process involves several stages, which are usually defined as the following: discovery, drafting, revising, and editing. Depending on what the writing task is, the stages vary in length and difficulty. For example, if a writer has difficulty narrowing a topic or deciding what to write about, a longer discovery time is helpful. Discovery time provides an opportunity to explore several possibilities about the subject and ways you might approach it. On the other hand, if you have the topic clearly defined, then you could begin with other discovery techniques, such as free writing or outlining. All writing requires several drafts, especially if you are incorporating outside sources into the paper. When you are writing a paper for publication, the revision and editing time is more lengthy than when the purpose of the paper does not require a polished final copy for a wide audience.

Discovery Stage

During the discovery stage, which is the beginning of writing, we discover what we know, what we need to find out, and how to begin to organize the information. There are several ways to accomplish this.

To begin, you need to decide on the subject of your writing. This may sound simplistic; for example, a teacher may suggest you write a description of a favorite place. Knowing that the subject is a favorite place, however, may not furnish much help as you begin to write. You may find several techniques helpful as you attempt to visualize the finished piece: brainstorming, clustering, outlining, and freewriting. The type of discovery technique varies with the subject and with the writer. Some find an outline most beneficial, while others use clustering to generate ideas for writing. A combination of activities is usually the most helpful.

All of the discovery techniques use informal writing as a way to explore the subject, recall details, and begin to organize. These exploratory activities are essential to writing a paper of substance—one that is interesting and thoughtful.

Brainstorming: Creating a list of thoughts or topics that come to mind when one thinks about a subject is brainstorming. The list may contain single words, short phrases, and questions, but not complete sentences. Because the writing is informal, spelling and coherency do not matter. What does matter is the effort to

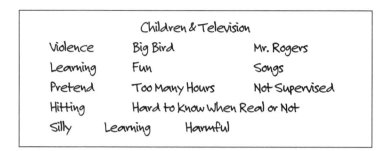

Figure 1.1   Brainstorming

explore the topic. Figure 1.1 is a list Jessica, a student, wrote when beginning a paper on children and television. She knew only the broad topic and did not know how she would narrow it. She wrote the general topic at the top, then wrote the thoughts that came to mind. One idea leads to another when you do this, and it is important not to limit yourself to what you think you should be noting. Brainstorming takes time; you need to think and explore, and it is important not to rush through this process. Time spent on brainstorming results in more interesting in-depth writing.

When you finish brainstorming, read over the brainstorming list. You can now begin to select a direction, narrow the topic, and find a focus for the paper. The topic that emerges from the brainstorming becomes another brainstorming until a clearer idea of what to write about emerges. For instance, Jessica's topic could be the hours children watch TV, or the effect of TV on violent behavior, or the development of children's television shows, or the content of shows whose intended audience is children. It may take several attempts at brainstorming before a well-defined topic emerges.

Clustering: A discovery technique that uses a phrase or word as the starting point is clustering. You write the topic in the middle of an empty sheet of paper, circle it, concentrate on it for a while, then write what comes to mind. Circle each topic and subtopic, and connect the circles by lines. This process helps you to connect one idea with another. You continue until the page is covered. This technique is illustrated in Figure 1.2.

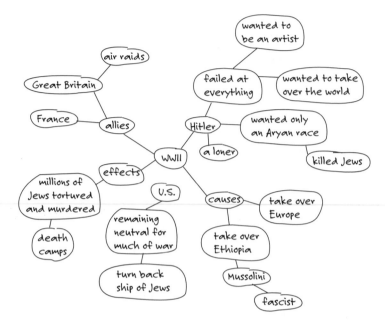

Figure 1.2   Clustering

The difference between brainstorming and clustering is the connections that are made among thoughts. In brainstorming, there may be few or no connections. In clustering, the ideas are more linear—that is, they follow one train of thought.

Outlining: Outlining is a way of organizing thoughts from the brainstorming and clustering activities. One needs to have a wealth of ideas before organizing. Too often, writers try to use outlining as a means of beginning to write, without first exploring the topic. By doing so, they miss the possibilities that add depth and breadth to a topic. As you work on an outline, more ideas will occur to you; this, too, helps you develop the topic.

Many people associate Roman numerals and letters with outlining; however, there are other ways to outline. A working outline consists of major points with topics listed under each. The subtopics are not necessarily in the order in which they will appear in the paper, but listing them serves as a reminder that they need to be covered. The "working" designation reflects the fact that ongoing changes and additions will occur as you write the paper. An outline serves as a flexible guide. An example of a working outline based on the clustering in Figure 1.2 follows:

Hitler

> his life his youth
>> often failed at things
>> abused by father
>> his family background
>> an artist
>> personality
> how he acquired political power
>> built confidence—in himself & the German people
>> set up a national program
>> methods of persuasion
> war
>> feared naval attacks
>> attempt to wipe out those he feared
>> sense of grandeur
> his failure

Freewriting: Writing everything one can think of in connection with a given topic is termed freewriting. You can use this method at any time during the writing process to generate ideas. For instance, if an assignment is to write about Stonewall Jackson, you would write the topic at the top of a page and begin to write what you know about him. Freewriting differs from brainstorming in that the subject is already chosen and the writing focuses on that topic. The writing is "free" in the sense that it is free from all restraints normally associated with writing: spelling, complete sentences, sequence of ideas, punctuation, complete thoughts, support for statements. The purpose is to write as much as possible. Some ideas are formed as questions that may occur or perhaps as half truths or barely remembered facts. Writing quickly helps keep you focused and helps you generate more thoughts. Internal editing, such as debating whether to include something or trying to organize the material as you write, is detrimental to a useful outcome. Freewriting tends to go off on tangents, and yet these often become the main idea or thesis of the paper.

Writers need to let their mind take over and not worry about how the writing looks or if they are doing it "right."

The Writing Activity here provides an opportunity to practice all four discovery techniques.

Writing Activity: Implementing Discovery Techniques

To practice using discovery techniques, imagine you are assigned a paper to write on your favorite place. What place will you choose? How will you begin?

Begin by brainstorming. Write down every place that comes to mind. It might be somewhere you like to be by yourself; someplace from your past; a country, building, park, or room; a particular place in a building or location. Write as many places as you can—at least five.

Clustering comes next. Take each place you have listed and cluster ideas around it, one place to a sheet of paper. Keep in mind that you are selecting your favorite place, so think of what you like about each one. Now you need to select one of these places.

Freewrite on the selected topic, including everything you associate with this place. You might write about feelings, descriptions, activities, people, events.

When you have written everything you can think of, make an outline of the information—adding or deleting as you develop the organization. At this point you are ready to begin drafting, an activity you will do later.

In the "favorite place" discovery activity, the subject is well known to you, and you do not need to include outside information and resources. Many writing tasks, however, require you to amass additional information by interviewing, reading, viewing films, taking notes, posing questions—all necessary before you can produce a final draft. You will be using discovery techniques throughout the information-gathering process: sorting through notes, examining what questions are unanswered, checking for undeveloped sections.

Drafting Stage

Drafting is the first attempt at putting the information from discovery activities into a coherent form. Expect the first draft to be incomplete and rough. Do not concern yourself with punctuation and spelling at this point; that comes later. Drafts are plural. How many one writes depends on several things: the length of the draft, the difficulty of the task, one's familiarity with the subject, and the available time. First drafts are still part of the planning stage. Often you need to return to discovery techniques to develop sections or discover gaps in information. Outlining a draft, even though you outlined the ideas before you wrote the draft, helps with continuity and development. For example, you may think you have sufficient examples; but when you outline, you may realize that some areas are not yet developed well enough. Outlining at this point works best if you use a numbering system, because numbering makes it easier to see if the points you made are supported.

Revising Stage

Revising is often thought of as the last thing we do before turning a paper in for a grade. But revising should begin right at the outset of a writing assignment, when we discuss our work and share it in revising groups or with a partner. Of course, you can revise at any point without receiving assistance from others, but revising on your own has limitations. We are too close to what we write to have the necessary objective view. Others can provide that needed objectivity.

Revising is much more than putting in commas or choosing a different word. The main purpose of revising is to clarify and explain to your audience. By sharing your work with others while you are in the process of writing, you gain an audience that can tell you if your ideas are clear, if you need more information or details, and if your tone and style fits the subject and purpose. All this is difficult to know on your own.

During the discovery stage, particularly when we are outlining and devising questions, input from others is valuable. Too often, we assume that what we think and write is clear to readers because we know what we mean. The best way to respond well to another's paper—that is, to be the most helpful—is to ask questions. For example, the following questions help the writer to see the writing from an audience viewpoint:

1. What do you mean?
2. How did you feel?
3. Why do you conclude that?
4. Do others agree with you?

The particular questions asked in a revising group will depend on the type of paper. A paper that uses outside resources calls for questions about the validity of the references, the balance of opinions, and the development of ideas. Questions about a paper on one's favorite place will focus on descriptions, details, and a sense of why it is a favorite.

Response guide sheets help direct the readers in a writing group to areas of particular importance to the writing task. For example, the response guide shown in Figure 1.3 was used for descriptive writing. Response guides accompany many of the writing assignments later in this book.

Revising groups are most helpful if response guides are followed. Otherwise it is easy for discussion to veer off the topic, and the result may be that you do not receive or provide adequate help with the writing. To begin, each one of you in turn reads his or her paper out loud to the others. The reason for this is that hearing the paper read aloud helps us concentrate more on what the paper is about and the points the author makes. When we listen to rather than read the paper, we concentrate on meaning and coherence rather than on mechanics.

The goal of the response group is to help one another improve the writing. If each listener responds to the paper, either orally or with written notes, then each author receives several suggestions from people with different viewpoints. Everyone, regardless of writing ability, has something to offer. After the revising session, you decide what suggestions you want to incorporate into your paper. No writer is obligated to make changes suggested by group members; however, it is in your best interest to consider them in a thoughtful way.

Revision is hard work for everyone, both writers and listeners. You need to come to the response group with a complete

---

Response Group's Guiding Questions

1. What is your overall impression of the paper?
2. Share with the author what you understand is the purpose of the paper.
3. In what ways is the paper interesting? What details could be added to strengthen the images?
4. What words and phrases are especially effective?
5. Where is the paper vague? Or confusing?
6. Authors want their paper to come alive in the mind of the reader (or listener). How could the author make this paper come alive more vividly?
7. Where should the author more fully develop the writing?
8. What do you like best about the paper?

Figure 1.3   Sample Response Guide

draft—one you have read aloud to yourself before coming to the group so that you have already caught redundancies, careless mistakes, and unnecessary words. You also need to have an open mind, to be ready to consider what others have to say about your writing.

Listeners need to give thoughtful responses and questions, helping writers consider how to improve the paper and yet offering praise to encourage them. Each person is at one time a writer and the rest of the time a listener in every group meeting.

Editing Stage

Editing occurs when you have a finished draft—one you consider ready to turn in. You have revised your paper based on the group's comments and on your own ideas from reading the paper with careful attention. You return to the response group you have been working with and again read your paper to the others in the group. After you read your paper, discussion follows, in which you review what changes you made and group members give you further recommendations that could improve your paper.

When everyone has had an opportunity to read, the members pair off to exchange papers and proofread them. Full attention is now on spelling, punctuation, word usage, paragraphing, and format. If there is any doubt or question, a style handbook is used as a reference. You may want to ask your partner for verification and suggestions as you are editing. Often the easiest way around awkward punctuation is to rewrite the sentence; consequently, there is a great deal of discussion between writing partners.

An editing guide can be useful as a reminder of what to look for. Figure 1.4 is one example. You will find editing guides with many of the writing assignments in later chapters.

Editing Guide

Word usage

Where do redundancies occur?

Where are words too general?

Look specifically for subject–verb agreement.

Suggest alternatives for clichés.

Punctuation

Ask the writer what in particular you should check.

Check for run-on sentences.

Where might semicolons be appropriate?

If the paper includes references, use a style guide to ensure correct punctuation.

Spelling

Read slowly to catch errors. If there is any doubt, check it out.

Transitions

Where might additional transitions help create a smoother and more cohesive paper?

Figure 1.4   Sample Editing Guide

In the writing process, the purpose of leaving editing until the last is to ensure that other steps are not slighted. The result is a more developed, interesting paper—a paper well worth the effort that goes into writing as a process.

Purposes of Writing

Writing assignments cover a variety of audiences and purposes. Not all writing is the same: Because of different purposes, writing varies in form and appearance. What variety of purposes does writing serve? Think of all the writing you have done in the past week; remember, even a note left for a roommate or family member is writing. Make a list of every incident of writing—at home, at work, at a friend's place—regardless of how informal or recreational.

When the list is complete, alongside each item note what your purpose was for writing each piece. No doubt, some were to inform, to help you remember, to explain, to create, or to communicate. Though we may not realize it, writing is an integral part of our lives.

Depending on what happened last week, the list of purposes might include

1. Informing
2. Remembering
3. Persuading
4. Explaining
5. Organizing
6. Communicating
7. Comparing
8. Arguing
9. Creating
10. Understanding
11. Entertaining

Writing for college fulfills many of the same purposes. The most informal college writing is note taking. Generally, the audience for our notes is ourself and we use our own brand of shorthand, which others may have trouble reading. The purpose is to help us remember what we have read or heard. Later, when we read over the notes or rewrite them, the purpose is understanding.

Writing clearly, so that others (and we ourselves) understand the message, is imperative regardless of the purpose. To accomplish clarity, a writer must use details, examples, and specific words. Details help flesh out the thought, concept, or image a writer has in mind and make it accessible to readers. There is a difference between writing, "I've gone to many different schools" and "During my growing-up years, I attended schools of all shapes and sizes: square brick buildings with wide hallways that housed grades 1 through 12 in large rooms with high ceilings; large spread-out newer buildings easy to get lost in; and some schools that had no windows, but where the walls could be moved around to change the size and shape of rooms."

Examples help, too, in creating pictures and understanding in readers' minds. If one is explaining that schools are a microcosm of the local society, examples provide a reality that readers understand and find interesting. How do students act in one setting versus another? How do school rules and regulations reflect the local culture? The more specific you are, the more easily a reader can relate to your ideas.

The same is true at the word level. Inexperienced or careless writers rely on vague words whose meaning is imprecise. The following sentences contain underlined words that convey little meaning because they are not specific enough:

> There is <u>very</u> little to do here.
> It is <u>much too</u> warm.
> I was <u>so</u> mad at the clerk.
> I had a <u>good</u> time last night.

Including detail allows readers to understand better what you had in mind. We cannot assume readers know what we mean. We must provide words that clarify our meaning.

Writing Activity: Using Specific Words in Descriptions

Rewrite each of the sentences above, changing each one to a specific description that gives readers a real sense of how you feel. For example, you should not only change the word "good" but elaborate on what a good time might be.

Using vague, general words interferes with meaning and leaves readers with little understanding of what you were thinking. As you write you have an image or picture in your mind, regardless of what the topic is. Your purpose is to transfer that image from mind to paper so that readers have similar images in their minds. Is there a piece of writing you've read that you have remembered long afterwards? Whether fiction or nonfiction, such as a report, the piece probably employed vivid images that you could picture clearly. That's a mark of a successful writer.

Writing Activity: Using Detail

To practice writing with clarity, write a paragraph describing an animal without naming the particular kind it is. First picture the animal in your mind, noting specific details. Then transfer that image to words. When your description is completed, exchange papers with a partner and each draw what is described. How close did you come? What additional information would have helped? Concrete drawings are fairly easy; but how would you describe an emotion, such as fear, or a general noun such as trust?

When reading your partners' papers throughout the course, check for detailed descriptive language that provides readers with necessary information. This kind of specificity is important in test answers, essays, reports, autobiographical writing—in all writing intended for other readers as well as oneself.

Patterns of Writing

Writers use various patterns of development to organize their writing to achieve the results they want. A pattern is a framework for presenting thoughts and information. For example, if you use a cause-and-effect pattern, you organize your material in a way that establishes causal links between ideas; a reader easily understands the points you are making. A different pattern of development would present the material in another way to emphasize other points. You need to choose the pattern that highlights your thesis and purpose in the strongest way. The following list briefly introduces the patterns. Chapters 3 through 10 explain each pattern of development in depth and provide you with opportunities to use it in writing activities. After you have been able to practice using various patterns, you will choose which pattern best fits your style as well as the purpose and audience for a given piece of writing. The writing you will do in your future career requires that you understand the patterns well enough to choose the most effective one for making your ideas clear to readers. Often, too, you will wish to combine patterns to strengthen the effect.

Description: Learning how to write good description is imperative to all types of writing; however, when description is used as a pattern of organization, the description itself provides readers with a keen sense of the writer's purpose. Detailed description can provoke reactions of joy, sadness, guilt—any human emotion.

Narration: Anecdotes are at the heart of narration, which is telling a story and is used in nonfiction as well as in fiction. You can use narration in any type of paper to explain and illustrate; as an organizer, narration follows the pattern of storytelling, using conflict and resolution.

Classification: A pattern of classification is used frequently in problem solving, because classifying—sorting things into categories—forces us to examine evidence and make decisions. Describing each class requires details and examples.

Comparison–contrast: The comparison–contrast pattern distinguishes important features to help identify what is alike and what is different between people, countries, or any other subject matter. It is an important pattern for bringing to light points that could go unnoticed or unexamined.

Definition: In the definition pattern the writer explains what he or she knows about a subject in such a way as to enlarge and enhance readers' understandings. Definition includes interpretation and clarification. This pattern of development can be very important in business and government settings, in scientific writing, and even in personal relationships.

Process analysis: A process analysis pattern is a sequential explanation of how to do something. This is a useful pattern for getting something done; usually it involves explanation by an expert to a novice. Computer manuals, recipes, instructions for putting furniture together, and guidelines for operating new equipment are all examples of process analysis writing.

Argumentation–Persuasion: We attempt to persuade every time we write for an audience other than ourselves. Argumentation and persuasion are both designed to convince; these strategies appeal to readers' emotions and concerns. We could use the argumentation–persuasion pattern in letters to the editor or to family members, any time we wish to convince a reader to take a particular action. While persuasion uses emotional language, argumentation assumes there is a controversy and emphasizes logic, adding additional information from knowledgeable sources.

Cause-and-effect: Examination of the consequences of actions is the basis for a cause-and-effect pattern. This pattern of development is frequently used in writing about history and related subjects. To examine the causes of events is difficult and requires serious thinking. Well written cause-and-effect papers are a tremendous help in understanding events.

The above list is only a quick overview; each pattern will be explored later on. Every pattern can be useful in helping you achieve your desired purpose. Learning the different strategies gives you the ability to select how to organize your writing based on the audience.

The following writing assignment is practice for implementing the writing process stages in your own writing.

WRITING ASSIGNMENT: DESCRIPTIVE WRITING

Return to the discovery activities for the "favorite place" topic. Read over the clustering, outlining, and freewriting you did, elaborating on one or all of them. Write a first draft and put it away for a day. Then read it over and make revisions and additions by asking yourself the following questions:

1. What have I left out?

2. Where could I add more details?

3. Where could I be more descriptive and specific?

You may have to work on the draft two or three times until you feel you have your description ready to bring to your response group. Be sure to read the essay aloud to yourself before reading it aloud to the group members. That way you avoid having members discuss errors that you made in haste and could easily correct on your own. Because this activity is a practice for future papers you will write, one reading in a response group is all that is required, and further revisions are not necessary.

2

Reading–Writing Connections

The connections between reading and writing have a significant bearing on our ability to read with understanding and to write with clarity and style. Writing in response to reading helps us gain skill in taking notes, summarizing, recalling, and understanding. In choosing readings for this book, I particularly sought selections that would be interesting to students with varied backgrounds and experiences; that would illustrate different styles and voices; and, finally, that would relate to the themes of the book.

Reading what other writers have created will help you improve your own writing in several ways. The readings serve as models for your writing by illustrating how a writer organizes material and uses examples to support his or her points. Also, you will gain insights on how writers set up persuasion and argumentation. The styles and points of view vary among the readings and provide examples of different ways to present information and interest readers. The readings demonstrate how many ways there are to use forms of writing, varieties of language, style, and voice to create strong work that appeals to different audiences.

Writing Reading Responses

For many readings in this book, you are asked to write responses. Writing about the readings will help you read with more attention and focus—a process sometimes referred to as close reading. The responses are not summaries but reactions to the reading, whether it is an essay, a story, a reminiscence, or a poem. There are three types of responses: (1) personal responses, (2) focus on content, and (3) analysis of the writer's craft. For the readings in this book, you first write a personal response. Second, you focus on the content by answering questions about the reading. These questions are designed to encourage thinking and class discussion. The last type of response, analysis of the writer's craft, draws attention to the reading's effect, vocabulary, sentence structure, examples, purpose, and intended audience.

Personal Responses

The first item, your personal reaction or response, you write while reading the selection or immediately afterward. Keeping paper and pencil handy while reading, even if it is a short piece, helps you to record thoughts while you read. If you wait, many of your initial reactions will fade. Do not ask yourself if your response is "right," because all responses are right as long as they are prompted by the reading. You might think of something seemingly unconnected to what you have just read, but if you can explain how your response relates to the material in the reading, it is acceptable. Avoid general statements, because they do not show depth of thinking. If you write something about liking an idea, continue with the reason why. A helpful technique is to add "because" at the end of each comment and then go on to finish the sentence. For example, "The boy reminded me of my brother *because. . . .*"

Guiding Questions

For those of you who have not had experience with reader response, guiding questions may be a help. The questions are only a guide, and once you become familiar with reader response you probably won't need them. The following questions provide a structure you can use to get started:

1. What ideas or images come to mind as you first begin the reading?
2. What experiences have you had that are similar to those described in the text?
3. What have you read or seen that relates to this reading?
4. What particular phrases do you like or dislike? Certain phrases, for example, may evoke a pleasant or a bad memory.
5. In what ways do you agree or disagree with the author?

6. What would you like to read or view as a follow-up?
7. What are your overall feelings and thoughts about the piece?

Because each of us has had different experiences, individual readers will have somewhat different responses. There are similarities, of course, but our interpretations will vary. An important aspect of reader response is sharing your responses with others in a group. Doing so gives you additional insights and points of view. You do not have to agree or come to a consensus with everyone in the group; however, it is important to listen to one another and respect others' views. Discussion leads to deeper understanding of the piece.

For practice, read the following piece by Teresa Paloma Acosta and write a personal response, keeping in mind the guiding questions listed above. Even though the reading is short, your response does not have to be. Remember to respond to specifics as well as giving an overall view.

My Mother Pieced Quilts

TERESA PALOMA ACOSTA

they were just meant as covers
in winters
as weapons
against pounding january winds

but it was just that every morning I awoke to these   5
october ripened canvases
passed my hand across their cloth faces
and began to wonder how you pieced
all these together
these strips of gentle communion cotton and flannel nightgowns   10
wedding organdies
dime store velvets
how you shaped patterns square and oblong and round
positioned
balanced   15

then cemented them
with your thread
a steel needle
a thimble

20 how the thread darted in and out
galloping along the frayed edges, tucking them in
as you did us at night
oh how you stretched and turned and rearranged
your michigan spring faded curtain pieces
25 my father's santa fe work shirt
the summer denims, the tweeds of fall

Personal Response

When you finish, share your responses in small groups. Do you disagree with some of the responses? If so, in what way? How did you
change your ideas about the poem after listening to others? What can
you add now to your response? Often, listening to others makes you
think of more to write. How did the sharing increase your understanding of the poem?

There are many different ways to respond to a reading. No one way
is more right than another. In the following example, Jessica, a student,
wrote a series of images that flashed into her mind as she read:

Thoughts on Reading "My Mother Pieced Quilts"

Barricades in World War II—weapons and covers
A blanket made from vines covering a person—interspersed with
    bits of flannel and broken pumpkins
A mosaic being made by the gods—cemented and shaped patterns
A rabbit darting in and out
Faded canvas
Dirt under my fingernails—cracked floors
Stacked checker pieces
Scotland Highlands—heather, tartans, gypsies
Swimming lessons—mother plunging me into the water
The dead after a plague—stretched out they lay
Stomach ache

Another student might write a response that followed the poem line
by line, commenting on how the fabric pieces are tied to memory, the
hard work the mother went through to create the quilt, or any of the

many images in the piece. Any way you respond is appropriate, as long as you think about the piece and make a serious effort to connect it to your own impressions.

Content Focus

Responding to content means examining the information the author provides to a reader. Content responses are not recall-type questions, but more general. For example, in "My Mother Pieced Quilts," content questions would focus on ideas like the following:

1. Acosta relates the quilt pieces to her history. What article or belonging in your family tells a story?
2. Quilts are an American art. Why is that? What are the special connections between quilts and the history of America?
3. If your family has handmade quilts, describe their origins and their meaning to you.
4. Describe the history of Acosta's family, using details from the poem.

Writer's Craft

Analysis of the writer's craft is often guided by questions; however, readers may focus on areas not addressed in the questions. For example, if you are especially interested in how tone and style convey meaning, then you may look closely at how the author's tone and style accomplish that. The following are examples of questions designed to help you focus on the writer's craft:

1. Acosta weaves descriptions throughout the poem as she tells about how her mother made the quilts. Find examples where she goes from one description to another.
2. Her descriptions use few adjectives or adverbs. For example, instead of an adverb she uses the phrase "michigan spring"—what does that mean to you? Where else does she convey vivid descriptions with minimal words?
3. As you wrote your personal responses, what phrases elicited your own memories? Describe a place you remember from your youth, using the same type of descriptive imagery Acosta does.

Responding to the readings throughout this text in these three ways—personal response, content focus, and writer's craft—will help you understand and react to each piece and will increase your knowledge of how other writers use words and style for effect.

The following selection is different in style and intent from Acosta's. As you read it, think about your responses to the piece. The essay is written by Andy Rooney, who contributes personal opinions on a wide array of topics for CBC's *60 Minutes.*

Advertising

ANDY ROONEY

1   My grandfather told me when I was a small boy that if a product was any good, they shouldn't have to advertise it.

2   I believed my grandfather at the time, but then years later my mother said that when *she* was a little girl he had told her that they'd never be able to build an automobile that would go up a hill. So I never knew whether to believe my grandfather or not.

3   Like so many things, I've really never made up my mind about advertising. I know all the arguments for it and against it, but the one thing I'm sure of is that there ought to be some sanctuaries, some places we're safe from being advertised at. There ought to be some open space left in the world without any advertising on it, some pieces of paper, some painted surfaces that aren't covered with entreaties for us to buy something.

4   Advertising doesn't belong on license plates, for instance. Of the fifty states, twenty-seven of them have slogans trying to sell themselves to the rest of us. It's offensive and wrong. The license plate has an important function and it's a cheap trick to tack something else on it. Most of the legends the states put on aren't true anyway.

5   Rhode Island, for instance, say it's the "Ocean State." There are fifteen states with more ocean than Rhode Island has. If they want to say something on their plate, why don't they explain why they call Rhode an island when it isn't one?

6   Florida says it's the "Sunshine State." I like Florida, but why don't they also say that Miami has more rain than any city in the whole United States except for Mobile, Alabama?

7   North Carolina says it's "First in Freedom." It doesn't say anywhere on the license plate who they think is *second* in freedom. South Carolina? Michigan?

Connecticut says it's the "Constitution State." I called the li- 8
cense bureau in Connecticut and no one could tell me why they
call it the Constitution State. Connecticut is not the Constitution
state, of course. *Pennsylvania* is the Constitution state. And Pennsylvania calls itself the "Keystone State." Does anyone really care?

Maine says it's "Vacationland." How would you like to drive 9
a garbage truck for eight hours in Augusta with a sign hanging
on the back that says "Vacationland"?

New Hampshire plates carry the pretentious legend "Live 10
Free or Die." Some religious organization that apparently wasn't
willing to die if they couldn't be free objected and taped over
those words on all their license plates. The state said this was il-
legal and the case went to the Supreme Court. The Court ruled
that the religious order did have the right to block out those
words. New Hampshire would have saved us all a lot of time
and money if they'd never put them on in the first place.

New Mexico calls itself "Land of Enchantment." This is not 11
the kind of slogan that gets the work of the world done.

Hawaii says it's the "Aloha State." Hawaii ought to get over 12
its palm-tree mentality and removing "Aloha" from its plates
would be a good start. What sensible state would want to con-
jure up a picture of dancing girls draping flower ropes over the
necks of visitors every time anyone thought about it?

Wisconsin "America's Dairyland"? Never mind that, Wis- 13
consin, if you're dairyland why don't you tell us on your license plates what ever happened to heavy cream? That's the
kind of stuff we'd like to read about when we're driving along
behind a car from your state.

And then Idaho. How would you like to work hard, save 14
your money and decide, when the kids were educated and the
house paid for, to buy yourself a Mercedes-Benz. You plunk
down your $28,000, the dealer screws on the license plate and
there you are with your dream car, you drive away, and affixed
to the bumper is the sign that says "Famous Potatoes."

"If a state is any good," I imagine my grandfather would 15
have said, "it shouldn't have to advertise."

License-plate advertising is a small part of what we're faced 16
with when we're driving. On the highways, trucks are turned
into rolling billboards. The companies that own them look on it
as easy advertising, too cheap to pass up. On major highways

the commercials come along more often than on a late-night television movie.

17   On city streets, the billboards on Coca-Cola and Pepsi trucks are often double-parked while the driver makes deliveries. In most cities now, taxis and buses carry advertising. When you're paying a buck and a half a mile, you shouldn't have to carry a sign pushing cigarettes.

18   In California there's a company called Beetleboards. What Beetleboards will do for you is paint your Volkswagen, apply a commercial motif from a sponsor who is paying them and pay you twenty dollars a month to drive around in it.

19   And if you can understand business advertising their products on our roads, how do you account for the private citizens who use the back end of their cars to tell us about themselves or about some private campaign of theirs? A typical car or van in a parking lot outside a tourist attraction in Washington, D.C., will announce, through the decals attached to it somewhere, that the owner is insured by Allstate, boosts the Northern Virginia Ramparts—a team of some sort, I guess—is against forest fires because he has a little Smokey the Bear stuck to his car, gives to the International Convention of Police Chiefs and believes in God because his bumper sticker tells us so.

20   If someone has to take pride in having people know what insurance company gets his money, he's in trouble for things to be proud of.

21   A third of the cars on the road have reading matter stuck to them somewhere trying to sell the rest of us a place, an opinion or a way of life. Sometimes it looks as though half the cars in the United States have been to a roadside stand in South Carolina called South of the Border, and for some reason the entrepreneurs who have made tourist attractions out of caves love to slap "Visit Secret Caverns" on visitors' bumpers.

22   One of the most incredible commercial coups of the century has been pulled off by the designers who have conned women into thinking it's chic to wear a piece of apparel on which the maker's name is imprinted as part of the design.

23   The French luggage maker Louis Vuitton may have started the trend when he made the brown LV the only design on his product, but the women's fashion designers have taken it over. Bill Blass makes towels with his name all over them. Why would anyone want to take a shower and buff themselves dry on a

piece of cloth bearing Bill Blass's name? Why would a woman go around with the name "Bloomies" on the seat of her underpants? Is there something I don't understand here?

Why would I or anyone else want to lay me down to sleep   24
with my head on a pillowcase embossed with the signature of Yves Saint Laurent?

The first time I remember seeing a designer's name on some-   25
thing, the name was Pucci. It seemed amusing enough but now they're all doing it. Halston, Calvin Klein and Diane Von Furstenberg must all be wonderfully famous and talented, but if I buy anything of theirs I'd prefer to have it anonymous. If I got a scarf with Diane Von Furstenberg's name on it, which is unlikely, my first inclination would be to send it out to the cleaners to have them try to get it out.

The advertisers are coming at us from all directions all the   26
time. If we were deer, a closed season would be declared on us to protect an endangered species. It just seems wrong to me that we're spending more time and money trying to sell some things than we are making them in the first place. I'm an all-American consumer but there are just certain times and places I don't want to be sold anything.

Personal Response

You may want to use the response questions given on pages 20–21. In any case, respond to the essay with detail. Do not give a summary or a statement about whether you cared for the piece or not.

After writing your responses, share them in a group. Then write a paragraph summarizing the group's responses to the essay.

Content Focus

1. What is Rooney objecting to? Be specific.
2. How might you generalize his comments?
3. He mentions only a few types of advertising. Using the same approach he does, what other types of ads can you describe?
4. Do you think he is being fair to the advertising industry? Or is his viewpoint too biased? Explain your answer.

Writer's Craft

1. What is Rooney's thesis? How does he convey it to the reader?
2. He uses humor to catch reader interest and explain his views. In what ways is the humor effective?

3. His first sentence catches a reader's interest and sets the tone for the essay. How does his writing style create a consistent voice?
4. How serious do you think Rooney is? How can you tell?

Writing Portfolios

Keep your responses from all of the readings in a portfolio or folder. A writing portfolio is indispensable in any writing class or for any writing project, because you can return to previous work for use in future assignments. Keeping a folder for all of your writing is especially important in this course, because all of the readings and writing activities may be used in future assignments. In addition to class work, you may want to add newspaper or magazine articles that you find interesting—not necessarily entire articles, but notes you have written based on your reading. Actually, notes are more helpful than pages of information. You can recall the content at a glance and decide quickly if it is what you need for a particular writing task. You save time by not having to reread or skim the entire article.

Taking Notes, Summarizing, and Paraphrasing

In addition to writing responses, the abilities to take notes, write summaries, and paraphrase are vital for connecting what you read to what you write. Note taking, summarizing, and paraphrasing are all useful when you read articles or books. You take notes for the sections when you need to remember details; summarize sections when you need to know the main ideas; and paraphrase when you are including a section in a piece of writing. Learning these skills will help you remember what you read, use ideas from other authors' works in your own writing, and organize your writing effectively.

Taking Notes

As a college student, you probably consider note taking as second nature; you take notes constantly during lectures and when gathering information for reports. However, you may not have thought about *why* taking notes is so helpful.

The reason is that as a memory aid, the act of writing is at the top of the list. Also, when you write notes, several activities are involved: reading; writing; rereading; and, if you want to memorize specific information like dates and names, reading the notes aloud so that hearing is involved as well. The more senses used, the more we remember and the longer we remember it. Highlighting does not serve the same purpose as note taking. You may highlight as you read to focus your attention on the text, or as a preliminary step in remembering what you read, but you remember far longer if writing is used. Highlighting requires little selection or decision making on the part of the reader; and if you tend to highlight long passages, it likely is no help at all. Writing notes, in contrast, requires that you read carefully, decide what you want to remember, and be selective in what you choose to write. No one is willing to copy long passages that are not necessary to remember.

Summarizing

An important skill for writing is the ability to summarize. When we are writing reports, research papers, or any paper in which we want to use outside sources, good summaries are indispensable. Summaries are brief, much shorter than the original piece. "To make a long story short" is good advice to heed.

To summarize a piece of writing, begin with its title, author, and publication data. Then write the main points, omitting the supporting evidence. Write what you need to know from the article, depending on what your purpose is. You may not have to summarize the whole piece. Always write summaries in your own words, taking care not to misrepresent the author's viewpoint. Be selective, but don't distort the original meaning.

If you have difficulty in putting the summary in your own words, follow this procedure: Read a paragraph, cover it with your hand (or turn away from the computer screen or darken it), then summarize the passage without looking at the text again. Do this repeatedly until you are in the habit of not using the author's words. If you are actually looking at the work while summarizing, you may be tempted to use the same words as the author. For practice, summarize Andy Rooney's "Advertising" essay and share your summary with other group members, discussing how and why you wrote what you did.

Paraphrasing

Paraphrasing is different from summarizing in that you do not condense the piece. The two are similar, however, in that we put the author's thoughts in our own words. A major problem some beginning writers have with paraphrasing is a tendency to change only a few words of the original text. The material must be completely rephrased, meaning that the entire selection is in your own words—different words. Obviously, there will be key terms that you will have to include in the paraphrasing; but outside of these you need to rephrase. As with summaries, it is easier to paraphrase correctly if you do not continue to look at the author's words. What points is the author making? What examples does the author use?

Using summarizing and paraphrasing correctly will eliminate any risk of plagiarizing—that is, of claiming others' words as your own. Most people plagiarize unintentionally because they do not know how to put material in their own words. Plagiarizing is a serious offense and can result in unpleasant consequences, so it is important to practice summarizing and paraphrasing until they are second nature to you. Chapter 7 will explain the skill of documenting (recording the sources of) the summaries and paraphrases that you include in your papers.

To practice summarizing and paraphrasing, read the following piece, "The Gettysburg Address" by Abraham Lincoln. President Lincoln gave the Gettysburg address during the Civil War, at the site of the Battle of Gettysburg in Pennsylvania, on November 19, 1863. The occasion was the dedication of a part of the battlefield as a cemetery for the men who died there. The speech is remembered both for its stirring message and for its lyrical quality, notably its use of parallelism and contrasts. Lincoln wrote five versions of the speech.

The Gettysburg Address

ABRAHAM LINCOLN

1   Four score and seven years ago our fathers brought forth on this continent, a new nation, conceived in Liberty, and dedicated to the proposition that all men are created equal.

2   Now we are engaged in a great civil war, testing whether that nation, or any nation so conceived and so dedicated, can

long endure. We are met on a great battlefield of that war. We have come to dedicate a portion of that field, as a final resting place for those who here gave their lives that that nation might live. It is altogether fitting and proper that we should do this.

But, in a larger sense, we can not dedicate—we can not 3 consecrate—we can not hallow—this ground. The brave men, living and dead, who struggled here, have consecrated it, far above our poor power to add or detract. The world will little note, nor long remember what we say here, but it can never forget what they did here. It is for us the living, rather, to be dedicated here to the unfinished work which they who fought here have thus far so nobly advanced. It is rather for us to be here dedicated to the great task remaining before us—that from these honored dead we take increased devotion to that cause for which they gave the last full measure of devotion—that we here highly resolve that these dead shall not have died in vain—that this nation, under God, shall have a new birth of freedom—and that government of the people, by the people, for the people, shall not perish from the earth.

WRITING ASSIGNMENT: PARAPHRASING AND SUMMARIZING

First, paraphrase the speech. As an example, approximately the first ten lines are paraphrased below. Continue with the entire piece.

> The founders of the United States created a union based on liberty and the belief that all people are equal. Now a civil war is testing the idea that a nation based on that premise can last. We are meeting on a battlefield of this civil war to dedicate an area for the men who died so that the ideals may live on. It is right that we do this; however, it isn't we but the men who gave their lives who have made this land holy.

This paraphrasing is only an example; you may want to write your own before going on to paraphrase the rest of the speech.

Next, summarize the speech. You could begin with some background material: Abraham Lincoln gave the Gettysburg address at the site of a battle, dedicating the land to the memory of the men who died there. Continue summarizing the speech.

Compare and discuss in groups both your paraphrasing and your summaries. Although individuals will have some differences, you may want to change, delete from, or add to your own summary or paraphrase. The purpose of this activity is not to come up with identical paragraphs but to consider what effective paraphrases and summaries are. Both paraphrasing and summarizing are essential writing skills, especially when you are using outside sources in your papers. These and the other essential skills and practices covered in the last two chapters will assist you in the reading and writing assignments in this book and also in your writing for other college courses.

PART
Two

Writing about Ourselves

We all have interesting and important stories to tell based on our experiences. When people share their stories, we learn about courage, pain, humor—in short, we learn about human history.

We have all heard older men and women talking about what their lives were like when they were growing up. Remember the times you listened with close attention to stories your parents, grandparents, aunts and uncles told? These stories help us to understand others' situations, others' experiences, and other people themselves. For example, when we read about World War II, the facts about battles, politics, and great suffering are important but may not seem real to us. The insight we gain from personal accounts is tremendous. What was wartime food rationing like in the United States? What did the "war effort" mean to people not in the service? What was it like to take part in antiwar demonstrations during the Vietnam War? What prejudices shaped American thought in regard to that conflict? When events of historic significance are told through personal experiences, they become more realistic and memorable. An example is the discovery and subsequent publishing of journals written by pioneer women. These journals offer us insight into what life was like for families during those early years in the American West. The same is true whenever people talk about themselves, the things that have affected them, and their impressions of everyday life—whatever the time period. Listening to people's stories helps us enter into their experiences, and understand the times in which they lived.

Similarly, our own experiences add to others' understandings of how people view the world. It is important to collect our own stories in writing so that they are not lost. Our experiences, if we save them by writing, are a legacy we can hand down to the next generation. What stories do you want to pass along to others? What is important for them to know? You could write about the historic significance of your time, your point of view, your beliefs. Memories are a rich source for ourselves, for our family, and—if we are willing to share beyond this familiar circle—for readers everywhere.

In Part Two we search back for early memories from our childhoods, writing short pieces to practice writing descriptions and using details and examples. Then we move to memories from adolescence and write a final-draft narrative of an experience. The readings in these next two chapters provide you with a view of other writers' memories. Through writing on topics you know well, you will sharpen the skills you need for creating meaning for readers—skills important in all types of writing.

3

Childhood Memories

An interesting way to begin thinking about our stories is to go back to our earliest memories. How far back can you remember? Sometimes it is difficult to know if we actually remember or if we are recalling stories others have told about us. Our own memories tend to be internal, not so much our fitting others' expectations as reflecting our own view of our world.

Early Memories

To illustrate, the following is an early memory of my own:

> Grandma called to me, "Grandpa's coming!" My Grandpa worked on the Great Northern Railroad and was often gone overnight, so his homecoming was an event. I started to run up the hallway to the front door, then decided what fun it would be to hide from him. I ducked behind the drapes that separated the living room from the dining room. I was quivering with excitement and finally couldn't stand the anticipation any more. I ran from behind the drapes just as he was opening the front door. He dropped his leather bag and swooped me up in his arms. He smelled of cigars, and his scratchy beard rubbed against my cheek. I put my arms around his neck and hugged him as hard as I could.

I know that's my own memory—who else would know about how I felt or what I did, or even care? I was only two or three years old; my grandfather died when I was three. Why do I remember that moment? I have no idea, but there is no question about its importance in my life. You have memories like that, too. Such moments make up the fabric of our early life.

When we search for early memories, it can be difficult to distinguish between what we really remember and what family members have told us. One thing that sometimes separates the two is that a genuine early memory is so simple—like my example. Recalling these early incidents can bring back a flood of memories long forgotten—snippets from our past.

Writing Activity: An Early Memory

Write about your earliest memory. Thinking of your earliest memory often takes a while, because you have to dig deeply into memories you haven't explored lately. This will not be a polished piece of writing, but it is designed to give you an opportunity to experience memory writing. (The writing assignment in the next chapter will take you through the entire writing process, including final polishing.)

To begin, imagine yourself as a small child and think of where you are and who the people are in your life. Most people recall an experience from when they were five to six years old. Using freewriting, describe what you remember. Now think back to when you were even younger—perhaps three or four. Take your time. Some people find it helpful to close their eyes as they picture themselves as a young child. Freewrite again with this earlier memory. Like my example, your memory may be more a snippet than a story. Read over what you have written; then concentrate on remembered smells and sounds, adding these sensory details to your piece. You may wish to share your memory pieces in your group, each person reading his or her piece aloud in turn.

Richard Brautigan, a well-known poet and prose author from the 1970s, wrote the following lines about his early memories:

Lint

RICHARD BRAUTIGAN

1   I'm haunted a little this evening by feelings that have no vocabulary and events that should be explained in dimensions of

lint rather than words. I've been examining half-scraps of my childhood. They are pieces of distant life that have no form or meaning. They are things that just happened, like lint.

Personal Response

Write your response to Brautigan's words, writing as quickly as possible to capture your feelings and reactions. Compare his thoughts with how you view your own early memories.

Remember, people's responses vary considerably. The following responses illustrate how two students reacted to "Lint." They are included here to show you how responses can differ. The writing is informal, as responses should be, and the pieces are printed here just as the students wrote them—complete with organizational problems and repeated words. Yet both are considered thoughtful responses. Your responses should be as individual as these two are.

This seems to me to be about the memories that a person remembers because the memories mean nothing, yet for some unexplainable reason stay in the mind. These memories are nothing like the events that make one a memorable person in the minds of others, instead like lint the memories are pieces of some larger part that for some reason are left over after many years have gone by. Like the author says these memories are things that "just happened" in one's life and although you understand what happened there is no good way to describe these happenings to someone else. These are things one must simply think about and feel. (Stephen Arnold)

When Richard Brautigan wrote "Lint" he did an excellent job of linking childhood memories and lint. Lint isn't just lint. It was once part of a sweater, shorts or even a pair of sox. Childhood memories are more important than lint because they aren't just memories. Together they are both a small part of something very important. Your clothes keep you warm and protect you while your memories make you the person you are. Richard says that he is haunted by feelings that have no vocabulary. In my mind this means that his feelings about his memories can't be described with words alone. Bad feelings. Another powerful line is "They are pieces of distant life that have no form or meaning." Richard recalls the scraps of his childhood in a sad way. He means that childhood memories are like the remains of the child that he used to be. In the last line he sums it all up by saying, "They are things that just happened like lint." Just as the lint in your pocket was an important part of your clothes, his memories are an important part of his childhood. (Jared Savage)

Content Focus

1. Brautigan compares memories to lint. What is lint? What use does it have? Think of as many ways as possible to describe lint. To expand the image of lint in your mind, share your list with others.
2. What are the connections between lint and memory?
3. What do you think Brautigan means when he writes that the memories have no form or meaning? Meaning for whom? In what ways are the memories important to him?
4. What does the author mean by "half-scraps of childhood"?
5. What images, besides lint, does this piece evoke?

Writer's Craft

Memories and lint seem an unlikely comparison, yet the very oddity strikes a chord, especially when we think of early memories that are but "half-scraps." Comparisons such as this create a lasting impression in readers' minds. For practice, compare one of your memories with something it reminds you of. The comparison should help a reader understand how you feel about the memory. Perhaps it is a light, vague feeling of happiness; what can you compare that to? Or a painful memory? Try to write several ideas for the comparison, then choose the one that best describes the memory.

Point of View

Most of us have heard stories of what we said or did when we were youngsters. Usually they relate humorous or embarrassing incidents, not ones that we actually remember ourselves. The stories are not from our viewpoint—not really our stories. But when you write your own story it is your vision, your truth. Viewpoint dramatically shapes a story. A child's view of the world is often at odds with adults' views. For example, you might remember feeling bad because your actions were misunderstood when you were trying to be helpful. Someone else might see the same situation as one where you were deliberately being destructive or bad. A former student, Mark Meisner, now an English teacher, wrote the following story relating such an experience.

I Didn't Mean to Be Bad

MARK MEISNER

I was in first grade at Holy Innocents Catholic Grade School. 1
Sister Kay was my teacher. She was unlike anyone I had ever
met. She did not just walk; she danced. She did not just talk; she
sang. She did not merely teach; she created. I adored Sister Kay,
and I wanted her to notice me.

Each week, Sister Kay chose students to be responsible for 2
various classroom tasks like washing chalkboards, clapping
erasers, sweeping the floor, emptying the trash, and watering
the plants. I yearned to be chosen. Everyone wanted to be chosen, of course, and I too desperately wanted an opportunity to
impress Sister Kay. After weeks of waiting, fingers crossed
under my desk, the day came. Although I did not get the cov-
eted eraser-clapping position, Sister Kay did ask me to water
the plants. Here was my chance.

The plants were to be watered after school on Friday, and 3
I waited all week. As it turned out, Sister Kay left early that
day—disappointing until I realized that she trusted me—me,
alone in the classroom. As I rifled through the supply closet in
search of the watering can, my gaze fell upon a can of shellac
left over from an art project we had done earlier in the week. I
remembered how the shellac made the wooden plaques gleam.
After dutifully watering the plants, I shook the can as vigor-
ously as my first-grade body could manage. It took two fingers
to hold down the spray nozzle. The mist fell on the leaves, creating rainbows in the afternoon sun. I stepped back to admire
my work.

On Monday, I waited for Sister Kay to notice my master- 4
piece. She said nothing. Each day I admired the rigid stems
and glistening leaves. As the days passed, the stiff leaves
gradually lost their bright green hue until they were the color
of mud. Shiny mud. I sensed that something was terribly
wrong. That's when Sister Kay approached me. I didn't mean
to be bad.

Writing Activity: Point of View

If Mark's teacher had written this story, it would have had a different viewpoint. Write a paragraph about some incident in your own life, one that happened recently or a while ago. First write it from your viewpoint, then rewrite it from another's viewpoint. Share your paragraphs in a writers' group and help one another adhere first to one point of view and then to the other. How does the vocabulary change? The details and descriptions?

Using Senses to Recall Details

When you are writing about experiences, focusing on each sense individually will help you recall details. Concentrating on one sense at a time can evoke a wealth of images.

❑ What do you see? What colors are there? What about the size and shape of things? Are other people around?
❑ What do you hear? People talking? Noises from cars or machinery? Birds, wind, water?
❑ Describe the senses of touch: smooth, cold, bumpy, sharp, rough?
❑ What about the senses of smell and taste? Depending on your memory, some senses are more helpful than others; work at recalling as many details as possible.

We rely on sight the most when recalling an incident, but smell is more closely connected with memory. That's why even a small whiff of an odor can bring back strong memories. I love the smell of cigars because I associate it with my grandfather. Are there certain fragrances that remind you of someone? People's houses have their own individual smells; your memory of the smell of a house may seem pleasant or not, depending on what you thought of the people who lived there.

To help strengthen the connections between smells and memories, try the following activity.

Writing Activity: Using the Sense of Smell

Find many different things to smell. For example, try spices, smelling each one and writing down what each reminds you of.

Take your time, giving each fragrance a chance to awaken your memories. Find other sources: pine needles, candies, soaps, cedar chips, foods, rivers, pools. The idea is to consciously locate smells that are associated with your background. The connections may surprise you. But memory doesn't stop there. As soon as you think of a place, you may remember what happened there, how you felt, the people who lived there—memories that might have stayed buried without the trigger of a smell. Additional aids to recalling memories come from thinking about holidays and other events that are often connected to smells.

The following piece, "Freedom to Breathe," is written by Aleksandr Solzhenitsyn, a Russian who was imprisoned in his homeland shortly after World War II for speaking out against Josef Stalin. Solzhenitsyn is well known for many works, including *One Day in the Life of Ivan Denisovich* and *The Gulag Archipelago*. For his writings against the Soviet government, he was charged with treason and exiled from Russia. After Mikhail Gorbachev became premier, Solzhenitsyn's citizenship was restored. This selection is an excellent example of how a writer can create strong visual images in a reader's mind by using sensory details.

Freedom to Breathe

ALEKSANDR SOLZHENITSYN

Translated by Michael Glenny

A shower fell in the night and now dark clouds drift across 1
the sky, occasionally sprinkling a fine film of rain.

I stand under an apple tree in blossom and I breathe. Not only 2
the apple tree but the grass round it glistens with moisture; words cannot describe the sweet fragrance that pervades the air. I inhale as deeply as I can, and the aroma invades my whole being; I breathe with my eyes open. I breathe with my eyes closed—I cannot say which gives me the greater pleasure.

This, I believe, is the single most precious freedom that prison 3
takes away from us: the freedom to breathe freely, as I now can.

No food on earth, no wine, not even a woman's kiss is sweeter to me than this air steeped in the fragrance of flowers, of moisture and freshness.

4   No matter that this is only a tiny garden, hemmed in by five-story houses like cages in a zoo. I cease to hear the motorcycles backfiring, radios whining, the burble of loudspeakers. As long as there is fresh air to breathe under an apple tree after a shower, we may survive a little longer.

Personal Response

Read the entire piece before responding so as to capture the mood.

1. What feelings do you have?
2. What are your first impressions?
3. Now read the selection again, more slowly, responding to phrases and images.

Content Focus

Solzhenitsyn uses the senses to create descriptions. The descriptions evoke a strong emotional response.

1. In what way do the descriptions evoke feeling in the reader?
2. What words in particular transform "freedom" from an abstract concept into a powerful reality?

Writer's Craft

Instead of writing "I love the freedom I now have," Solzhenitsyn makes us feel his freedom, smell it, experience it as we never could without this vivid description. Choose an abstract word such as *love, happiness, honor,* or *peace,* or some similar term, and describe it through a series of images. You may write these in list form. Share the images you create with your writing group, reading the list but not telling the group members what word you are describing. Through discussion, revise your list to make stronger images.

Writing Activity: Refining Descriptive Writing

Look at the "favorite place" piece you wrote in Chapter 1. With Solzhenitsyn's writing in mind, revise your piece again. Where can you use comparisons to strengthen the descriptions? Elaborate the piece by explaining why and how the place is a favorite. You need to persuade the reader that you have strong reasons for feeling the way you do.

Description Pattern of Development

In descriptive passages writers try to take the images and ideas they have in their minds and create similar impressions in the minds of readers. Description is important in all types of writing, whether you are writing a portrait of a favorite place, a recollection of an early memory, an essay on *Hamlet*, an explanation of macroeconomics, or an analysis of disagreements over the Common Market. Even when writing argumentative papers, you want the audience to see and understand the issue as you do—not an easy task unless you learn to use details, examples, and descriptions.

Tone and style in descriptive writing are created by the examples and the language an author chooses. The following reading by Bailey White describes an event in the life of a six-year-old girl. Bailey White is a regular commentator on *All Things Considered*, a National Public Radio program.

Turkeys

BAILEY WHITE

Something about my mother attracts ornithologists. It all 1
started years ago when a couple of them discovered she had a rare species of woodpecker coming to her bird feeder. They came in the house and sat around the window, exclaiming and taking pictures with big fancy cameras. But long after the red cockaded woodpeckers had gone to roost in their sticky little holes in the red hearts of our big old pine trees, and the chuck-will's-widows had started to sing their night chorus, the ornithologists were still there. There always seemed to be three or four of them wandering around our place, discussing the body fat of hummingbirds, telling cruel jokes about people who couldn't tell a pileated woodpecker from an ivory bill, and staying for supper.

2   In those days, during the 1950s, the big concern of ornithologists in our area was the wild turkey. They were rare, and the pure-strain wild turkeys had begun to interbreed with farmers' domestic stock. The species was being degraded. It was extinction by dilution, and to the ornithologists it was just as tragic as the more dramatic demise of the passenger pigeon or the Carolina parakeet.

3   One ornithologist had devised a formula to compute the ratio of domestic to pure-strain wild turkey in an individual bird by comparing the angle of flight at takeoff and the rate of acceleration. And in those sad days, the turkeys were flying low and slow.

4   It was during that time, the spring when I was six years old, that I caught the measles. I had a high fever, and my mother was worried about me. She kept the house quiet and dark and crept around silently, trying different methods of cooling me down.

5   Even the ornithologists stayed away—but not out of fear of the measles or respect for a household with sickness. The fact was, they had discovered a wild turkey nest. According to the formula, the hen was pure-strain wild—not a taint of the sluggish domestic bird in her blood—and the ornithologists were camping in the woods, protecting her nest from predators and taking pictures.

6   One night our phone rang. It was one of the ornithologists. "Does your little girl still have measles?" he asked.

7   "Yes," said my mother. "She's very sick. Her temperature is 102."

8   "I'll be right over," said the ornithologist.

9   In five minutes a whole carload of them arrived. They marched solemnly into the house, carrying a cardboard box. "A hundred two, did you say? Where is she?" they asked my mother.

10   They crept into my room and set the box down on the bed. I was barely conscious, and when I opened my eyes, their worried faces hovering over me seemed to float out of the darkness like giant, glowing eggs. They snatched the covers off me and felt me all over. They consulted in whispers.

11   "Feels just right, I'd say."

12   "A hundred two—can't miss if we tuck them up close and she lies still."

I closed my eyes then, and after a while the ornithologists 13
drifted away, their pale faces bobbing up and down on the black
wave of fever.

The next morning I was better. For the first time in days I 14
could think. The memory of the ornithologists with their whispered voices and their bony, cool hands was like a dream from
another life. But when I pulled down the covers, there staring
up at me with googly eyes and wide mouths, were sixteen fuzzy
baby turkeys and the cracked chips and caps of sixteen brown
speckled eggs.

I was a sensible child. I gently stretched myself out. The 15
eggshells crackled, and the turkey babies fluttered and cheeped
and snuggled against me. I laid my aching head back on the pillow and closed my eyes. "The ornithologists," I whispered.
"The ornithologists have been here."

It seems the turkey hen had been so disturbed by the elabo- 16
rate protective measures that had been undertaken in her behalf that she had abandoned her nest on the night the eggs were
due to hatch. It was a cold night. The ornithologists, not having
an incubator to hand, used their heads and came up with the
next best thing.

The baby turkeys and I gained our strength together. When I 17
was finally able to get out of bed and feebly creep around the
house, the turkeys peeped and cheeped around my ankles,
scrambling to keep up with me and tripping over their own big
spraddle-toed feet. When I went outside for the first time, the
turkeys tumbled after me down the steps and scratched around
in the yard while I sat in the sun.

Finally, in late summer, the day came when they were ready to 18
fly for the first time as adult birds. The ornithologists gathered. I
ran down the hill, and the turkeys ran too. Then, one by one, they
took off. They flew high and fast. The ornithologists made V's
with their thumbs and forefingers, measuring angles. They consulted their stopwatches and paced off distances. They scribbled
in their tiny notebooks. Finally they looked at each other. They
sighed. They smiled. They jumped up and down and hugged
each other. "One hundred percent pure wild turkey!" they said.

Nearly forty years have passed since then. In many ways the 19
world is a worse place now. But there's a vaccine for measles.
And the woods where I live are full of pure wild turkeys. I like

to think they are all descendants of those sixteen birds I saved from the vigilance of the ornithologists.

Personal Response

1. In the first paragraph, White sets the tone for the rest of the essay. How does she accomplish this?
2. Obviously, the style is humorous, but what does she do to achieve that mood?
3. How would you describe the ornithologists on the basis of the first paragraph alone?
4. What events in your own life does this essay bring to mind?

Content Focus

1. What does "I was a sensible child" convey about the girl's personality?
2. Why was it necessary to move the turkey eggs into the house?
3. Could this stratagem really work?

Writer's Craft

White uses humor to describe an entertaining event from her childhood. Do you think the anecdote is true? White exaggerates in an effective manner to bring humor to the telling, yet the story triggers memories for a reader.

Writing about an event in a humorous manner without overdoing it is not easy, but this kind of gentle humor is a worthwhile ability to develop if you enjoyed White's story.

WRITING ASSIGNMENT: A CHILDHOOD MEMORY

Write about a memory from your childhood. You may wish to use one of the very early memories you worked on previously; a memory of your later childhood might be easier to develop, however. Think of an episode that is important to you, for whatever reason. It might involve a person who meant a lot to you, or an experience that upset or pleased you, or a historic event. The only criterion is that it is important to you that you describe the memory.

Begin with a discovery activity: Jot down ideas. Keep thinking back—what do you see in your mind's eye? Recall colors, movement, sounds. Try to think of yourself in the time frame, not as an adult looking back but as a child experiencing where you are, what you see, what you are doing. If the first memory you choose does not seem clear, go on to another. You are really searching around in your mind for those "half-scraps," and several may come to mind before you choose one to write about. Try the discovery ideas from Chapter 1: brainstorming, clustering, freewriting—use as many as necessary to acquire the details that flesh out your story.

When you have enough substance from one particular memory to write about the experience, write a first draft. Concentrate on sensory details. Also—although this may seem like an odd bit of advice—do not attempt to start from the beginning. First of all, beginnings are difficult to write. The first line should encourage others to read the whole story, but when you are struggling to find just the right words, it is difficult to start at all. Always begin with the part you know best and feel the most strongly about. You do not have to explain the background situation—perhaps not at all, but certainly not when you begin to write. You can fill it in later. Trying to begin with what you expect to be the first line makes starting difficult and often inhibits writers to the point that they can't get going.

Remember to compose quickly when writing a first draft. Then read over what you wrote, adding more details. Now take one sense at a time—sight, smell, sound, touch, taste—and concentrate on just that one, adding details as you remember them. Make sure you create images in readers' minds—images that are sharp and understandable. For instance, if you are writing about a fish you caught, what did it look like? Just stating its length does not create a clear picture for a reader. Picture the fish in your mind's eye and describe it as if you were a camera.

You are writing a memory piece, not a narrative paper. (You will do that in the next chapter.) This piece does not need a strong beginning or ending; it must, however, make the memory come alive in the mind of the reader. Readers should understand not only what you experienced but what your emotions were.

Descriptive writing helps you to write effective papers of many types: classification, persuasion, comparison, cause and effect, and argumentation—all forms of writing you will use in college and in your future jobs. What you have learned from this chapter about selecting details to create moods, using sensory images, and making interesting comparisons will be the foundation for the narrative writings you will do in the next chapter.

4

Creating Believable Stories

Stories drawn from childhood memories take many forms. You might connect a string of memories or events together, relate a family story you heard as a child, describe cultural traditions, or choose one memory to develop fully. The phrase *telling a story* does not necessarily mean "writing fiction"; rather, it designates a narrative form. In the readings throughout this chapter, authors use various styles and patterns to share their stories based on memories. The culminating writing assignment in this chapter is your own story based on memories.

Writing Narratives

Narration is telling stories, and we use the narrative form for many purposes. For instance, telling a story to support a point is the most effective way to persuade an audience. We are more likely to respond to a news broadcast calling for help for flood victims if we hear the story of one particular person or family, rather than learning only general information about the crisis. We respond on a personal level because through a story we understand the necessity to ease pain and suffering better than when we hear only facts and statistics. Effective narration helps us write convincing descriptions, definitions, arguments—any type of writing, except strictly technical material.

When you write a story based on your life and experiences, even if the story is not directly about you, the point of view is yours. Because you are writing about real events, another person may say, "That's not how it happened." Pay no attention— because no two people see or remember an incident in exactly the same way. For example, when two people see a movie, they may differ not only as to what they thought about it but as to what actually happened: the characters' motives, personalities, and actions. Even an immediate happening can be seen in more ways than one. A car drives by; one person notices the make and condition of the car, another person notices the people in the car, and perhaps a third notices only which way the car turned after driving on. In writing, your job is to take readers by the hand and show them your vision of life.

Include examples in your story. Henry James said that an ounce of examples is worth a ton of generalities. Rather than write that a person was always angry, give examples of the anger. Describe how you knew the person was angry. You've probably heard the admonishment to show, not tell. In other words, rather than making a statement, allow readers to come to their own conclusions from the concrete evidence you provide. For example, don't write that you were happy or sad, or that a newly acquired belonging was special; explain the how and why in detail, and let readers come to share your emotion themselves.

Creating Settings

Settings help readers place themselves right alongside of you. They let readers see, smell, touch, and hear what you do. Because we as writers see settings clearly in our own minds, we sometimes forget to explain to readers. If someone told you she spent summers in North Dakota when she was a child, you would know the setting was that state. What you would not know would be the golden fields of ripe wheat, the blue flowers of flax waving like a sea, the hot sun, the constant dry wind.

Settings are made up of the following details:

❑ *Locations:* A country, a town, a building, a particular room, outdoors, a specific place outside such as a tree house.
❑ *Time:* Could be evening or daytime, or a specific hour or even minute; year and/or month; or a time of year such as a season.
❑ *Environment:* A season, such as winter or fall; weather conditions, such as rain, clouds, storms, ice, sunshine, wind. These details are important for the action or mood.

Settings are created by details of color, temperature, sound, shadows, and smells. A setting may be crucial to a story, as in "The Portrait" by Thomás Rivera; or the story may not depend on any particular place, as in Garrison Keillor's "Who Do You Think

You Are?" (Both these stories appear below.) However, some mention of where and when the story takes place helps readers to share your experience.

Writing Practice: Detailed Settings

Using one of your childhood memories from Chapter 3, write a few paragraphs adding details of the setting. Then rewrite the same piece without any setting. Compare the two versions to see where and when the details enhance the story.

Writing Dialogue

We want written dialogue to sound "real"; but if we were to write what people actually say, it would seem disjointed and repetitive. In actual conversation we talk with our hands, facial expressions, and body language as much as with words. As an exercise, write down what people say, capturing the words verbatim as much as possible. You will discover that real-life conversation is informal, especially among friends and family, and does not translate well to the printed word.

Dialogue is important, however. It helps make characters, real or imagined, come alive for readers. The words people speak, and when and how they say them, tell a lot about their character: how they interact with others, what they are thinking, and why they behave in the way they do. We can tell a lot about people just by listening to what they say in given situations.

In general, do not attempt to write dialect—written representations of people's accents. There may be times when dialect is appropriate to your story, but only if it is your own; don't try to imitate others' speech. Dialogue should, however, be appropriate for the social position and age of the person. In word choice, hesitations, and sentence length, you can create feelings, style, and mood.

Using dialogue helps to carry the story line along; a reader finds out what will happen from the words characters say, rather than from a statement inserted into the story. For example, if a character is anxious to get started, you might have him say, "Hey, let's get going," rather than writing, "He was anxious to be on his way." Action conveyed through dialogue is more immediate and vivid.

Also, dialogue helps readers know the characters in a personal way. Dialogue comes from the character, not from someone else telling the reader about that person, and thus gives the character vitality. We like to speak for ourselves, and we should give the people in our stories a chance to do that, too.

In the narrative "The Portrait," Tomás Rivera uses dialogue to tell a story—not a story about himself, but one he remembers from his childhood. Tomás Rivera grew up in Texas and as a boy had to alternate his schooling with working as a migrant laborer. Eventually he became the chancellor of the University of California–Riverside. He wrote poetry and fiction; his best-known novel is *And the Earth Did Not Devour Him (Y no se lo tragó la tierra)*.

The Portrait

TOMÁS RIVERA

1   As soon as the people returned from up north the portrait salesmen began arriving from San Antonio. They would come to rake in. They knew that the workers had money and that was why, as Dad used to say, they would flock in. They carried suitcases packed with samples and always wore white shirts and ties; that way they looked more important and the people believed everything they would tell them and invite them into their homes without giving it much thought. I think that down deep they even longed for their children to one day be like them. In any event, they would arrive and make their way down the dusty streets, going house to house carrying suitcases full of samples.

2   I remember once I was at the house of one of my father's friends when one of these salesmen arrived. I also remember that that particular one seemed a little frightened and timid. Don Mateo asked him to come in because he wanted to do business.

3   "Good afternoon, traveler. I would like to tell you about something new that we're offering this year."

4   "Well, let's see, let's see . . ."

"Well, sir, see, you give us a picture, any picture you may 5
have, and we will not only enlarge it for you but we'll also set it
in a wooden frame like this one and we'll shape the image a little, like this—three dimensional, as they say."

"And what for?" 6

"So that it will look real. That way . . . look, let me show 7
you . . . see? Doesn't he look real, like he's alive?"

"Man, he sure does. Look, vieja. This looks great. Well, you 8
know, we wanted to send some pictures to be enlarged . . . but
now, this must cost a lot, right?"

"No, I'll tell you, it costs about the same. Of course, it takes 9
more time."

"Well, tell me, how much?" 10

"For as little as thirty dollars we'll deliver it to you done with 11
inlays just like this, one this size."

"Boy, that's expensive! Didn't you say it didn't cost a lot 12
more? Do you take installments?"

"Well, I'll tell you, we have a new manager and he wants 13
everything in cash. It's very fine work. We'll make it look like
real. Shaped like that, with inlays . . . take a look. What do you
think? Some fine work, wouldn't you say? We can have it all
finished for you in a month. You just tell us what color you
want the clothes to be and we'll come by with it all finished one
day when you least expect, framed and all. Yes, sir, a month at
the longest. But like I say, this man, who's the new manager,
he wants the full payment in cash. He's very demanding, even
with us."

"Yes, but it's much too expensive." 14

"Well, yes. But the thing is, this is very fine work. You can't 15
say you've ever seen portraits done like this, with wood inlays."

"No, well, that's true. What do you think, vieja?" 16

"Well, I like it a lot. Why don't we order one? And if it turns 17
out good . . . my Chuy . . . may he rest in peace. It's the only picture we have of him. We took it right before he left for Korea.
Poor m'ijo, we never saw him again. See . . . this is his picture. Do
you think you can make it like that, make it look like he's alive?"

"Sure, we can. You know, we've done a lot of them in soldier's 18
uniforms and shaped it, like you see in this sample, with inlays.
Why, it's more than just a portrait. Sure. You just tell me what
size you want and whether you want a round or square frame.
What do you say? How should I write it down?"

19   "What do you say, vieja, should we have it done like this one?"

20   "Well, I've already told you what I think. I would like to have m'ijo's picture fixed up like that and in color."

21   "All right, go ahead and write it down. But you take good care of that picture for us because it's the only one we have of our son grown up. He was going to send us one all dressed up in uniform with the American and Mexican flags crossed over his head, but he no sooner got there when a letter arrived telling us that he was lost in action. So you take good care of it."

22   "Don't you worry. We're responsible people. And we understand the sacrifices that you people make. Don't worry. And you just wait and see, when we bring it, you'll see how pretty it's gonna look. What do you say, should we make the uniform navy blue?"

23   "But he's not wearing a uniform in that picture."

24   "No, but that's just a matter of fixing it up with some wood fiber overlays. Look at these. This one, he didn't have a uniform on but we put one on him. So what do you say? Should we make it navy blue?"

25   "All right."

26   "Don't you worry about the picture."

27   And that was how they spent the entire day, going house to house, street by street, their suitcases stuffed with pictures. As it turned out, a whole lot of people had ordered enlargements of that kind.

28   "They should be delivering those portraits soon, don't you think?"

29   "I think so, it's delicate work and takes more time. That's some fine work those people do. Did you see how real those pictures looked?"

30   "Yeah, sure. They do some fine work. You can't deny that. But it's already been over a month since they passed by here."

31   "Yes, but from here they went on through all the towns picking up pictures . . . all the way to San Antonio for sure. So it'll probably take a little longer."

32   "That's true, that's true."

33   And two more weeks had passed by the time they made the discovery. Some very heavy rains had come and some children,

who were playing in one of the tunnels leading to the dump, found a sack full of pictures, all worm-eaten and soaking wet. The only reason that they could tell that these were pictures was because there were a lot of them and most of them the same size and with faces that could just barely be made out. Everybody caught on right away. Don Mateo was so angry that he took off to San Antonio to find the so and so who had swindled them.

"Well, you know, I stayed in Esteban's house. And every day 34 I went with him to the market to sell produce. I helped him with everything. I had faith that I would run into that son of a gun some day soon. Then, after I'd been there for a few days, I started going out to the different barrios and I found out a lot that way. It wasn't so much the money that upset me. It was my poor vieja, crying and all because we'd lost the only picture we had of Chuy. We found it in the sack with all the other pictures but it was already ruined, you know."

"I see, but tell me, how did you find him?" 35

"Well, you see, to make a long story short, he came by the 36 stand at the market one day. He stood right in front of us and bought some vegetables. It was like he was trying to remember who I was. Of course, I recognized him right off. Because when you're angry enough, you don't forget a face. I just grabbed him right then and there. Poor guy couldn't even talk. He was all scared. And I told him that I wanted that portrait of my son and that I wanted it three dimensional and that he'd best get it for me or I'd let him have it. And I went with him to where he lived. And I put him to work right then and there. The poor guy didn't know where to begin. He had to do it all from memory."

"And how did he do it?" 37

"I don't know. I suppose if you're scared enough, you're ca- 38 pable of doing anything. Three days later he brought me the portrait all finished, just like you see it there on that table by the Virgin. Now tell me, how do you like the way my boy looks?"

"Well, to be honest, I don't remember too well how Chuy 39 looked. But he was beginning to look more and more like you, isn't that so?"

"Yes, I would say so. That's what everybody tells me now. That 40 Chuy's a chip off the old block and that he was already looking like me. There's the portrait. Like they say, one and the same."

Personal Response

1. Think about things you have sold or bought. What do you think about the salesman's appeal?
2. Have you had the satisfaction of something working out like it did for Don Mateo? Put yourself in the situation and think how you would react.
3. Why do you think Rivera chose this story to tell?

Content Focus

1. Who is talking to whom in each of the blocks of dialogue?
2. Describe the salesman. What information shaped your opinion?
3. What time and place is the story set in? How do time and place shape the story?
4. In what ways did you find the ending satisfying—or unsatisfying?

Writer's Craft

Through this short story Rivera tells much about the people involved. How does he accomplish this? What makes the people come alive for the reader? Most of the story is told through dialogue. How does this work as a vehicle for the story line?

Writing Activity: Family Stories

In "The Portrait" the author, Tomás Rivera, does not play a major role but retells a story from his childhood. Write a story about your family where you do not play a major part. What liberties does this give you? What restrictions does this create for you?

Write another family story that has been handed down from past generations. The setting will probably be important for the reader's understanding. How does this story influence your family today?

Both of these stories are only first drafts and are not intended to be taken to the final-draft stage. Keep them in your writing folder, however, because at a later time you may want to revise and expand them.

Connecting Incidents to Create a Narrative

"Who Do You Think You Are?" by Garrison Keillor begins differently than any of the other readings. Keillor's style and tone are consistent with those of his monologues on his weekly show on National Public Radio.

Who Do You Think You Are?

GARRISON KEILLOR

It has been a quiet week in Lake Wobegon, my hometown was such 1
a sweet line all those years on the radio, the standard opening of each week's story, a pleasant, modest *useful* sentence, considering how many writers stew over their opening lines (e.g., "Ray opened the refrigerator door and bent down to look for the margarine"), and most stories stop there and wind up in the wastebasket, brilliant stories wasted because the first sentence wasn't as brilliant as what would soon follow, so the writer quit and his masterpiece, his *In Our Time*, his *Great Gatsby*, his *Collected Stories of John Cheever*, never got written because the first sentence opened like a rusty gate, and is it so different for you and me? The marvelous work we could do if only we didn't have to *begin* it but could start in at the middle. The things we could accomplish if only we didn't know what we are doing until later.

It has been a quiet week in Lake Wobegon gets you right in 2
there, into the dim recesses of the Chatterbox Cafe, the air lit up with the smell of hot caramel rolls, where three heavy men in dark-green shirts hunker in the back booth under the Allis Chalmers calendar ("Krebsbach Farm Implement / New & Used Since 1912 / JUniper 5610") and drink black coffee, refilled by Dorothy in her big pink uniform, who doesn't ask if they'd like more (Do bears pee in the woods?), she just pours, as they commiserate on the lousy world situation and console each other with a few beloved old jokes about animals in barrooms. There was this man who trained his dog to go around the corner to Bud's Lounge with a dollar bill under his collar and get a pack of cigarettes and bring them home, until one day

the man only had a five, so he put it under the dog's collar and sent him down, waited an hour, and no dog, so he got mad and went to Bud's and there was the pooch sitting up on a stool drinking a vodka gimlet. He said, "You've never done this before!" The dog looked straight ahead and said, "I never had the money before."

3   One problem with *It has been a quiet week in Lake Wobegon* is that you couldn't go straight from that into talking about dreams of boundless grandeur and the many-rivered generosity of life, but, then, it was that way when I lived there, too. Dreams we did not discuss, they were embarrassing in normal conversation, especially big ones. We sat at supper, Dad at one end, Mother at the other, children in the stanchions along the sides, and talked quietly about the day's events. We might discuss the immediate future such as a history test the day after tomorrow or Bible camp next June, but the distant future, 1964, 1980, was inscrutable, due to the imminence of the Second Coming. And there was to be no grandeur. Once, just to see how it would sound coming out of my mouth, I said I was going to college someday. "College" rhymes with "knowledge." I was ten years old and words were as good as food in my mouth. I chewed my food fast so as to clear the way to be able to say more. "I'm going to go to college," I stated. My sister laughed: Who d'ya think *you* are? She was right, I didn't know.

4   What I didn't dare mention was my other dream of going into the show business, a faint dream because we were Christian people and wouldn't dream of doing immoral things, though I hoped to find a way around this. I mentioned S. B. to Mrs. Hoglund, the piano teacher, and she told me the story of the famous Swenson Sisters, who hailed from nearby Kimball, a girls' quartet who sang at summer resorts including Moonlite Bay and who, one cold winter day in 1954, won the St. Paul Winter Carnival Outdoor Talent Contest, and the next week boarded the morning Zephyr to Chicago and then the Super Chief to Hollywood. They signed a contract with Fairmont Pictures to make a movie called *Minnesota Moon* but then the producer, Leo Lawrence, took a deep drag on his stogie and growled, "Kids, I love this script, it's beautiful, I loved every bit of it except the cows and the lakes and the farmers—we're going to change them to camels and desert oases and thousands of

Bedouins galloping hard over the desolate sands," so the movie became *Moon over Morocco* and the Swenson Sisters became the Casablanca Quartet, dressed in vast black robes, their faces veiled, and their career went down like a concrete block and by 1955 they were back at Gull Lake, singing at Hilmer's Supper Club (Beer & Setups, Fish Fry—All U Can Eat Friday Nites), and their dream was just an old black shell of a burned-down house. What's more, they, who had gone away innocent and filled with shining hope, returned home four hardened women with dark-crimson lipstick who smoked Luckys and drank vodka gimlets and when they laughed, they laughed a deep laugh, like men, laced with pain, and so of course men would have nothing to do with them, and they fell into unnatural forms of love. There ended the story; she would say no more. *They tried to go too far,* and it should be a lesson to the rest of us: not to imagine we *are* somebody but to be content being who we are, Minnesotans.

I'm very proud to be a Minnesotan and have been proud   5
since I was a kid and first traveled to see our beautiful State Capitol building in St. Paul. Our fourth-grade class got up at six o'clock and rode a schoolbus down to meet the governor. We had studied state government for a month, the duties of governor, lieutenant governor, secretary of state, and other state officers, and the legislature and the state commissions and boards, which didn't prepare us for the grandeur and sheer magnificence of the great white temple spread on the crest of a gentle hill, the bank of steps rising to the pillars, the golden horses and golden chariot high above, and the dome, the largest anywhere in the Christian world, so it appeared. We camped in the bus, eating liverwurst sandwiches and drinking green Kool Aid, waiting for our 11:00 A.M. appointment. Mrs. Erickson said that she was trusting us to be on our best behavior indoors, but she didn't have to worry, we were stunned, we shuffled along with the dumb dignity of the barely conscious. Indoors was even more magnificent, such opulence as a child might imagine from fairy tales but never associate with our modest prairie state, long vast echoey marble halls, marble statues, oil paintings, and a room with a gold ceiling and a rug three inches thick, and there was the governor of Minnesota, the leader of our people, physically present in the room with us.

6   We formed a straight line and gravely filed one by one past Mrs. Erickson, who whispered our name to a grim-faced man, who then whispered it to the governor, who shook our hands and said, "Hello, Stanley, it's good to meet you." This was thrilling, until suddenly, when Mrs. Erickson whispered *Shirley,* Shirley clapped her hand over her mouth and rushed away to the toilet, but her name had gone into the pipeline and when the governor shook Billy's hand he said, "Hello, Shirley, it's good to meet you." He smiled the same warm smile and went right on calling all the rest of the class by the wrong name, including Elaine, who was called Robert. I was called John. He was the governor but he wasn't what you'd call bright.

7   It was so amazing how many kids (mostly girls) later defended him, saying he was a busy man, had a lot on his mind, had to run the state, etc. We boys said, No, he's dumb. How can you look at a boy and say, Hello, Shirley. The girls said, How do you know Shirley isn't a boy's name, too? Show us where it says Shirley *can't* be a boy's name. How do *you* know? Who do you think *you* are? You're not so smart.

8   Who do you think you are? You're from Lake Wobegon. You shouldn't think *you're* somebody.

9   You're no better than the rest of us.

10   Some of our teachers, however, such as Miss Heinemann, believed that we were good enough and could be improved with proper instruction, and so she set Shakespeare's sonnets in front of us, *Macbeth,* Wordsworth, Chaucer, and expected us to read them and to discuss what was on the page, and if any of us had been so bold as to aspire to a life in literature, she'd have been pleased as punch. The higher the better.

11   She strolls the aisles between our desks, swishing past in her dull-brown dress, talking about metaphor, the use of language to mean more than what we know it to mean, whereby common things, such as a rose, a birch tree, the dark sky, rain falling, come to mean something else for which there isn't an exact word. She talks about literature as being urgent, impulsively bold, unavoidable, like stopping your car on the highway at night and stepping out and walking alone into dark damp woods because it's unbearable to only know what's in your headlights. Art calls us out of the regulated life into a life that is dangerous, free. I re-

membered that when I was chosen class poet, to participate in the winter homecoming program and, after the procession of Queen Aileen to the throne and the singing of her favorite song, to stand and recite her favorite poem. Her favorite song was "Vaya Con Dios" but she didn't have a favorite poem, she said, so I said, "That's okay, Aileen, I'll choose a real good one for you." I had in mind a few lines from Whitman's "Song of Myself," beginning:

> I tramp a perpetual journey, (come listen all!)
> My signs are a rain-proof coat, good shoes, and a staff cut from
> the woods,
> No friend of mine takes his ease in my chair,
> I have no chair, no church, no philosophy,
> I lead no man to a dinner-table, library, exchange,
> But each man and each woman of you I lead upon a knoll,
> My left hand hooking you round the waist,
> My right hand pointing to landscapes of continents and the
> public road.

> Not I, not any one else can travel that road for you,
> You must travel it for yourself.

But first I had to show it to Miss Heinemann for her approval. 12 She was incredulous. "Aileen *Heidenschink* chose this? This is her favorite poem? Aileen?" No, not exactly, Miss H., it's one that I thought might be one that—

"I think that on Aileen's big day you might come up with 13 something more appropriate than this. Really. *I have no church, no philosophy?* Aileen is Catholic. Her family will be sitting there. Think."

I *was* thinking, that the Queen's Favorite Poem was a rare 14 occasion when Art had a chance to lift its hairy head and call my classmates toward a higher spiritual life, but Miss Heinemann didn't see it that way; she said, "Don't be mean to Aileen. Find something she'll enjoy, like 'Invictus.' Or else don't do it," which disgusted me, idealist that I was, and also was a huge relief, because the thought of reciting Walt Whitman to a gym full of Lake Wobegon made me sick with fear. So I bowed out as Homecoming Poet on the issue of artistic freedom, keeping my principles intact and taking a big load off my mind at the same time.

Personal Response

1. Keillor talks about hometown cafés. What can you remember about similar cafés or stores that were part of your childhood?
2. Reflect on his comment that "words were as good as food in my mouth." What experiences have you had that are comparable to Keillor's in "Who Do You Think You Are?"
3. How do you feel about your hometown and your state?

Content Focus

1. Keillor covers a lot of subjects. How does he connect them together?
2. What makes his account of his experiences realistic?
3. How does the humor carry the story along?
4. What do you think Keillor's choice of the Whitman poem tells you about Keillor as a boy?

Writer's Craft

1. How does Keillor create a consistent tone throughout the piece?
2. Look at the variety of sentences, especially the variation in length. What is the effect of sentence length on the style?
3. Keillor tells several short stories in one narrative, yet they are connected by a theme. How might you use this technique in your own writing?

Writing Activity: Weaving Incidents Together

Using one theme from your childhood memories, connect three or four incidents together in narrative form. Your theme could be learning how to do an activity, such as riding a bicycle, Roller-blading, canoeing, or any activity that required several experiences before you mastered it. Or it could be incidents involving a brother or sister. Whatever you choose, begin the narrative with a general statement about the theme. Then follow with the examples, ending with a statement about the experiences.

Writing Memories as Fiction

Writing memories as fiction has many advantages. Fiction allows you to expand beyond facts, and you may create a story that is closer to the truth than the reality was. That may sound odd; but often we need an illustrative anecdote to show a point, and there isn't one that actually happened. By creating one, you can show how someone felt or reacted. Also, if you write about something that happened a long time ago, you will inevitably have gaps in the story. By making up probable actions and dialogue, you build the story so readers understand the people and the place. Ben Logan, who wrote the novel *The Land Remembers*, describes fictionalized memories as "feeling-level truth." By making up details or an incident, we help readers understand the larger truth about the remembered past.

Fiction also allows us more freedom. You might want to write about something that you know would not be enough for a complete story; or you may want to write about an interesting person but may need to make up events about his or her life. Changing the person's name allows you to do that. Truth and fiction go hand in hand for creating wonderful stories.

Narration Pattern of Development

The final writing assignment for this chapter will be to write a narrative based on your memories. Writing narration is much like telling a story and is used in many types of writing. In persuasive or argumentative writing, examples strengthen the thesis and points of the paper. These examples are stories about people—narrations—that support the argument. We understand and empathize with any thesis better when explanations include personal stories. Whether you are writing an argument about a highway bypass, the effects of the Vietnam War, Napoleon's rise to power, women writers in the eighteenth century, or safety measures in a manufacturing plant, narration will be an essential part. For this reason, learning how to write effective narration helps you both in your work for college classes and for job-related writing.

Narration depends on details. We want readers to recognize the importance of the story; and to do that, they need to see and feel what the person in the story does. Only details accomplish that kind of identification. If you are writing a report on the need for increased safety measures in the workplace, for example, a story of what happened or could happen to an individual, and how that might affect the person's life, can illustrate the proposal you are making.

Chronological order, or a direct sequence of events, is often used in narrations; however, you may use flashback, or explain events in an order that is not sequential, depending on the topic and what you want to achieve. Always be sure to let the reader know what time frame you are using so there is no misunderstanding. Tags at the beginning of sentences help readers follow the sequence: "afterwards," "earlier," "a few years ago," "three weeks later"—whatever fits the situation.

When you relate an incident, as you will do for your next writing assignment, your narration needs to explain what happened, when, and how, and why it is important to you; narration is more than recounting a memory. The next reading, "The Christmas Sled" by William Olien, a college biology instructor, is an example of this type of writing.

The Christmas Sled

WILLIAM C. OLIEN

1   We called it "The Pit" and no urban planner ever designed a place half as enticing for kids to play and explore; the remnant of a dry river bed left long ago when the Red Cedar River decided to change course on its way to meet the Grand River. What was left of the old valley and yet untouched by city development was bounded on the north end and west side by neighborhoods of 1920's to 1950's houses, on the south end by the embankment of busy Kalamazoo Street, and on the east, the far side from our house, by a dark and mysterious woods. Going out by the kitchen back door, I walked along the clotheslines, past the big black oak tree at the end of our yard (which I would climb in summer to watch my mother hanging the laundry) and over the broad, rough field that led to the thin line of trees at the first, higher edge of the valley. The path led to the right and then

sharp to the left as it took me around the trees and down the short incline to a smaller field that bordered the most wonderful spot in a seven-year-old's world, the main valley, The Pit.

There were dozens of paths leading and twisting down the banks of the pit and these made terrific sledding runs in winter, as I soon found out. The far bank of the pit was steeper and brushier than our side and was crowned by the shadowed woods, so no one went sledding from that side. But on our side, there were always kids in bright winter coats, hats, and mittens. A declaration of motion in pure reds, blues, yellows, greens, and whites against the starkness of winter, they lined up to jump on their sleds one after another and slid, racing and swerving, down the long runs to the bottom, slowing in a long glide along the valley floor as far as speed could carry, ending with the final crunch and squeak when sled runners could slide no farther. Gravity bound again, they tromped back up to the top for another run, dragging their wonderful sleds behind them, new from Christmas, with varnished wooden tops and bright red steel runners. We moved into the neighborhood in January and it did not take long for me to be convinced that what I needed most in life was a sled. 2

When I pointed out to my parents that I did not have a sled, as though they may have overlooked this limiting fact, my mother suggested that I try coasting with a cardboard box. I took the box she gave me and tried some trial runs on the "pony" hill that ran from the upper to the lower field above the pit. Being impatient to try sledding in something, I found more truth to her prediction of fun than I had expected. It was not long before the pony hill no longer thrilled, and I was ready to take my box to the big runs, the ones leading all the way down to the bottom of the pit. I made lots of trips down the hill by box that winter. But fun as it was, I admired the kids racing by on their runner sleds while I trudged back uphill after each run. My craving increased to experience the speed and grace of those sleds in their flights for myself. Occasionally, I was lucky enough to borrow a sled for a few runs down the hill. A taste of pure heaven. 3

One day someone brought an aluminum saucer sled to the pit, a kind of sled that I had not seen before. They seemed to be having a great time careening down one of the more open trails. After watching them for awhile, in between coasts in my box, 4

I asked if I could have a turn in their saucer. I was young enough to assume they would of course say yes, and indeed they did. "Sure, have a try," one said. Now I wonder if, besides being generous, they were also open to a little entertainment in seeing how I would do. My turn came and I climbed onto the saucer at the edge of the hill, dug in my heels to steady myself, grabbed the canvas straps at each side firmly, and wondered how in the world you steered this thing. Someone gave me a push and off I went like a streak of uncontrolled lightning. It was great at first since I was facing forward and could see where I was going, but a bump about halfway down sent me spinning. Off I went to the side of the trail. Flying backwards, I crashed into a bush and ended in a heap somewhere in the middle of a mass of long, stiff shoots that bent down into the snow. I was not happy. Shaken, but not hurt, I tromped back up the hill, gave them their sled back, and left with a certainty that saucer sleds out of control on dumb brushy hills were not for me.

5   On a day in late winter I met a new boy at the pit. He was a couple of years older than I and he looked like he knew what he was doing. His sled was long, sleek, and well used, with a wooden top and steel runners built for business. He was looking over the various coasting runs and seemed to be considering which one to try first. When he saw me staring at his sled, he asked me which runs were best. I said I would show him if he gave me a ride. He agreed and we spent the rest of the afternoon going down one run after another, with the intention of trying all of the trails. He would lie flat on the sled and I lay on his back, hanging onto his shoulders. "Ready?" he asked. "Set," I returned, and we tore down the hill like winged fury. It was great fun as we worked our way, trail by trail, down the length of the pit.

6   Finally, we reached the end of the pit and came to a steep trail near the edge of the dark woods; a trail seldom used for sledding. We stood for a minute looking down the tortured path that cut between bumps, bushes, small trees, and who knew what else under the cover of snow. Steep and twisting, the trail taunted us to come, to try it with our long sled and the weight of two boys (one smaller). "Want to try it?" I asked. "Well," he said, "It's kind of rough looking. I dunno, it might be a little too much for you." "It's not too much for me," I said. "It

looks super. Come on, lets try it!" "Okay," he said, "we'll try it.
But don't blame me if you get scared. We'd better start off from
over there." He brought the sled over to the top of the trail and
set it down carefully. Then he slid it back and forth a couple of
times to make a take-off track, leaving the front of the sled jut-
ting out just over the crest of the slope. He climbed on first, then
I climbed on top, as usual. This was going to be great! In a second we would be having the best run of the day! "Ready?" he
asked. "Ready" I said. He reached out and dug his mittened
hands into the snow, first pushing us back a bit, and then snap-
ping us forward, stroking a couple of more times to give us
speed. By the time he grabbed the steering bar, we were nearing
the first curve.

I do not remember a lot about the ride down, except that   7
there were some fast spots, some bumps, some curves, a lot of
wind and snow in the face, and exhilaration in the lungs. I
loved it. Before I knew it, we were gliding along the smooth run
at the bottom. We finally eased to a stop and I jumped off. "That
was great!" I said and gave a whoop. "Yeah," he said, "but that
one even scared me a little!" I was surprised by that, a bigger
kid scared of something that I wasn't. He may have been kid-
ding, or maybe he had just had enough. It had been fun, but I
am sure that I wore that boy out. At any rate, that was our last
run of the day. It was getting late, time to go home for dinner.
We said good-bye. I don't know if he was from out of town and
visiting someone in our neighborhood, or if he lived across
busy Kalamazoo Street and was trying out our pit for a change
of pace from sledding at the golf course over there (more remnant of the old river valley). Whatever the case, I do not remember seeing him again. But that afternoon certainly increased my
desire for a sled of my own.

Winter ended and I had different adventures in our pit with   8
the neighborhood kids. Through the spring, summer, and fall,
we ate cherries from the neighbor's tree and raspberries from
the fence row, played cowboys with cap guns and construction
with trucks and shovels, and discussed various great issues of
the day (great to us anyway). All of that time, though, the idea
of sledding down those paths next winter was not far from my
mind. How great it would be to sled like the boy who had carried me down the hill on his back, away from the dark woods,

around the bushes and bumps, and then to glide over the smooth long run at the bottom of the hill till you came to stop. My greatest wish was that Santa would bring me a sled at Christmas, a sled with bright red steel runners and a varnished wooden top. That was all a long time ago now (ancient times to my kids), but I still have my sled and can't wait to fly on it again one day soon, with kids on my back.

WRITING ASSIGNMENT: TELLING A STORY

Your final assignment for this chapter is to write a narrative based on a real-life experience. You may write your memories in a factual style, as William Olien did in "The Christmas Sled," or fictionalize the memories as Garrison Keillor and Bailey White do.

You may choose from one of the following:

❑ Write a series of events or recollections connected by a common theme;
❑ Elaborate on one of your memories;
❑ As a bystander, write about a family story;
❑ Trace an interest or object throughout your childhood;
❑ Write a piece of family history; or
❑ Choose from additional ideas your instructor may offer.

The paper is to go through the entire writing process; this means you will work with your writing group as you produce drafts, revise, and edit.

To begin, read over all your writing from this and the previous chapter and choose two or three ideas you might want to develop into a longer piece. You may find it useful to discuss possible choices with your writing group. Often, the process of explaining and discussing your writing helps ideas become more focused.

As before, do not attempt to write the beginning of your story at the outset. Instead, start with the part you have strong feelings about or the strongest recollection and develop the narrative from there. Consider various time orders and experiment by using one, perhaps chronological; then add flashbacks. Or begin with the present and switch to previous times. The time order depends on how you want to tell the story.

Write the entire first draft; then add necessary details. Include dialogue, active verbs, and sentence variety. Read the draft aloud, listening for redundancies and attending to word choice and details. Rewrite the draft and share it with your writing group. After reading aloud, each person will be revising based on a response guide filled out by the other members. Reading your paper aloud to the group is essential; do not hand it to the members to read. If the members begin by reading your draft, they will have difficulty focusing on the content and will tend to go directly to editing. The effect will be that you will skip the revision step and cut yourself off from valuable assistance.

If certain parts of your paper were troublesome to you, tell the people in your group in advance. If you don't share writing problems with them, they may not comment on the aspects with which you would most like help. The response guide here will help the writing group members focus on areas that develop strong narratives.

Response Guide for Story

1. What is the overall tone or mood of the story?
2. Where could the writer add more detail to make the experiences more real or vivid to a reader?
3. What words are too general?
4. List all clichés. Help the writer think of another way to express the same idea.
5. How could the writer make the paper more interesting?
6. What needs to be added?
7. What did you like best about the paper?

Writer's name _____

Names of people in response group _____

_____

_____

_____

_____

Revise your story based on the group's suggestions. When you believe you have a final draft, meet with a group or a partner for editing. The editing guide here is provided as a reminder for particular mechanics and grammar. Use your style handbook to look up questions about usage and punctuation.

Editing Guide for Story

1. Circle every vague word. Discuss what words might be substituted.
2. Check paper for sentence variety.
3. Check every semicolon. Make sure semicolons separate complete sentences.
4. Check "and" and "but." Remember they are preceded by a comma only when used between complete sentences.
5. Find "everyone" and similar words. Remember such words are singular and the related pronoun must also be singular.
6. Check spelling, commas, and incorrect use of "you."

PART
Three

Friendships

Friends—the word conjures up feelings and images that range from our earliest friendships to our present ones. Feelings associated with friendships may be of joy and contentment—good feelings; however, we may think, too, of separations or broken or discarded friendships. Friendship means giving and taking, so while we think of people who are our friends, we look also at the kind of friend we are to other people. From our own experiences and those of others, we realize that the concept of friendship is multilayered and intricate.

In this part of the book, you will share your thoughts, feelings, and experiences about friendships with others and hear their views and experiences. Through the readings and discussions, you will explore several aspects of friendships—across generations, genders, levels of commitment, and intensity of relationships. What expectations do you have for friends? What can they expect from you? How does one's concept of "friends" change over time? This topic is rich with material for a variety of writings. The classification, comparison–contrast, and definition patterns of development are explained in Part Three. As in the preceding chapters, many of the writing activities are short; their aim is to provide you with practice in exploring, sorting out your thoughts, and considering other ways of looking at the concept of friendship.

5

What Does "Friend" Mean?

What does it mean to say someone is a friend? You may use the word casually, to mean someone you are acquainted with. For instance, you might say you have a friend who plays cricket; what you mean by "friend" is someone you talk to once in a while and really do not know well at all. On the other hand, if you call someone a friend, you may be referring to a person whose friendship you cherish. We all have friends who fill a variety of roles in our lives, just as our friendships with others involve different levels of commitment.

Characteristics of Friends

In identifying a person as a friend, we would all probably describe many similar characteristics, although there could be differences. How would you describe a person whom you consider your friend?

Writing Activity: Being a Friend

Write what "friend" means to you—either in a list format or in a narrative paragraph. Compare what you wrote with others' descriptions and further discuss what being a friend means. What differences are there among the descriptions? What accounts for the differences? A common definition of a friend is "someone who is there for me." What does this mean? What does being there entail? What responsibilities do you require in a friendship, and what can friends require of you?

Responsibilities between Friends

The question of mutual responsibilities, commitment, and interests between friends has been around for a long time. Aesop, a Greek slave who died about 565 B.C., is credited with fables that teach moral lessons, each ending with a proverb—advice based on the moral. No one knows how many of the fables Aesop actually wrote himself; many are probably re-telling of stories handed down for generations. Around 300 B.C. Demetrius, an Athenian, collected about two hundred of the fables into written form, preserving them for all future generations. Read the following paraphrase of one of Aesop's fables dealing with friendships, and then write a personal response.

Two friends were deer hunting in the woods when they suddenly saw a large bear. Frightened, they ran to a tree and tried to scramble up the trunk. The first man was able to climb up to a strong limb but did not look back to see if his friend needed help. The second man fell to the ground and lay motionless, hoping the bear would not attack him. The bear came up to him, then bent down, whispered in his ear, and ambled away. The first man climbed down from the tree and asked his friend what the bear had said. The friend responded, "He told me that a friend in need is a true friend."

Write a personal response to the fable. What is the moral of the fable? Then discuss the fable in writing groups, using your responses as starting points. Consider the following questions:

1. What needs could friends expect to fulfill for one another?
2. Responsibilities to friends depend somewhat on circumstances. Give examples of when one should help a friend and when not.
3. Fables were created to make points about human behavior and are deliberately short, to the point, and simplistic; however, they are applicable to actual life situations. Apply the lesson or moral of this fable to modern situations by sharing experiences you have had where friends did or did not stand by you in adversity. Also, consider times when you did or did not stand by others.

Writing Activity: Illustrating Morals

After the group discussion, write a short paper based on an experience that illustrates the fable's moral. Or you may take the opposite stance and illustrate why the moral is not a valid one. You may write about an experience of your own or use someone else's experience. In either case, use specific examples to make your point clear. When describing how you felt, avoid words that are vague. For example, don't simply say you were "mad," but explain in detail how you felt and why.

Critique one another's papers with the following points in mind:

1. How does the author support claims?
2. What words are specific and help readers to understand the author's points?
3. What words and phrases could be more specific and/or colorful?
4. Where would additional examples and details strengthen the paper?

Differences and Similarities among Friends

Often shared interests are the beginning of friendships. We meet and become friends with people through activities: orchestra, softball, art, swimming, drama, racquetball, biking—any activity where there is opportunity to get to know others. Yet although there is a common interest, we may have different personalities, values, and experiences. In what ways do these differences shape the friendships?

Writing Activity: Describing Friends

Describe a friend you believe to be quite different from you. Through examples, illustrate how the differences enhance or weaken the relationship. Then write about a friend who is similar to you. Be specific in relating the ways in which you two are similar. In writing groups share and discuss what you wrote. Summarize what conclusions the group arrived at.

The next reading is a poem Jan Kippenhan wrote as a birthday gift to her friend. First read it to yourself, then read it aloud.
Write a personal response.

I Have a Friend

JAN KIPPENHAN

I have a friend
bold   bumptious
         buoyant

       with forces that explode
5   in frenzies of pain
      or rockets of joy
      her battered basket overflows
      with the fabric of her life
      a generous jumble of
10   black, white
      blood-red
      she lays her soul bare
      asks me to sort, advise
      and thinks me so wise
15   when I speak from her heart.

I have a friend
warm   caring
         embracing

      I go in silent supplication
20   seeking solace
      in her warm affection
      and friendly bias
      she sweeps away the bluegrey mist
      that chills the brittle reeds
25   trembling in my basket
      weaves patches to keep
      the soil from seeping away

beams nourishing rays
to dark roots
and renews the flower.   30

Personal Response

A reader can respond to a poem in much the same way as one would respond to a story or essay. A student wrote the following response after reading "I Have a Friend." As you read it, remember this is casual writing as all responses should be. The original is handwritten, not typed.

I love this poem. This is the perfect description of a good friend. One can go through life and never have a friend as special as this. Others will argue that friendships like this will form, but they are just few and far between. I agree with the second statement. I have had friends like this. They are, however, very few and far between.

The first part of the poem describes the role of being a friend. Often times I find that it is more difficult to be a friend than it is to have friends. This is because you have to give so much of yourself. To be a good friend, one has to be there all the time. A friend has to be able to put her problems aside to help the other when they need it. This is not always easy to do. Friends will often come to me, lay all their hurts and problems out, and want an instant opinion or solution. The satisfaction of knowing I helped someone in a situation when he or she came to me for guidance is a feeling beyond compare. The funny thing is that this satisfied feeling can give faith and comfort to the problems lying inside myself.

The second part of the poem deals with the aspect of what a friend is. A friend is someone who cares. A person who knows my innermost secrets and insecurities and will not reveal them to anyone. True friends often know what their counterpart is thinking before they themselves even realize it. This has happened to me many times. My best friend can always guess my true thoughts. No matter how big an act I put on or no matter how much I deny it, he always knows what's going on in my head. (Michele Turck)

Content Focus

1. In what ways are the two friends different? How are the friends compared?
2. What does each one bring to the friendship? How does each help the other?

3. Kippenhan uses images to describe her friend: "forces that explode," "rockets of joy," "a generous jumble." What kind of person is she describing? Do you know someone who resembles her friend?
4. Words the author uses to describe herself are quite different in tone and connotation. What do you think she is like?

Figurative Language

Figurative language, such as Kippenhan uses, creates images and responses in a reader's mind. Although we find this type of language more often in poetry, it is appropriate in many types of writing. Comparisons (called similes) such as "as strident as a goose" say a lot in a few words, and for those of you who have been chased by a goose, the image is clear and powerful. A simile uses "as" or "like" in the comparison. Kippenhan uses, rather than similes, a technique in which the thing being described is called something else (called metaphor). In her poem, the friend's life "is" a battered basket. A metaphor does not use "as" or "like." Both simile and metaphor work the same way—they create a picture or image that explains a great deal. You get a sense of a person whose life is "a generous jumble" or "brittle reeds."

Writing Activity: Comparing Characteristics

Divide a sheet of paper vertically in half. On the left side, in a list, jot phrases, images, or words that describe a close friend. On the right side, do the same for another friend or for yourself—preferably for someone who is quite different from the first person. Pair up the phrases as much as possible so as to create a series of comparisons. Write a short narrative piece using the two lists. Some people may like to use a poetic form, but a narrative form also works well.

Variety of Friendships

Having a variety of friends enriches our lives. Author Judith Viorst classifies her friends into categories in the following reading, "Friends, Good Friends—and Such Good Friends."

Friends, Good Friends— and Such Good Friends

JUDITH VIORST

Women are friends, I once would have said, when they to-   1
tally love and support and trust each other, and bare to each
other the secrets of their souls, and run—no questions asked—
to help each other, and tell harsh truths to each other (no, you
can't wear that dress unless you lose ten pounds first) when
harsh truths must be told.

Women are friends, I once would have said, when they share   2
the same affection for Ingmar Bergman, plus train rides, cats,
warm rain, charades, Camus, and hate with equal ardor Newark
and Brussels sprouts and Lawrence Welk and camping.

In other words, I once would have said that a friend is a   3
friend all the way, but now I believe that's a narrow point of
view. For the friendships I have and the friendships I see are
conducted at many levels of intensity, serve many different
functions, meet different needs and range from those as all-the-
way as the friendship of the soul sisters mentioned above to
that of the most nonchalant and casual playmates.

Consider these varieties of friendship: 4

1. Convenience friends. These are the women with whom, if   5
our paths weren't crossing all the time, we'd have no particular
reason to be friends: a next-door neighbor, a woman in our car
pool, the mother of one of our children's closest friends or
maybe some mommy with whom we serve juice and cookies
each week at the Glenwood Co-op Nursery.

Convenience friends are convenient indeed. They'll lend us   6
their cups and silverware for a party. They'll drive our kids to
soccer when we're sick. They'll take us to pick up our car when
we need a lift to the garage. They'll even take our cats when we
go on vacation. As we will for them.

But we don't, with convenience friends, ever come too close   7
or tell too much; we maintain our public face and emotional
distance. "Which means," says Elaine, "that I'll talk about being
overweight but not about being depressed. Which means I'll

admit being mad but not blind with rage. Which means that I might say that we're pinched this month but never that I'm worried sick over money."

8   But which doesn't mean that there isn't sufficient value to be found in these friendships of mutual aid, in convenience friends.

9   2. Special-interest friends. These friendships aren't intimate, and they needn't involve kids or silverware or cats. Their value lies in some interest jointly shared. And so we may have an office friend or a yoga friend or a tennis friend or a friend from the Women's Democratic Club.

10   "I've got one woman friend," says Joyce, "who likes, as I do, to take psychology courses. Which makes it nice for me—and nice for her. It's fun to go with someone you know and it's fun to discuss what you've learned, driving back from the classes." And for the most part, she says, that's all they discuss.

11   "I'd say that what we're doing is *doing* together, not being together," Suzanne says of her Tuesday-doubles friends. "It's mainly a tennis relationship, but we play together well. And I guess we all need to have a couple of playmates."

12   I agree.

13   *My* playmate is a shopping friend, a woman of marvelous taste, a woman who knows exactly *where* to buy *what*, and furthermore is a woman who always knows beyond a doubt what one ought to be buying. I don't have the time to keep up with what's new in eyeshadow, hemlines and shoes and whether the smock look is in or finished already. But since (oh, shame!) I care a lot about eyeshadow, hemlines and shoes, and since I don't *want* to wear smocks if the smock look is finished, I'm very glad to have a shopping friend.

14   3. Historical friends. We all have a friend who knew us when . . . maybe way back in Miss Meltzer's second grade, when our family lived in that three-room flat in Brooklyn, when our dad was out of work for seven months, when our brother Allie got in that fight where they had to call the police, when our sister married the endodontist from Yonkers and when, the morning after we lost our virginity, she was the first, the only, friend we told.

15   The years have gone by and we've gone separate ways and we've little in common now, but we're still an intimate part of each other's past. And so whenever we go to Detroit we always

go to visit this friend of our girlhood. Who knows how we looked before our teeth were straightened. Who knows how we talked before our voice got un-Brooklyned. Who knows what we ate before we learned about artichokes. And who, by her presence, puts us in touch with an earlier part of ourself, a part of ourself it's important never to lose.

"What this friend means to me and what I mean to her," says 16 Grace, "is having a sister without sibling rivalry. We know the texture of each other's lives. She remembers my grandmother's cabbage soup. I remember the way her uncle played the piano. There's simply no other friend who remembers those things."

4. Crossroads friends. Like historical friends, our crossroads 17 friends are important for *what was*—for the friendship we shared at a crucial, now past, time of life. A time, perhaps, when we roomed in college together; or worked as eager young singles in the Big City together; or went together, as my friend Elizabeth and I did, through pregnancy, birth and that scary first year of new motherhood.

Crossroads friends forge powerful links, links strong enough 18 to endure with not much more contact than once-a-year letters at Christmas. And out of respect for those crossroads years, for those dramas and dreams we once shared, we will always be friends.

5. Cross-generational friends. Historical friends and cross- 19 roads friends seem to maintain a special kind of intimacy— dormant but always ready to be revived—and though we may rarely meet, whenever we do connect, it's personal and in- tense. Another kind of intimacy exists in the friendships that form across generations in what one woman calls her daughter– mother and her mother–daughter relationships.

Evelyn's friend is her mother's age—"but I share so much 20 more than I ever could with my mother"—a woman she talks to of music, of books and of life. "What I get from her is the bene- fit of her experience. What she gets—and enjoys—from me is a youthful perspective. It's a pleasure for both of us."

I have in my own life a precious friend, a woman of 65 who 21 has lived very hard, who is wise, who listens well; who has been where I am and can help me understand it; and who rep- resents not only an ultimate ideal mother to me but also the per- son I'd like to be when I grow up.

22   In our daughter role we tend to do more than our share of self-revelation; in our mother role we tend to receive what's revealed. It's another kind of pleasure—playing wise mother to a questing younger person. It's another very lovely kind of friendship.

23   6. Part-of-a-couple friends. Some of the women we call our friends we never see alone—we see them as part of a couple at couples' parties. And though we share interests in many things and respect each other's views, we aren't moved to deepen the relationship. Whatever the reason, a lack of time or—and this is more likely—a lack of chemistry, our friendship remains in the context of a group. But the fact that our feeling on seeing each other is always, "I'm *so* glad she's here," and the fact that we spend half the evening talking together says that this too, in its own way, counts as a friendship.

24   (Other part-of-a-couple friends are the friends that came with the marriage, and some of these are friends we could live without. But sometimes, alas, she married our husband's best friend; and sometimes, alas, she *is* our husband's best friend. And so we find ourself dealing with her, somewhat against our will, in a spirit of what I'll call *reluctant* friendship.)

25   7. Men who are friends. I wanted to write just of women friends, but the women I've talked to won't let me—they say I must mention man–woman friendships too. For those friendships can be just as close and as dear as those that we form with women. Listen to Lucy's description of one such friendship:

26   "We've found we have things to talk about that are different from what he talks about with my husband and different from what I talk about with his wife. So sometimes we call on the phone or meet for lunch. There are similar intellectual interests—we always pass on to each other the books that we love—but there's also something tender and caring too."

27   In a couple of crises, Lucy says, "he offered himself, for talking and for helping. And when someone died in his family he wanted me there. The sexual, flirty part of our friendship is very small, but *some*—just enough to make it fun and different." She thinks—and I agree—that the sexual part, though small, is always *some*, is always there when a man and a woman are friends.

28   It's only in the past few years that I've made friends with men, in the sense of a friendship that's *mine*, not just part of two couples. And achieving with them the ease and the trust I've

found with women friends has value indeed. Under the dryer at home last week, putting on mascara and rouge, I comfortably sat and talked with a fellow named Peter. Peter, I finally decided, could handle the shock of me minus mascara under the dryer. Because we care for each other. Because we're friends.

8. There are medium friends, and pretty good friends, and 29 very good friends indeed, and these friendships are defined by their level of intimacy. And what we'll reveal at each of these levels of intimacy is calibrated with care. We might tell a medium friend, for example, that yesterday we had a fight with our husband. And we might tell a pretty good friend that this fight with our husband made us so mad that we slept on the couch. And we might tell a very good friend that the reason we got so mad in that fight that we slept on the couch had something to do with that girl who works in his office. But it's only to our very best friends that we're willing to tell all, to tell what's going on with that girl in his office.

The best of friends, I still believe, totally love and support 30 and trust each other, and bare to each other the secrets of their souls, and run—no questions asked—to help each other, and tell harsh truths to each other when they must be told.

But we needn't agree about everything (only 12-year-old girl 31 friends agree about *everything*) to tolerate each other's point of view. To accept without judgment. To give and to take without ever keeping score. And to *be* there, as I am for them and as they are for me, to comfort our sorrows, to celebrate our joys.

Content Focus

1. What principle do you think Viorst used when defining her categories of friends? In what ways do her examples fit the classification scheme?
2. What values are apparent in each of the categories?
3. If you were making a list in which to classify your friends, what overall scheme would you use?
4. Which examples could fit into more than one category?

Writer's Craft

1. Viorst begins her essay with what she "once would have said" friends were. In what ways does this set up interest for a reader? It is a technique you could use in several types of writing for a variety

of audiences: "What used to be, but now. . . ." Brainstorm topics where this technique would be particularly useful.
2. The pattern of writing is classification. What other patterns could one use to write an essay on friends?
3. What connections are there between the pattern and the author's purpose?

Classification Pattern of Development

To use a classification pattern in writing a paper is to bring related information together and categorize it by type. Judith Viorst does this in her essay by describing several degrees of friendships and then dividing kinds of friendship into categories. In classification the categories or groups must be mutually exclusive—that is, each item or description must fit into only one of the categories. That way one can compare and analyze the groups.

To use a simple example, if you had to sort a large number of buttons in various colors, designs, and sizes, you would need to select a system that clearly designated into which group each button would go. If you used color, you would need to decide to what degree different shades of color would fit into one designated group, and there might be a necessity for a multicolored group. Designs could be a controlling factor, or uses, or style. Size might be a determining factor, if the sizes clearly fell into distinct groups.

What system an author uses depends on the purpose of the writing. What would you say is Viorst's purpose? Does her classification system serve that purpose? For example, if her purpose were to illustrate how geographically spread out her friends are, her design would look quite different. Or one could describe friends according to the period of one's life in which one knew them. Viorst refers to this criterion in "crossroads friends," but only as one attribute. You could design an entire essay using a chronological classification: friends you had before going to school, in elementary grades, in middle school, in high school, at work, and at college. Each group would be further defined depending on your own experience. If you worked at several jobs before attending college, you might have more job-related categories; other categories might include friendships before or after marriage or children. Your own experience and information would determine how you defined the categories. The classification system used depends on what points you are making in your paper; in other words, on your purpose.

Organizing material into a classification form has many applications. Analysis of the information necessary for creating the categories often shows patterns that would otherwise go unnoticed. For example, suppose a law-enforcing agency classifies all the robberies in the area for a selected time period—a month or a year. In creating the categories, law-enforcement officials must analyze the information in a systematic way, and patterns emerge. These patterns can provide the police and the public important information about the robberies.

Another example is classifying job duties. Jobs might be categorized by time of day or working shifts—what is best to do in the morning, and so forth; or they could be classified by level of difficulty or by customer needs. In other words, a situation can be examined in several ways, and each analysis provides additional information.

When you write a classification essay, remember to make the categories you design reflect the purpose of your paper. Also, each description must fit in only one of the categories, according to the way you define them. The following student paper is an example of how one student, Brad Bucki, used categories to identify his friends—and also to write a strong description of his best friend.

STUDENT PAPER

FRIENDS

Brad Bucki

I have no clue how or why it turned out this way. Eight years ago I would rather have been dead than have this happen. Even today I wonder how I let that snot-nosed brat from fourth grade do the things he did to me; name calling and daily pummelings were normal for me. After five years of this

constant abuse, I had to retaliate. I was now bigger and stronger than he was; this was going to be
the sweetest revenge of my life. That fateful night
it happened; I won my first fight and made a new
best friend all with one swing.

No one truly knows why or how people pick the
friends they do. The simple fact is that it is
unavoidable. At some time or another each person
on this earth will have a friend. Of course, most
people will have many friends throughout their
lives. Be it a best friend, a classmate from second
grade or the kid next door, friends have their own
special place in a person's life. When I was young
I considered every friend I had to be my best
friend. I just knew it would stay that way for our
entire life, no matter what. I was certain they
thought the same. As the years go sweeping by, the
reality sets in that this is an extremely narrow-
minded view of the world. Best friends become
ordinary everyday acquaintances and mortal enemies
become invaluable friends. I now realize, as much
as I do not want to admit it, friends can be
labeled and grouped into several categories based
on intensity and duration of the relationship.

1) The school buddies. These are the people I
sat next to in Mr. Alberti's history, study hall,
lunch or shared a locker with in freshman gym class.
After pure repetition, I began to learn their names
and faces. I give them the name buddies because as
the name implies these friends never get too close

to my feelings nor do I get too close to theirs. At
lunch, conversations covered a variety of subjects:
sports, cars, parties or the always popular girls.
Rarely did subject matter sway toward more serious
subjects. Even if it did, it was quickly dropped in
order to preserve the all important reputation. The
main purpose of the school buddy is to make the day
go by quicker; once the bell sounded we all went
our separate ways until the next morning. Scott,
the kid from history class, summed up the school
buddy relationship eloquently when he poured his
heart out to me and confessed, "Thank God, you're
my friend or there wouldn't be no one around here
to wake me up after class."

2) The sport friends. Much like the school buddies these friends are great for the social part
of life. For the most part, this group of friends
consisted of guys I met from playing sports since
fifth grade. I am positive that somewhere there is
a golden rule chiseled in stone which states it is
a serious crime to show emotion in the presence of
this group. They possess the unparalleled ability
to turn one's emotions or misfortune into information which will be held over one's head for as long
as possible. I have determined that the single most
important function of this group is to pick on one
another. It is impossible for two members of this
group to be within twenty feet of each other for
more than five minutes without teasing, picking or
harassing each other. This may seem terribly cruel

for friends to do, but in fact the opposite holds true. This teasing has definitely taught me how to handle myself in adversity, how to think quickly for an answer and when to walk away. Most importantly, although it is hard to admit, these friends are always right. Be it the shirt I am wearing, the classes I am taking, or the girl I am dating, this group never has a problem telling me their opinions on any subject. They show absolutely no remorse in telling the harsh truth no matter how much it's going to hurt me.

3) Stand the test of time friends. Even though time and distance will separate Shane and me, there will always be a special bond between us. The bond may be stretched and twisted, but it will never be severed. Good times and bad, we have been through it all, side by side. Who could ever forget the times we shared? Our innocent schoolboy crushes on Kim and Alison. The overnight camping expeditions into the mysterious woods behind my house. The two-hour rafting trip that took nine due to miscalculations in flotation capacity and poor navigation. All those sleepless nights before motorcycle races spent eating peanuts, drinking grapefruit juice and discussing the female gender. Those are all high points in our friendship, but friendships are defined by the low spots. Aesop once stated that genuine friends are proved through adversity. This was never more obvious than on May 7, 1989. That was the day Shane's dad was fatally

shot by a worker he had laid off from the family
business. In the following month, we spent many
nights on Old Man Johnson's hill staring at the
stars. I had absolutely no idea what to say. All I
could do was listen, offer advice, and most importantly, provide a shoulder to cry on. We have since
gone our separate ways, but we both know an irre-
placeable part of our lives is still on Old Man
Johnson's hill staring at the stars.

4) We're just friends! This group of friends
is comprised completely of members of the opposite
sex. These friendships can be just as intense and
meaningful as same-sex friendships. However they
do undeniably contain a small amount of attraction
between the two individuals involved. Both parties
also realize that it is in the best interest of
both to not act on this attraction and keep the
relationship purely a friendship. My good friend
Sara once described it as, "The you can look, but
you can't touch friendship." The most outstanding
trait of these friends is they can look past status,
money, shortcomings, and forgive the unforgivable.
They are always willing to lend an ear or give
advice, never passing judgment. They accept with
open arms the true me along with all my faults.

5) Why am I friends with you? This perfectly
describes my relationship between my best friend,
Greg, and me. For five seemingly endless years we
were mortal enemies. I hated everything he stood
for. He was loud and obnoxious; I was quiet and

reserved. He partied; I studied. I was in sports;
he was on drugs. Never once did I consider him for
a future friend. That all changed the day after
he and I had our battle royal. The next day he
appeared at my front door to apologize for everything he had done to me in the past. After he
finished, I told him exactly what I thought of
him, making sure not to leave out any adjectives
describing his character. In the next two weeks,
we talked a lot and discovered we had much more in
common than we ever thought possible. We both were
scared of the future. We had similar relationships
with our parents and brothers. We both enjoyed
hunting, fishing, snowmobiling, and especially
girls. Eventually I realized he was not the rich
spoiled bully he came across as. He realized that
I was not the stuck-up preppy he viewed me as. We
both realized we were two similar people trying to
get through life the best we knew how. I admire
Greg; not only has he put his own life back in
order, but he has taught me a lot about my own
life. He has shown me how to let loose and have a
good time and how to approach life with a relaxed
attitude. Greg has opened my eyes to the vast world
around me and forced me to look at life in a new
and interesting way. I now know that there is life
outside of school and sports. People I deemed undesirable two years ago are now some of my closest
friends. I consider Greg my one true friend in
this world. He stands for everything I value in a

friendship. He accepts me for who I am. He is always
willing to listen to my problems no matter how
trivial or insignificant they may seem. He respects
my opinions and feelings even if he disagrees with
them. I know that no matter what happens to us in
the future, there will always be a special spot in
my heart for that snot-nosed kid from fourth grade.

The beginning of Brad's paper is especially effective because
it captures a reader's attention. Brad successfully ties the beginning and ending together. His use of details and specific examples create a believable experience for readers.

WRITING ASSIGNMENT: CLASSIFICATION PAPER

Your final assignment for this chapter is to write a classification
paper. You may wish to use the broad topic of friends; but,
rather than classifying them in groups as Judith Viorst or Brad
Bucki did, consider the following options:

❑ Classify friends by the time period you knew them.
❑ Classify places and situations where you met friends.
❑ Classify intergenerational friends.
❑ Classify your parents' friends.

If you wish to choose a topic other than friends, check with
your instructor.

When writing your paper, keep in mind Brad's effective and
lively beginning. How can you catch the reader's interest?
Viorst does it by explaining what she used to believe; Brad
makes us curious about what he is referring to with the first sentence. A deadly beginning would be "My friends fall into five
categories. Here they are." A reader's response might be "Who
cares?" As mentioned earlier, when you are writing a paper, it is
best not to begin composing with the beginning. As you work
on the paper, try out different beginnings. It takes time and practice to develop an effective first paragraph. Try out several with
your writing group to get their reactions.

To begin, freewrite about your topic and begin to form categories. This will take time, and probably you will change your initial idea several times. After you have an outline or sketch of the basic direction, begin composing a first draft. Let it sit for a day and then come back to the work. Read it aloud only to yourself. Make changes; fill in gaps; try out examples to see if they fit in the categories you selected. If they don't fit, redefine the categories. Rewrite a second draft before you meet with the writing group. By then you are far enough along so that the suggestions the members will give you can be helpful. Remember to tell the group what in particular you need help with. Follow through with all the steps in the process, as this paper should reflect your best work. A suggested response sheet and editing guide are provided for your use.

Response Guide for Classification Paper

1. What is your first response to the paper?
2. In what ways do the categories fit the examples?
3. How could the categories be strengthened? Look especially for consistency among categories.
4. Where would additional examples be helpful?
5. Where could the author use specific/figurative/concrete words?
6. How could the beginning be improved?
7. How could the conclusion/ending be stronger?
8. In what ways is the tone appropriate and consistent?
9. What should the author focus on in revision?
10. What do you like best about the paper?

Writer's name _____

Names of people in response group _____

_____

_____

_____

Editing Guide for Classification Paper

1. Check closely for correct pronoun use.
2. Check the author's use of semicolons. Are there places where you think a semicolon would help with the flow of the reading?
3. If in doubt about a spelling, look in the dictionary.
4. Correct use of commas can be difficult. Go over the paper carefully and consult your style handbook.
5. Apostrophes can be troublesome, usually because they are left out. Carefully read the paper, looking for omissions.
6. Do the sentences begin in much the same way? How could the author add interest by varying the beginnings? How about sentence length—are nearly all the sentences long, or all short? A variety helps with flow and interest.

6

Friends across
Generations and Time

Most of us, when asked to consider friendships, think first of friends who are part of our daily lives—friends we interact with frequently. They tend to be more or less in our age bracket, although there are exceptions. We may have a friend much older or younger, perhaps a relative who has become close or someone we work with. Intergenerational friends bring a richness to our lives through their stories and experiences. In this chapter we'll read accounts of these and other special friendships, share our own experiences, and compare friendships.

Unwilling Friends

Sometimes friendships are thrust upon us as we are forced unwillingly into a close relationship. Novelist and playwright Laura Cunningham describes such a situation in her essay "The Girls' Room." After reading the essay, write your personal response.

The Girls' Room

LAURA CUNNINGHAM

1   When I heard she was coming to stay with us I was pleased. At age eight I thought of "grandmother" as a generic brand. My friends had grandmothers who seemed permanently bent over cookie racks. They were a source of constant treats and sweets. They were pinchers of cheeks, huggers and kissers. My own grandmother had always lived in a distant state; I had no memory of her when she decided to join the household recently established for me by my two uncles.

But with the example of my friends' grandmothers before   2
me, I could hardly wait to have a grandmother of my own—
and the cookies would be nice too. For while my uncles provided a cuisine that ranged from tuna croquettes to Swedish
meatballs, they showed no signs of baking anything more ele-
gant than a potato.

My main concern on the day of my grandmother's arrival   3
was: How soon would she start the cookies? I remember her
arrival, my uncles flanking her as they walked down the apartment corridor. She wore a hat, a tailored navy blue suit, an ermine stole. She held, tucked under her arm, the purple leather
folder that contained her work in progress, a manuscript entitled
"Philosophy for Women." She was preceded by her custom-
made white trunk packed with purses, necklaces, earrings,
dresses and more purple-inked pages that stress "the spiritual
above the material."

She was small—at 5 feet 1 inch not much taller than I was—   4
thin and straight, with a pug nose, one brown eye (the good eye)
and one blue eye (the bad eye, frosted by cataracts). Her name
was "Esther in Hebrew, Edna in English, and Etka in Russian."
She preferred the Russian, referring to herself as "Etka from
Minsk." It was not at once apparent that she was deaf in her left
ear (the bad ear) but could hear with the right (the good ear). Because her good ear happened to be on the opposite side from the
good eye, anyone who spoke to her had to run around her in circles, or sway to and fro, if eye contact and audibility were to be
achieved simultaneously.

Etka from Minsk had arrived not directly from Minsk, as the   5
black-eyed ermine stole seemed to suggest, but after many
moves. She entered with the draft of family scandal at her back,
blown out of her daughter's home after assaults upon her dignity. She held the evidence: an empty-socketed peacock pin. My
cousin, an eleven-year-old boy, had surgically plucked out the
rhinestone eyes. She could not be expected to stay where such
acts occurred. She had to be among "human beings," among
"real people" who could understand. We seemed to understand.
We—my two uncles and I—encircled her, studied her vandal-
ized peacock pin and vowed that such things would never happen with "us."

She patted my head—a good sign—and asked me to sing the   6
Israeli national anthem. I did, and she handed me a dollar. My

uncles went off to their jobs, leaving me alone with my grand-mother for the first time. I looked at her, expecting her to start rolling out the cookie dough. Instead she suggested: "Now maybe you could fix me some lunch?"

7   It wasn't supposed to be this way, I thought, as I took her order: "toasted cheese and a sliced orange." Neither was she supposed to share my pink and orange bedroom, but she did. The bedroom soon exhibited a dual character—stuffed animals on one side, a hospital bed on the other. Within the household this chamber was soon referred to as "the girls' room." The name, given by Uncle Abe, who saw no incongruity, only the affinity of sex, turned out to be apt, for what went on in the girls' room could easily have been labeled sibling rivalry if she had not been eighty and I eight. I soon found that I had acquired not a traditional grandmother but an aged kid sister.

8   The theft and rivalry began within days. My grandmother had given me her most cherished possession, a violet beaded bag. In return I gave her my heart-shaped "ivory" pin and matching earrings. That night she stole back the purse but insisted on keeping the pin and earrings. I turned to my uncles for mediation and ran up against unforeseen resistance. They thought my grandmother should keep the beaded bag; they didn't want to upset her.

9   I burned at the injustice of it and felt the heat of an uncomfortable truth: where I once had my uncles' undivided indulgence, they were now split as my grandmother and I vied for their attention. The household, formerly geared to my little-girl needs, was rearranged to accommodate hers. I suffered serious affronts—my grandmother, in a fit of frugality, scissored all the household blankets, including what a psychiatrist would have dubbed my "security" blanket, in half. "Now," she said, her good eye gleaming, "we have twice as many." I lay under my narrow slice of blanket and stared hopelessly up at the ceiling. I thought evilly of ways of getting my grandmother out of the apartment.

10   Matters worsened, as more and more of my trinkets disappeared. One afternoon I came home from school to find her squeezed into my unbuttoned favorite blouse. Rouged and beribboned, she insisted that the size 3 blouse was hers. Meanwhile, I was forced to adapt to her idiosyncrasies: she covered

everything black—from the dog to the telephone—with white doilies. She left saucers balanced on top of glasses. She sang nonstop. She tried to lock my dog out of the apartment. The word that explained her behavior was "arteriosclerosis." 11
She had forgotten so much that sometimes she would greet me with "You look familiar." At other times she'd ask, "What hotel is this?" My answer, shouted in her good ear, was: "We're not in a hotel! This is our apartment!" The response would be a hoot of laughter: "Then why are we in the ballroom?"

Finally we fought: arm-to-arm combat. I was shocked at her 12
grip, steely as the bars that locked her into bed at night. Her good eye burned into mine and she said, "I'll tell." And she did. For the first time I was scolded. She had turned their love to disapproval, I thought, and how it chafed.

Eventually our rivalry mellowed into conspiracy. Within 13
months we found we had uses for each other. I provided the lunches and secret, forbidden ice cream sundaes. She rewarded me with cold cash. She continued to take my clothes; I charged her competitive prices. I hated school; she paid me not to go. When I came home for lunch I usually stayed.

Our household endured the status quo for eight years: my 14
uncles, my grandmother and I. Within the foursome rivalries and alliances shifted. I became my grandmother's friend and she became mine. We were the source of all the family comedy. When she said she wanted a college diploma we gave her one— with tinfoil stars and a "magna magna summa summa cum laude" inscription. We sang and performed skits. We talcum-powdered hair and wearing one of her old dresses, I would appear as her "long-lost friend." We had other themes, including a pen pal, "The Professor."

Of course, living with an elderly person had its raw aspects. 15
When she was ill our girls' room took on the stark aura of a geriatrics ward. I imagined, to my shame, that neighbors could stare in through curtainless windows as I tended to my grandmother's most personal needs.

Yet, in these times of age segregation, with grandmothers 16
sent off to impersonal places, I wonder if the love and the comedy weren't worth the intermittent difficulties? Certainly I learned what it might be to become old. And I took as much comfort as my grandmother did in a nightly exchange of Russian

endearments—"Ya tebya lyublyu," "Ya tebya tozhe lyublyu—" "I love you," "I love you, too."

17   If I sold my grandmother blouses and baubles, maybe she gave me the truth in exchange. Once, when we were alone in the girls' room, she turned to me, suddenly lucid, her good eye as bright as it would ever be—a look I somehow recognized as her "real" gaze—and said, "My life passes like a dream."

Personal Response

Write what Laura Cunningham's experience brings to your mind. Your personal experience may not involve a grandmother; it could be any older person—perhaps someone in your neighborhood, a person you knew as a child, or a relationship in the present. Describe what the person is like, how the friendship formed, and how you and your friend are alike and different.

Content Focus

1. What does the term "generic brand" mean in relation to a grandmother or to any person?
2. From the details Cunningham gives of her first encounter with her grandmother, what do you think the grandmother will be like? What details in particular help form your opinion?
3. Although the situation must have been difficult for an eight-year-old child, the author tells the story with humor. How does this affect your reaction?
4. How did the little girl and the old lady become friends? What were the benefits the girl gained from the friendship?
5. How do you interpret "My life passes like a dream"?

Writer's Craft

1. Cunningham contrasts her expectations of a grandmother with the realities of "Etka from Minsk." How do the contrasts draw the reader into the essay?
2. Notice that Cunningham does not write, "You might think a grandma would bake cookies" but makes the experience realistic and immediate by describing what *she* thought. Using "you" separates the reader from the writer's response, and writers need to avoid the inappropriate use of "you." Use "you" only when you are directly addressing a reader. The most appropriate time to do this is when writing instructions or a process paper in which you want a reader to respond directly. For example, "Next, apply a primer to the book-

case" is directed to the reader. Unless you do want the reader to follow specific directions, avoid using "you."

3. Cunningham uses only a few examples to illustrate the relationship; in some instances, in fact, she alludes only briefly to particular events. How do these brief mentions create a strong image of the grandma and the young girl?

Writing Activity: Expectations of Friends

Write a short paper about a time when your expectations of a person did not come true. You might consider a time when you thought you would really like a person but discovered that what you expected did not fit the reality of the situation; or the reverse could be true. In either case, explain in detail what your expectations were and then what the outcome was. Examples of specific behavior help readers to understand and appreciate your experience.

Unlikely Friendships

In "The Girls' Room" the friendship developed because the two protagonists were related and were forced into close proximity. In the following reading, written by Charles Kuralt, neither reason applies. Kuralt traveled around the United States gathering stories, often from interviews with people he met. Here he describes an unlikely friendship that developed from a chance meeting.

Mr. Misenheimer's Garden
(Surry County, Virginia)

CHARLES KURALT

We've been wandering the back roads since 1967, and we've been to a few places we'll never forget. One of them was on Route 10, Surry County, Virginia. We rolled in here on a day in the spring of 1972 thinking this was another of those little roadside rest stops. But there were flowers on the picnic tables. That was the first surprise.

2   And beyond the tables, we found a paradise, a beautiful garden of thirteen acres, bright with azaleas, thousands of them, and bordered by dogwoods in bloom, and laced by a mile of paths in the shade of tall pines. In all our travels, it was the loveliest garden I'd ever seen. It made me wonder how large a battalion of state-employed gardeners it took to keep the place up. The answer was it took one old man, and he was nobody's employee. Walter Misenheimer, a retired nurseryman, created all this in the woods next to his house, created it alone after he retired at the age of seventy. He was eighty-three when I met him and was spending every day tending his garden for the pleasure of strangers who happened to stop.

3   WALTER MISENHEIMER: I like people, and this is my way of following out some of the teachings of my parents. When I was a youngster, one of the things they said was, "If you don't try to make the world just a little bit nicer when you leave here, what is the reason for man's existence in the first place?" I have tried to give it to the state. The Parks Department says it is too small for them. The Highway Department says it is too big for them.

4   KURALT: What's going to happen to this place after you're gone?

5   MISENHEIMER: Well, I imagine that within a very few years, this will be undergrowth, or nature will take it over again.

6   KURALT: You mean, it's not going to survive?

7   MISENHEIMER: I doubt it.

8   KURALT: That's a terribly discouraging thing, isn't it?

9   MISENHEIMER: Well, that's the way I see it now.

10   We watched for a while as people enjoyed the beauty of Walter Misenheimer's garden. And we left, and a few years later somebody sent me a clipping from the Surry County paper. It said Walter Misenheimer had died. I wondered what would happen to his garden. I wondered whether the Virginia sun still lights the branches of the dogwood, which he planted there.

11   Well, it does. Some stories have happy endings. Walter Misenheimer's garden does survive, and so does his spirit, in Haeja Namkoong. It seems that she stopped by the garden just a few months after we did, eleven years ago.

HAEJA NAMKOONG: We slowed down and saw a sign and picnic   12
tables and a lot of flowers blooming. We came to the picnic
table, found a water spigot, helped ourselves, and we were
sort of curious as to what this place was all about. Finally,
we saw the old man sort of wobbling around and coming
'cross the lawn, saying "Hello," and just waving to us to
stop. I guess he was afraid we were going to leave.

To please the old man, and herself, Haeja Namkoong stayed   13
the afternoon with him, walking in his garden. It made her remember, she says, something she wanted once.

HAEJA: I grew up in a large city in Korea, and I have never re-   14
ally seen rice grow. I always dreamed about living in the
country, about a small, little cabin in the wilderness, with
lots of flowers. That's what I dreamed about, but I guess
that was just childhood dreams.

When the sun went down that day, the young woman said   15
good-bye to the old man and headed home to Boston, but the
roadside Eden called her back. That is, Walter Misenheimer
did. He phoned her, long distance, and asked her to come for a
little while and help in the garden.

HAEJA: He was sort of pleading with me, "Please come down.   16
Just help me for a couple of weeks."

A couple of weeks only, and then a few more, and then it was   17
Christmas. Haeja Namkoong was twenty-six. She had no family. Neither did Walter Misenheimer and his wife.

HAEJA: From wildflowers to man-grown shrubberies, he taught   18
me. I was interested in learning the whole thing. I was out
here almost every day with him.

They became as father and daughter working in the garden,   19
and in time Haeja Namkoong was married in the garden.

HAEJA: He was very proud to give me away. I guess he never   20
thought, since he didn't have any children of his own, he
would give someone away.

21   Brown earth was coaxed by the gentle old man into green growth and flowering red and pink and white. The earth rewards every loving attention it is paid. People repay such love, too, in memory.

22   HAEJA: I was very, very close to my mother. But other than my mother, I can't remember anyone that loved me so much and cared for me so much as Mr. Misenheimer.

23   The garden is still here. Walter Misenheimer died in 1979 and left it to Haeja Namkoong. She pays a caretaker, Ed Trible, to help keep it beautiful for anybody who passes by. Haeja and her husband and their children live in Richmond now, but they return on weekends to work in the garden.

24   HAEJA: So, knowing how much the garden meant to him, I want to keep it up and carry on.

25   Walter Misenheimer told me that he expected when he was gone the garden would soon be overgrown. He might have known better. His garden shows that something grows from seeds and cultivation. And if what you plant is love and kindness, something grows from that, too.

26   HAEJA: Look at this purple one.
27   CHILD: I like the red.
28   HAEJA: Aren't they pretty?

Personal Response

Respond to the unexpected friendship that developed between Misenheimer and Haeja. Think about such friendships in your life. What is the connection between the garden and the friendship?

Content Focus

1. Why did the friendship develop?
2. Why Haeja and not someone else?
3. What attracted Kuralt to this story?
4. What do you think the author meant by "He might have known better."

Writer's Craft

1. Kuralt intersperses interview questions and answers with narrative. How does this technique work?
2. The piece is short; if more were added, how would the piece be more or less effective?
3. Interviews bring a feeling of familiarity to readers—a sense of being there. Where in your past writing activities for this course would an interview approach be effective?

Writing Activity: Unlikely Friendships

Write a short piece relating the unlikely friendship between two people. These people may be real or fictional; the friendship may span historical time or be in the present. For example, you might write about an imagined friendship between poets Anne Sexton and Emily Dickinson; between one of your parents and a historical figure such as a president; or between two present-day people you know. Use Kuralt's format, combining quotes and narrative. Where necessary, create fictional interviews.

Distance, Time, and Friends

In spite of our best intentions, we do lose track of friends or, for various reasons, change friends. Rachel Killough, a student, describes the changing stages of friendships.

STUDENT PAPER

FRIENDSHIPS

Rachel Killough

Remember that friend you had when you were four? You know, that partner in curiosity? The ever faithful confidant who would never tell on the person whose hand they witnessed in the cookie jar? Partner in crime, fellow pinky-swearer, the Best

Friend. Yes, that special someone that would share their cherry Tootsie Pop in exchange for a juicy secret. Unfortunately, those days don't last forever, but the sheer joy and mischief of the mighty bond does not have to end. At least it wouldn't . . . if it wasn't for the detestable fact that people change.

I have been alive only 18 years, but I have been through and witnessed quite a few friendships that have lasted and quite a few that have disintegrated. When you are young, an easy way to lose a friend is to move away or have them move away. It feels like being ripped away from a significant part of you, like maybe losing a thumb. One day you have it, the next day you try to climb a tree or throw a baseball, but it's not the same. Sometimes, however, the friends separate because of gender. Imagine for a moment. Here you are, holding hands with your best friend . . . Johnny. Now here you are . . . (let's just call you Jane). Suddenly, some annoying 3-ft-tall spectators from behind mention to Johnny that you happen to be a girl and obviously have cooties that you are intending to maliciously infect him with. Thus boy lets go, runs with friends and you stand there trying to figure out what a cootie is. Let's see, if you are a cootie holder, why not go and spend time with the other cootie holders. After all . . . there might be a new kind of Barbie or something that would be more fun than catching frogs. Soon, your company consists mainly of girls and stays that way for a good portion of your grade school years.

Middle school is a very trying time for friendships, especially when you and your friend have no classes together. Cliques become the new thing and people latch onto some kind of group. With so many new and different people, it is easy to grow apart. Here's an example: Josh "the jock" is seen talking to Seth "the smoker." Josh's friends take no hesitation in informing Josh that Seth is a total loser, and to avoid further persecution, Josh avoids Seth from then on. Seth is hurt and angered, so he goes back to his "group" of smokers and convinces them that all jocks are bastards and that they think everybody else is below them. The "smoker friends" indeed are angered by this and convince themselves that fighting is the only way to successfully vanquish this "lower class" mentality that these jocks have of them. Sometimes a fight is started, but most of the time a bitter resentment is carried over throughout the rest of the students' school lives.

High school is the final test of a friendship if it has made it this far. Many people have said that high school is the final phase a person must go through to develop an attitude and personality they will have for the rest of their life. This is true in many ways. A good, close to home example is partying or drug use in general. If you start off trying to fit in freshman year by blending into the whole drinking scene, it won't be long before you find hanging out, watching movies, and drinking Pepsi with your loyal "goody" friends boring. I call this the "buddy shift." The funny thing is, in high school, the easiest people to become buddies with are the ones who can supply you with alcohol, marijuana, acid . . . you name it. No, no. The funny thing is, the number of kids who fall for it. Now that's funny.

A true friend is a friend that has seen you at your worst, but has stood strong to defend you against the odds. Always available for advice but takes heart that you will do the right thing. A true friend understands "No" without pushing for "Yes." But most of all, a friend accepts you for you, and not for your hair, skin, clothes, money or social standing. A true friend is hard to come by; once you have one, you may never afford to let them go.

Rachel Killough writes about some of the reasons that friendships change: distance, peer pressure, gender, maturity, and values. In addition, sometimes we lose friends because we neglect them.

Writing Activity: Changing Friendships

Write a short essay about changing friendships that you have experienced or observed. What conclusions can you draw?

We may lose friends because, in spite of good intentions, we forget to call them; or, as is the case in the essay by Edward Ziegler that follows, we may break off a relationship because of anger.

It Was a Good Barn

EDWARD ZIEGLER

An old friendship had grown cold. Where once there had 1
been closeness, there was only strain. Now pride kept me from
picking up the phone.

Then one day I dropped in on another old friend, who's had 2
a long career as a minister and counselor. We were seated in his
study—surrounded by maybe a thousand books—and fell into
deep conversation about everything from small computers to
the tormented life of Beethoven.

The subject finally turned to friendship and how perishable 3
it seems to be these days. I mentioned my own experience as an
example. "Relationships are mysteries," my friend said. "Some
endure. Others fall apart."

Gazing out his window to the wooded Vermont hills, he 4
pointed toward a neighboring farm. "Used to be a large barn
over there." Next to a red-frame house were the footings of
what had been a sizable structure.

"It was solidly built, probably in the 1870s. But like so many 5
of the places around here, it went down because people left for
richer lands in the Midwest. No one took care of the barn. Its
roof needed patching; rainwater got under the eaves and
dripped down inside the posts and beams."

One day a high wind came along, and the whole barn began 6
to tremble. "You could hear this creaking, first, like old sailing-
ship timbers, and then a sharp series of cracks and a tremendous roaring sound. Suddenly it was a heap of scrap lumber.

"After the storm blew over, I went down and saw these 7
beautiful, old oak timbers, solid as could be. I asked the fellow
who owns the place what had happened. He said he figured the
rainwater had settled in the pinholes, where wooden dowels
held the joints together. Once those pins were rotted, there was
nothing to link the giant beams together."

We both gazed down the hill. Now all that was left of the 8
barn was its cellar hole and its border of lilac shrubs.

My friend said he had turned the incident over and over in 9
his mind, and finally came to recognize some parallels between

building a barn and building a friendship: no matter how strong you are, how notable your attainments, you have enduring significance only in your relationship to others.

10   "To make your life a sound structure that will serve others and fulfill your own potential," he said, "you have to remember that strength, however massive, can't endure unless it has the interlocking support of others. Go it alone and you'll inevitably tumble.

11   "Relationships have to be cared for," he added, "like the roof of a barn. Letters unwritten, thanks unsaid, confidences violated, quarrels unsettled—all these act like rainwater seeping into the pegs, weakening the link between the beams."

12   My friend shook his head. "It was a good barn. And it would have taken very little to keep it in good repair. Now it will probably never be rebuilt."

13   Later that afternoon I got ready to leave. "You wouldn't like to borrow my phone to make a call, I don't suppose?" he asked.

14   "Yes," I said, "I think I would. Very much."

Personal Response

After reading this selection, respond with your experiences of friends you've disagreed with, friends you haven't seen for a while, and friends you have been meaning to contact. Pride kept Edward Ziegler from calling his friend. What has pride kept you from doing?

Content Focus

1. What caused the barn to collapse?
2. How does barn maintenance compare to friendship? Be specific.
3. Think about this quote: "No matter how strong you are, how notable your attainments, you have enduring significance only in your relationship to others." What does this statement mean to you? In what ways is it true; in what ways is it not?

Writer's Craft

Ziegler has used the technique of an extended metaphor. Where else have you seen this used? Think of films or TV shows; metaphor is used in the visual arts as well as in print. How successful is Ziegler's metaphor? Think of a different metaphor to describe one of your friends or a particular kind of friendship. To begin, think of what a friendship or a friend reminds you of; then use details of that object or situation to describe the friend. Using this extended metaphor, write a paragraph or two.

Stereotypes and Expectations

Friendships between people of different generations are often hindered by stereotypes—preconceived ideas of what it means to be old or young. The following poem by Ruth Harriet Jacobs illustrates how one woman perceives advancing years.

Becoming Sixty

RUTH HARRIET JACOBS

There were terror and anger
at coming into sixty.
Would I give birth
only to my old age?

Now near sixty-one   5
I count the gifts
that sixty gave.

A book flowed from my life
to those who needed it
and love flowed back to me.   10

In a yard that had seemed full
space for another garden appeared.
I took my aloneness to Quaker meeting
and my outstretched palms were filled.

I walked further along the beach   15
swam longer in more sacred places
danced the spiral dance
reclaimed daisies for women
in my ritual for a precious friend
and received poet's wine   20
from a new friend who came
in the evening of my need.

Personal Response

Respond on a personal level to your own "terror and anger" at changes, whether they are age-related or not. Many of you will remember your fears about entering middle school or high school. We tend to fear the unknown, and old age is an unknown. Respond, too, with experiences older friends and family members have had.

Content Focus

1. How does the stereotype of aging affect the poet's personal life? Even though Ruth Harriet Jacobs speaks of "the evening of my need," the mood of the poem is not sad.
2. What are the experiences Jacobs has that alleviate the "terror and anger"? Why does she feel comforted?
3. How might knowing that someone felt fearful and angry about growing older affect your friendship?

Writer's Craft

Jacobs alludes to, rather than explaining in detail, what has happened. This strategy works better in poetry than in prose, because readers of poetry don't expect a lot of detail—although the technique is appropriate in both. In what ways does this allusive approach affect the reader?

Comparison–Contrast Pattern of Development

Throughout this chapter, you have had the opportunity to read, discuss, and write about friendships between dissimilar people and friends you've had over time. Your final assignment for this chapter will be to write a comparison–contrast paper.

The comparison–contrast pattern is a way of explaining what we know or how we feel about a subject in a clear, organized fashion. It helps us to understand an issue by focusing on how alike or different the subjects or topics are. For example, if you were trying to decide whether to move into an apartment or live in a dorm, move from one apartment to another, or move from an apartment to a house, the issue would be more understandable if you compared the pros of cons of the different options. In writing a paper about a friendship, you could come to a deeper understanding of what that friendship means to you by comparing your own and your friend's personalities, values, dreams, or any attributes that define the two of you. By comparing two subjects, a writer gains insights that other patterns may not provide.

An entire paper may follow a comparison–contrast pattern, or the pattern can be used for only one section. This pattern is important in all academic subjects and areas of employment, especially when decisions have to be made or points must be articulated clearly and forcefully. Often test questions are framed in a comparison format: "Compare the issues in separation of church and state"; "Compare the issues in state funding of private schools"; "Explain the differences between the political parties' views on tax cuts." The comparison format allows a writer to state the major points clearly, explain how they differ, and make connections.

The following elements are key in successful comparison–contrast papers.

Thesis

A strong thesis, or position, is important when you are writing an information paper. A reader must know not only what you are writing about but your stand on the issue. For example, if you begin a paper with "I am comparing two of my friends who are very different," you have written an explanation, not a thesis. To develop a thesis you must state your opinion. The comparison–contrast paper then supports that thesis.

In a way, every paper can be thought of as "persuasion" (even though persuasion is covered separately in Chapter 9)—because your goal is always to convince your reader that your thesis is right. In the example mentioned above, you might argue that the reason the friends are different from each other is that you have different sides to your personality and need different kinds of friends. Or you might contend that having different kinds of friends helps you to learn and mature. If your paper compares friends from different times in your life, you could make a statement to the effect that "I've outgrown my childhood friends"; or you could assert that "My childhood friends are the only true friends I have, even though I don't see them anymore." Whatever your view or attitude, articulate it in your thesis statement.

Points of Contrast

At the beginning of the paper, usually in the first paragraph, explain what you are comparing and/or contrasting and in what ways. You may want to focus only on the differences (contrasts) or only on the similarities (comparisons). Usually, though, comparison–contrast subjects are discussed both ways. If you do use both, keep a balance between the two. That is, if you discuss four aspects that are the same, then you should have approximately four that differ. This is only a general guideline; you may have several points of difference and one outstanding area of similarity. The overall effect, however, should balance.

Organization

For the organization of the paper, you have two options. You can describe one subject in terms of all the points you have chosen, then do the same with the other subject; or discuss one point as it relates to both subjects, then go on to the next point. Use the organization option that works the best for you, but do not go back and forth between the two. For example, if you begin by discussing one point in relation to both subjects, stay with that method; don't then go on to describe several points about one subject before comparing again. A consistent approach is much easier for a reader to follow.

Transitions

In all writing, transitions are important for connecting thoughts and for providing a road map for readers. They are especially important in a comparison–contrast paper, because in this pattern you switch from subject to subject and from point to point. A transition is like a signal, letting the reader know you are now going to explain a different point or subject.

Transitions are not complicated, usually just a word or two. Some frequently used transition words are *however, but, by contrast, similarly, also, likewise, yet, while, however,* and *in addition.* Punctuate carefully when using transitions. Remember that transitional expressions are usually at the beginning of a sentence and followed by commas.

Conclusions

You must come to a conclusion that supports your thesis. You are comparing and contrasting for a reason. You are demonstrating to your readers, through the information you provide throughout the paper, that your view is logical. Repeating the thesis is not enough: Explain how your evidence leads to the view you have. In a way, you are saying, "See now why I believe what I do?"

WRITING ASSIGNMENT: A COMPARISON–CONTRAST PAPER

Your assignment is to write a comparison–contrast paper. You may want to compare two friends who are different from each other. Or, as Jan Kippenhan did in her poem "I Have a Friend" (Chapter 5), you might compare yourself and a friend. Other possible topics: how your friends have changed over time; your friends as they are, compared to what you would like your friends to be; friends of different ages; or how your own expectations of friends have changed. Any aspect of friendship makes an acceptable topic. If you wish, you may choose a topic other than friends; check with your instructor.

Begin by brainstorming possible topics. Try one or two by freewriting to see if the topic is strong enough for you to develop into a paper of approximately three pages. Write your thesis statement several times, until you arrive at a statement that accurately reflects your belief or attitude. The next step is to select the points for comparison–contrast. Again, this may take several tries before you arrive at the best points to support the thesis. Next, decide on the organizational pattern and begin drafting.

When you have developed a rough draft to the point that sharing with others is helpful, meet in writing groups to read and respond. The questions in the following response guide will help focus the discussions.

Response Guide for Comparison–Contrast Paper

1. How could the thesis take a stronger stand? Remember, a thesis needs to state the author's stance, value, or opinion.
2. Look for a clear description of what is compared and on what points.
3. Is the organization pattern consistent? How could it be improved?
4. Is each point developed enough to make a clear distinction between the areas compared? Suggest ways to strengthen each point.
5. Discuss the conclusion. Look for thesis support, evidence of logical connections, and a strong finish.
6. Listen for specific descriptions; watch out for redundant words and clichés.

This assignment requires a final copy. After you make revisions based on the group's suggestions, meet again in editing groups to read and proofread one another's papers.

7

Friendships and Gender

Having friendships with both men and women enriches our lives. The insights and attitudes of each gender have much to offer to persons of the opposite gender. A man will have many close friends who are men; however, he may also have several close women friends. The same is true for a woman. Friendships with both genders are valuable and important.

Society's Expectations

Society's idea of what is acceptable or not can interfere with close relationships, however. Misunderstanding, prejudice, and ignorance often cause problems. The three readings in this chapter illustrate the unhappiness that can result when misguided people make faulty assumptions and judgments.

The first reading is a short story by Paula Gunn Allen. Allen grew up in Cubero, New Mexico, as part of Laguna Pueblo. Her storytelling family, her multicultural background, and the dramatic physical setting of her homeland all contribute to the richness of her stories. In this story, the friendship between two girls is crushed by an adult's prejudice.

They Make Their Climb

PAULA GUNN ALLEN

It had been the apple tree. The long spring days there. With the   1
girl. They had watched the village going. They had watched the clouds. When they thirsted they climbed down from the branches and walked to the nearby spring. Took a long sweet drink.

2   Elena had taught Ephanie about the weeds. Which to eat. When they had gathered prickly pears in the summer, brushing carefully the tiny spines from the fruit before they ate. They had wandered the mesas and climbed the nearer peaks. Together they had dreamed. Sharing. They never talked about growing up. What that would mean.

3   They had ridden horses. Pretended to be ranchers. Chased the village cattle around the town. Suffered scoldings for it. Learned to be trick riders. Roy Rogers and Hopalong Cassidy. Maybe they could be stunt men in Hollywood if they got good enough at it. If they could learn to jump from the rooftop onto the horse's back. They had chased the clouds.

4   Or lying, dreaming, had watched them, tracing faces and glorious beast shapes in the piling, billowing thunderheads. On July mornings they had gone out from their separate homes, laughing, feet bare and joyful in the road's early dust. The early wind cool and fresh, the bright sunlight making promises it would never keep. They had lain together in the alfalfa field of Elena's father, quiet, at peace.

5   They were children and there was much they did not know.

6   In their seasons they grew. Walking the road between their houses, lying languorous and innocent in the blooming boughs of the apple tree. Amid the fruiting limbs. And had known themselves and their surroundings in terms of each other's eyes. Though their lives were very different, their identity was such that the differences were never strange. They had secret names for each other, half joking, half descriptive. Snow White and Rose Red, they named themselves, in recognition of the fairness of Elena, the duskiness of Ephanie. In recognition also of the closeness they shared, those friends.

7   The events that measured their shared lives were counted in the places that they roamed, and Ephanie always remembered her childhood that way. The river, the waterfall, the graveyard, the valley, the mesas, the peaks. Each crevice they leaped over. Each danger they challenged, each stone, each blade of grass. A particularity that would shape her life.

8   They had especially loved the shadows. Where they grew, lavender, violet, purple, or where those shadows would recede. On the mountain slopes and closer by, beneath the shading trees. And the blue enfolding distance surrounding that meant

the farthest peaks. Shared with them in their eyes, in their stories, but where, together, they had never been.

In all those years, in spite of distance, in spite of difference, in   9
spite of change, they understood the exact measure of their relationship, the twining, the twinning. There were photographs of them from that time. Because Elena's gold-tinged hair looked dark in the photograph's light, no one could say which was Elena, which Ephanie. With each other they were each one doubled. They were thus complete.

Jump.   10

Fall.   11

Remember you are flying. Say you are a bird.   12

She has said that, Ephanie. Had urged Elena to leap the   13
great crevices between the huge sandstone formations that shaped the mesas they roamed. Some of the leaps were wide and the ground far below. She had always done the leading. Elena, devoted, did what Ephanie decided. Or it seemed that way.

Ephanie didn't want to remember it that way. Wanted the   14
fact to be that Elena had gone on her own windings, ones not of Ephanie's making. And in some cases, that was true. There were some things that, no matter how Ephanie urged them, Elena would not do. Some ways in which she remained safe within her own keeping. Sometimes, when she had adamantly refused, Ephanie would give up and go back to her own home. And it also went, sometimes, the other way.

They did not argue. They did not fight. Elena would do what   15
was of her own wanting. And while it seemed that the dark girl was leading, the fair one did the guiding. And in her quiet, unargumentative, unobtrusive way, she kept them both safe within the limits of their youthful abilities, gave the lessons and boundaries that encompassed their lives.

Kept them safe. Or almost so. Except for that one time that she   16
hadn't. Kept them safe. Had missed some signal. Had turned aside in some way, away or toward, a split second too soon, too late. Had not known in time not to speak. Had not known what her words, in time, in consequence, would create.

Perhaps it had been the shadows that betrayed her. The   17
certain angle of light that somehow disoriented her. Perhaps so accustomed to being safe, she did not know the danger, any

danger that might tear the web of their being. Shredding. Shattering. Splintering.

18   Or maybe it was the sun. The bright, the pitiless, the unwavering sun.

19   But whatever had disturbed her knowing, her keeping in time with the turns and twists of their sharing, their lives, in that splitting second everyone had abandoned Ephanie. Everything had gone away.

20   It was on a certain day. They went hiking. Exploring. They went walking. It was an adventure. One they had planned for a long time. Ever since they were small. They planned to walk to Picacho. The peak. That rose, igneous formation, straight up from the surrounding plain. The arid floor of the semi-desert of their homeland.

21   They wanted to climb the peak. To go to the top. To see. Elena said they could see the next village. The one that was invisible from where they lived. She told Ephanie the story, one she had recounted before. Much of what Ephanie knew about the people and land around them she learned from Elena. She didn't hear much that others told her. Not for many years.

22   Not that others had not spoken. Had not told her stories, had not given ideas, opinions, methods. They had. Some part of Ephanie recorded what they told her. What they said. But she did not acknowledge it until later. Not for many years. She did not understand how that had happened. But it did.

23   They had planned in the last days before their journey very well. Deciding what to take. What would not be too heavy to carry. What would not get in their way. What to wear, for comfort and protection, in the heat, against the stone. Which shirts, which length pants, which shoes. They knew they would get thirsty. It was July.

24   They wore tennis shoes and jeans. Usually they went barefoot from spring well into fall. Every chance they got. But this journey was special. It signified accomplishing. That they were grown. That they knew something, could put it into use.

25   They took oranges. For the juice. They knew how to use them, slit the rind with a toughened thumbnail, in a circle. Peel the small circle of rind away from the flesh. Press finger into the fruit, firmly, gently. So as not to lose too much juice. The juice was precious. It would sustain them. Then put the opening thus made to

their mouths. Sucking. When all the juice was thus taken, they would split open the fruit and eat the pulp. And the white furry lining of the rind. Elena said it was sweet. That it was healthy.

Ephanie never ate an orange that way later. It didn't seem 26
right. She didn't know why she wouldn't. Like her dislike of spiders. Which made no sense either. She remembered how it had gone, that journey, and why they had learned to eat oranges that particular way. She didn't understand her unwillingness to follow that childhood ritual. Not for a long time. And she found the lining bitter. Peeled it carefully away from the fruit all of her adult life. Threw it away.

But she loved the smell of oranges. The orange oil that clung 27
to her hands when she was done. Its fragrance. Its echoing almost remembered pain. She would sniff it, dreaming, empty in thought, empty in mind, on her way to the faucet to wash it off her hands. And in the flood of water and soap she would banish what she did not know. Averting. Avoiding. Voiding. Pain.

They met in the early morning. While the cool wind blew 28
down from the mountain. The way they were going was into the wind. The earth sparkled. The leaves. The sun was just getting started. Like a light from elsewhere it touched their eyes, their hands. They shivered slightly, shaking. They began to walk. Taking the road that curved upward. Upward and out. They were leaving. They know that. They knew they would never return.

They didn't talk about that intuition, but walked, silent, amiable, 29
close. They listened to the soft padding of their footfall on the dusty road, watched their shadows move, silent, alongside of them. Elena told Ephanie how high the peak was. Much taller than it looked. They speculated about climbing it. Ephanie was afraid of heights that had no branches to hold on to, but she never let on. She had never let on.

The great isolate rock rose maybe a hundred feet from the 30
ground. Its top was slender, precarious. It stood alone, gray and silent, reaching into the sky. It was a proud rock. A formation. It brooded there on the plain between the villages. It guarded the road to the mountain. Sentinel.

The story it bore was an old one. Familiar. Everywhere. They 31
remembered the old tale as they watched the rock grow larger, approaching it. About the woman who had a lover. Who had died in a war. She was pregnant. Lonely, desperate, she went to

Picacho, climbed to the top, jumped to her death. That was one version, the one Elena's Chicano people told.

32   There was another version, one that Ephanie's Guadalupe people told. The woman was in love with a youth she was forbidden to marry. He was a stranger, and she had fallen in love with him somehow. Maybe he was a Navajo. Maybe he was a Ute. But her love was hopeless from the start. Then the people found out that she was seeing the youth secretly. They were very angry. They scolded her. Said the things that would happen to the people because of her actions. Shamed her. Hurt and angry, she had gone to Picacho. Climbed to the top. Jumped to her death.

33   Ephanie imagined that climb. The woman finding places to put her hands. Her feet. Tentative, climbing. Tentative but sure. Shaking. She climbed to the place where the rock was narrowest. Where the drop was straight and steep. Dizzy she had stood there, thinking perhaps, of her anguish, of her rage, of her grief. Wondering, maybe, if whether what she contemplated was wise. No one knew what she had been thinking. They must have wondered about it. They must have told themselves stories about what had gone through her mind as she stood, wavering, just on the edge of the narrow rock bridge that connected the two slightly taller peaks of the formation.

34   From there she could have seen the wide sweep of the land, barren, hungry, powerful as it raised itself slow and serene toward the lower slopes of the mountains to the north beyond Picacho and was there lost to the wilderness of tabletop hills, soaring slopes, green grasses, flowers, shadows, springs, cliffs, and above them the treeless towering peak. Where it became wilderness. Where it came home.

35   She could have seen that, looking northward. Where the mountain called Ts'pin'a, Woman Veiled in Clouds, waited, brooding, majestic, almost monstrously powerful. Or she could look southward, eastward, toward the lands the people tended, that held and nurtured them. But probably she had not looked outward. Had not seen the sky, the piling, moving, thunderheads. The gold in them. The purpling blue. The dazzling, eyesplitting white. The bellies of them pregnant, ripe with rain about to be born. The living promise of their towering strength. For if she had seen them, would she have jumped.

By the time they got to the foot of the peak it was late morn-   36
ing. The sun was high and the earth around them looked flat.
Sunbitten. The shadows had retreated to cooler places for the
long day. Ephanie, slender, sturdy, brown, and Elena, slender,
sturdy, hair tinged with gold, lightly olive skin deepened almost brown by the summer sun, sat down to rest amid the grey
boulders that lay in piles at the base of the peak. They ate their
oranges. Looked at the climb that faced them, uneasy. The gray
rock soared above their heads, almost smooth. Ephanie looked
at Elena for reassurance, thinking how beautiful her friend was,
sweating, laughing. Wanting to reach out and touch her face. To
hold her hand, brown and sturdy like her own. Reached and
touched the smooth brown skin, brushed tenderly back the
gold-streaked hair.

"When we get home," she said, "let's go to the apple tree and   37
cool off."

"I can't ," Elena said. "I have to go with my mother to town.   38
We're going to stay a few days at my sister's." She looked away
from Ephanie. Looked at the ground. Ephanie felt uneasiness
crawling around in her stomach. She shifted her weight away
from Elena. She didn't know why she felt that way. "Let's go on
up," she said.

They climbed. Elena went first. Finding places to put hands   39
and feet. They pretended they were mountaineers, climbing
Mount Everest. They didn't have ropes, but they knew about
testing rock and brush before trusting weight to them. They
climbed over the boulders and up the first stage of the climb.
That part was fairly easy. It was steep, but there was a broad
abutment that circled most of the peak, as though supporting
its slender, massive skyward thrust. The abutment was hard
packed dirt, light sandstone and the gray rock, probably vol-
canic, that formed Picacho.

They came to a resting place, high above the valley floor. It   40
was very hot. They sat and looked around them. The rest of the
peak rose above them along a narrow path that rose toward it
from where they sat. A sheer drop on either side. Dizzy. Can we
cross that. They looked into each other's eyes. Daring. Testing.
Their old familiar way. "I don't think I can get across that. It
makes me dizzy," Ephanie said. Elena said, since Ephanie had
admitted her fear, "just crawl across it. That's what I'm going to

do. I'm not going to try and walk across. We can crawl. It's not far." And she began crawling across the smooth sand that lay over the rock bridge that stretched between them and the smooth curving roundness of the farther peak. "Look down," Elena said. "It's really far."

41   Ephanie, on hands and knees, crept behind Elena. Feeling foolish, scared. Foolish in her fearfulness. Shaking. She did look down. It was a long way to the ground. She imagined falling. Smashing herself on the rocks below. How Elena would manage. Going home to tell them she had fallen. How the woman long ago had fallen. From here.

42   They got across the narrow bridge and stood up, clinging to the gray rock of the highest point that rose some three feet above their feet. They climbed up on it, scooting their bodies up and then turning to lie stomach-down on the flat peak. They looked down, over the back side of the peak. Saw the mountain a few miles beyond. "Let's stand up," one of them said. They stood, trembling slightly, and looked around. They saw the villages, one north of them, the other, just beyond it to the west.

43   They rested for awhile, wishing they hadn't left the rest of the oranges down below. They realized they still had to climb back down. The part they were always forgetting. As they examined the descent, Elena said, "Ephanie, there's something I have to tell you." She didn't look at her friend. She looked at her hands. Sweating and lightly streaked where the sweat had washed some of the dust of their climb away. "I can't come over to your place anymore."

44   The sun was blazing down on them, unconcerned. It was so hot. Ephanie look at Elena's hands intently. She didn't speak for a long time. She couldn't swallow. She couldn't breathe. For some reason her chest hurt. Aching. She didn't know why. Anything.

45   She tried to think, to understand. They had been together all their lives. What did Elena mean. She wondered if it was because she had more. Of everything. Dresses, boarding school, a bigger house. A store-owner for a father. A trader.

46   Elena's father had a small cantina that he owned. But he didn't make a lot of money at it. He drove a school bus, to make ends meet.

47   Elena's house had three rooms. Besides the kitchen. They were all used for sleeping. One of them they used as a living room too.

One of them was very small, hardly large enough for the tiny iron bedstead it held. Five or six people lived there, depending on whether her brothers were both there or not. They didn't have running water, and their toilet was outdoors. Ephanie thought maybe that was what was the matter. That they were growing up. That now that they were nearing adulthood, such things mattered. Were seen in some way that caused anger, caused shame.

When Ephanie didn't say anything for so long, Elena said, "It's because my mother thinks we spend too much time with each other." She looked at Ephanie, eyes shut against her. Not closed, open, but nothing of herself coming through them. Nothing in them taking her in. Ephanie sat, thinking she was dreaming. This didn't make any sense. What could be wrong. What could be happening. How could she not see Elena. Be with her. Who would she be with then, if not Elena.   48

She put out her hand. Took hold of Elena's arm. Held it, tightly. Swaying. She looked over the side of the peak. Thought about flying. Dropping off. She thought of going to sleep.   49

She moved so that she could put her hand on Elena's arm. Held her like that, staring. Trying to speak. Not being able to. There were no words. Only too many thoughts, feelings, churning in her like the whirlwind, chindi, dust devils on the valley floor below. "What are you talking about," she finally said. Her voice sounded strange in her ears.   50

Elena tried to back away, get loose from Ephanie's hand. Pulled away, but not completely. She looked at Ephanie. Her face was wet. Beads of sweat had formed along her upper. lip. She wiped them away with the back of her hand. Her eyes looked flat, gave off no light. Her light brown eyes that were flecked with gold. Her brown face had a few freckles scattered over it. They stood out now, sharp.   51

"You know," she said, her voice low. "The way we've been lately. Hugging and giggling. You know." She looked down at her hands, twisting against themselves in her lap. "I asked the sister about that, after school. She said it was the devil. That I mustn't do anything like that. That it was a sin. And she told my mother. She says I can't come over any more."   52

Ephanie sat. Stunned. Mind empty. Stomach a cold cold stone. The hot sun blazed on her head. She felt sick. She felt herself shrinking within. Understood, wordlessly, exactly what Elena   53 was saying. How she could understand what Ephanie had not understood. That they were becoming lovers. That they were in love. That their loving had to stop. To end. That she was falling. Had fallen. Would not recover from the fall, smashing, the rocks. That they were in her, not on the ground.

54   She finally remembered to take her hand off of Elena's arm. To put it in her pocket. She stood up again. Almost lost her balance. How will we ever get down, she wondered. She couldn't see very well. She realized her eyes were blurred with tears. "Why did you do that," she said. "How could you tell anyone? How did you know, what made you ask? Why didn't you ask me." And realized the futility of her words. The enormity of the abyss she was falling into. The endless, endless depth of the void.

55   "I was scared. I thought it was wrong. It is." Elena looked at Ephanie, eyes defiant, flat and hard, closed.

56   "Then why did we come today. Why get me all the way up here and then tell me?" Ephanie felt her face begin to crumble, to give way. Like the arroyo bank gave way in the summer rains. She didn't want Elena to see her like that, giving in to anguish, to weakness, to tears.

57   "I'm sorry." That was all Elena would say.

58   They got down from the peak the way they had come, using lifelong habits of caution and practice to guide them. In silence they walked the long way back to the village. Elena went inside when they came to her house. Ephanie went the rest of the way, not so far however long it seemed, alone. She went to the apple tree and climbed up into it. Hid her face in the leaves. She sat there, hiding, for a very long time.

Personal Response

Consider close friendships you have had or still have. Respond with your memories of adventures and secrets shared. Paula Gunn Allen writes about "shared closeness" and imaginative games. What memories do you think of when reading about the two girls? Perhaps the setting makes you think of related images. Do you know of any situations where adults interfered with friendships? As usual, read with attention and focus, then respond in any way you wish.

Content Focus

1. Describe the relationship between the two girls. How are Elena and Ephanie alike and different?

2. Why does Elena wait until they have climbed to the top of the rock formation to tell Ephanie that she can't see her anymore?
3. What clues are there that suggest this may happen?
4. How does the title relate to the story?
5. Why do the two girls make the climb?

Writer's Craft

All through the story Allen uses short sentences and sentence fragments. What effect does this have? How does this create a sense of movement and action? This is a fine illustration of using the form of words and sentences to express meanings in prose, much as happens in poetry. How is the mood created? How does the author use color, light, and shadow? How are images expressed, and what do they tell us?

Same-Sex Friendships

In our society it is difficult for men to express close friendships with other men without people jumping to the conclusion that theirs is a sexual relationship. Women can more easily hug each other, hold hands, and in other ways show affection without people assuming they are homosexual—despite the experience of the two girls in "They Make Their Climb." The following reading by Peter M. Nardi is from the introduction to the book *Men's Friendships*. Nardi addresses the problem of societal misunderstanding or stereotyping of men's close friendships. Men's friendships can, of course, be sexual—that is, homosexual; but here we are looking at friendships that are close but not sexual. Men are subject to suspicion and criticism when there is a close same-sex friendship. Read the following selection and write your responses.

Seamless Souls

PETER M. NARDI

When Montaigne described friendship as "souls that mingle 1
and blend with each other so completely that they efface the
seam that joined them," he was talking about his friendship
with another man. The images of friendships in both myth
and everyday life were historically male-dominated. They were

characterized in terms of bravery, loyalty, duty, and heroism (see Hammond & Jablow, 1987). This explains why women were often seen as not capable of having "true" friendships. But today the images of ideal friendship are often expressed in terms of women's traits: intimacy, trust, caring, and nurturing, thereby excluding the more traditional men from true friendship (see Sapadin, 1988).

2   Attempts to alter how men construct their friendships on a wider cultural level involve major shifts in the way men's roles are structured and organized. For one, friendships between men in terms of intimacy and emotional support inevitably introduce —in ways they never had done before—questions about homosexuality. As Rubin (1985, p. 103) found in her interviews with men: "The association of friendship with homosexuality is so common among men." For women, there is a much longer history of close connections with other women, so that the separation of the emotional from the erotic is more easily made.

3   Lehne (1989) has argued that homophobia has limited the discussion of loving male relationships and has led to the denial by men of the real importance of their friendships with other men. In addition, "the open expression of emotion and affection by men is limited by homophobia. . . . The expression of more tender emotions among men is thought to be characteristic only of homosexuals" (p. 426). So men are raised in a culture with a mixed message: Strive for healthy, emotionally intimate friendships, but be careful—if you appear too intimate with another man you might be negatively labeled homosexual.

4   Part of this has to do with what Herek (1987) calls "heterosexual masculinity," an idea that includes such personal characteristics as independence, dominance, toughness, and success. It also is defined by what it is not—not feminine and not homosexual. Thus, to be masculine in today's culture requires a distancing from any behavior that may indicate homosexuality, including emotionally close friendships with other men.

5   This certainly wasn't always the case. As a good illustration of the social construction of masculinity, friendship, and sexuality, one need only look to the changing definitions and concepts surrounding same-sex friendship during the nineteenth century (Rotundo, 1989; Smith-Rosenberg, 1975). Romantic friendships could be erotic but not sexual, since sex was linked to reproduction. Be-

cause reproduction was not possible between two men, the close relationship was not interpreted as being a sexual one: "Until the 1880s, most romantic friendships were thought to be devoid of sexual content. Thus a woman or man could write of affectionate desire for a loved one of the same gender without causing an eyebrow to be raised" (D'Emilio & Freedman, 1988, p. 121).

However, as same-sex relationships became medicalized and   6 stigmatized in the late nineteenth-century literature, "the labels 'congenital inversion' and 'perversion' were applied not only to male sexual acts, but to sexual or romantic unions between women, as well as those between men" (D'Emilio & Freedman, 1988, p. 122). Thus, the twentieth century is an anomaly in its promotion of female equality, the encouragement of male–female friendships, and its suspicion of intense emotional friendships between men (Richards, 1987). Yet, in ancient Greece and medieval Europe, chivalry, comradeship, virtue, patriotism, and heroism were all associated with close male friendship. Manly love, as it was often called, was a central part of the definition of masculinity (Richards, 1987).

Same-sex friendship between men was highly revered in an-   7 cient Greece and during the European Renaissance. Sherrod (1987, p. 231) writes: "Based on literary sources, we can assume that educated Europeans 500 years ago, like educated Greeks 2500 years ago, held a high regard for intimate friendships." Historical evidence also suggests a high level of intimacy and romantic friendships between young men during the nineteenth century. Rotundo (1989, p. 1) quotes Daniel Webster in 1800 calling his best male friend "the partner of my joys, griefs, and affections, the only participator of my most secret thoughts." He argues that such phrases were typical of middle-class men during their youth. Friendship, beyond the companionship of boyhood, evolved into one "based on intimacy, on a sharing of innermost thoughts and secret emotions . . . a friend was a partner in sentiment as well as action" (Rotundo, p. 1).

The romantic nature of male friendships in middle-class   8 nineteenth-century America can in part be explained by the absence of words and concepts for homosexuality. Physically affectionate relationships between men and even the sharing of beds were not uncommon between young men. Since the desire to engage in sexual acts between two men was seen as something beyond human nature, a sexual connection was not made with physical touch or sleeping together. Furthermore, when homosexuality was thought about, it was almost always in terms of a particular sexual act, not an identity or personal characteristic. Rotundo concludes:

> [A] man who wished to kiss or embrace an intimate male friend in bed did not have to worry about giving way to homosexual impulses because he would not assume that he had them. In the Victorian language of touch, a kiss or an embrace was a gesture of strong affection at least as much as it was an act of sexual expression. (p. 10)

9   However, as distinctions began to be made between homosexuality and heterosexuality in the late nineteenth century—a distinction that was now seen to be rooted in a person's biological and psychological urges, not something that was an external unnatural impulse—the stigma attached to same-sex touch and intimacy grew. By the turn of the century, a form of male relationships was gone: "Romantic male friendship is an artifact of the nineteenth century" (Rotundo, p. 21).

10   In contrast, contemporary society holds a set of social meanings and prohibitions about homosexuality to such a degree that ordinary touches, and certainly the act of "sleeping together," often are interpreted in homosexual terms when they occur between two men. Thus, studies of friendship today consistently argue that close friendship is rarely experienced by men in our culture.

11   Bell (1981) believes that gender images, identities, and roles significantly limit the display of certain emotions, especially those viewed as feminine. This leads, then, to restrictions in how friendships are socially constructed. As Allan (1989, p. 73) says, "Given the dominant images there are of what being masculine entails, it is not surprising that ties of friendship between males are based around sociability rather than intimacy."

12   The changing nature of and imagery associated with male friendships over time and across culture signify the close interaction that exists between the social structure at various historical moments and the articulation of gender roles and sexuality in terms of friendship. Some of the change can be traced to the

nature of the socioeconomic and political order, especially as expressed in the world of work. Hegemonic masculinity closely involved defining labor as either "men's work" or "women's work," thus resulting in a tension between the gender order and the class order (Carrigan, Connell, & Lee, 1987).

Some of the change in definitions about masculinity and inti- 13
macy can also be linked to the relationship between men and women in different historical periods. As Kimmel (1987, p. 14) stated it: "Although both masculinity and femininity are socially constructed within a historical context of gender relations, definitions of masculinity are historically reactive to changing definitions of femininity." Thus, when changes occurred in how work was organized and how the family was structured, women's roles entered the public sphere and femininity was redefined. Given the relational nature of gender, masculinity in turn began to be reconstructed.

The emergence of sexual political movements, such as gay 14
liberation and the women's movement, in the mid- to late twentieth century was a result of these structural changes and gender redefinitions in the nineteenth century. And these movements further threatened the traditional power relationship not only between men and women but also between men and men, leading to additional questioning of the hegemonic masculinity.

But whatever the actual forces are that have created alter- 15
ations in men's roles historically, they illustrate one important thesis, namely that as definitions about masculinity change, how friendships are organized by men also is affected. Not only can this be seen historically, but it also points out the importance of looking at men's friendships as equally variable today. If the argument holds that certain social structural elements have contributed to how friendship and gender are constructed over time, then that must also apply within any one time period as well. Variations within gender, based on location within the social structure, should be evident. Allan (1989, p. 71) reasons that "men's position within the social structure tends in the main to encourage the formation of sociable relationships with others, but, at the same time, to restrict the extent to which the self is revealed in them."

The failure of most of the literature on friendship to con- 16
sider the diversity within gender has led to the global differences

traditionally presented in the literature. Women's friends are seen as expressive and men's as instrumental. "Face-to-face" characterizes women's friendship patterns, while "side by side" describes men's. Caldwell and Peplau (1982), in their study of college students' friendships, found that both men and women desired intimacy in their friendships, but differed in what that meant. Men were nearly twice as likely as women to say they preferred "doing some activity" with their best friend and sought a friend who "likes to do the same things." Women chose "just talking" with a friend and someone who "feels the same way about things" as more important aspects of their intimate friendships.

17   Similar findings are reported when it comes to issues related to disclosure. Davidson and Duberman (1982, p. 817) claim that women disclose more personal information about self, yet "men *perceive* that they are being open and trusting, even though they report little investment in the personal and relational levels of the friendship." But Allan (1989, p. 66) warns that we must be careful in making conclusions about global gender differences in the absence of a more complex analysis of other social structural influences:

> There is, of course, a danger here of "reifying" gender differences by underplaying the other factors which shape people's friendships. . . . [I]n order to analyse friendship satisfactorily it is necessary to examine the range of social and economic factors that pattern an individual's immediate social environment, rather than focusing solely on any particular one. . . . [F]riendship is certainly influenced by gender, but exactly in what way depends on the interaction there is with the other factors that collectively shape the personal space for sociability that people have.

18   What is needed, therefore, is an analysis of the differences within each of the genders and the social forces that shape the ways friendship is organized.

References

Allan, G. (1989). *Friendship: Developing a sociological perspective.* Boulder, CO: Westview.

Bell, R. (1981). *Worlds of friendship.* Beverly Hills, CA: Sage.

Caldwell, M., & Peplau, L. A. (1982). Sex differences in same-sex friendships. *Sex Roles 8*(7), 721–732.

Carrigan, T., Connell, R., & Lee, J. (1987). Hard and heavy: Toward a new sociology of masculinity. In M. Kaufman (Ed.), *Beyond patriarchy* (pp. 139–192). Toronto: Oxford University Press.

Davidson, L., & Duberman, L. (1982). Friendship: Communication and interactional patterns in same-sex dyads. *Sex Roles, 8*(8), 809–822.

D'Emilio, J., & Freedman, E. (1988). *Intimate matters: A history of sexuality in America.* New York: Harper & Row.

Gilmore, D. (1990). *Manhood in the making: Cultural concepts of masculinity.* New Haven, CT: Yale University Press.

Hammond, D., & Jablow, A. (1987). Gilgamesh and the Sundance Kid: The mythology of friendship. In H. Brod (Ed.), *The making of masculinities: The new men's studies* (pp. 241–258). Boston: Allen & Unwin.

Herek, G. (1987). On heterosexual masculinity: Some physical consequences of the social construction of gender and sexuality. In M. Kimmel (Ed.), *Changing men: New directions in research on men and masculinity* (pp. 68–82). Newbury Park, CA: Sage.

Kimmel, M. (1987). Rethinking "masculinity": New directions in research. In M. Kimmel (Ed.), *Changing men: New directions in research on men and masculinity* (pp. 9–24). Newbury Park, CA: Sage.

Lehne, G. (1989). Homophobia among men: Supporting and defining the male role. In M. Kimmel & M. Messner (Eds.), *Men's lives* (pp. 416–429). New York: Macmillan.

Richards, J. (1987). "Passing the love of women": Manly love and Victorian society. In J. A. Mangan & J. Walvin (Eds.), *Manliness and morality: Middle-Class masculinity in Britain and America 1800–1940* (pp. 92–122). Manchester, England: Manchester University Press.

Rotundo, A. (1989). Romantic friendships: Male intimacy and middle-class youth in the northern United States, 1800–1900. *Journal of Social History, 23*(1), 1–25.

Rubin, L. (1985). *Just friends: The role of friendship in our lives.* New York: Harper & Row.

Sapadin, L. (1988). Friendship and gender: Perspectives of professional men and women. *Journal of Social and Personal Relationships, 5*(4), 387–403.

Sherrod, D. (1987). The bonds of men: Problems and possibilities in close male relationships. In H. Brod (Ed.), *The making of masculinities: The new men's studies* (pp. 213–239). Boston: Allen & Unwin.

Smith-Rosenberg, C. (1975). The female world of love and ritual: Relations between women in nineteenth-century America. *Signs, 1*(1), 1–29.

Personal Response

What personal experiences and knowledge would lead you to agree or disagree with Peter Nardi? Why might women have an easier time than men with close relationships? In what ways are your own views represented in our society, and to what extent? In what ways, if any, has homophobia affected same-sex relationships you have?

Content Focus

1. How are men's and women's roles changing?
2. How does this relate to friendships and societal expectations?
3. What would cause an increase of hegemonic masculinity?
4. What do you see as the present situation for men and women's roles and friendships?
5. Nardi quotes an author who cautions against drawing global conclusions about a complicated issue. Explain why Nardi endorses this caution.

Writer's Craft

Nardi uses many references in his essay. What effect does this have? In the writing assignment at the end of this chapter, you will be asked to include references for your sourced material. Examine closely Nardi's use of references so as to gain a sense of when to use them in your own writing. Nardi uses historical evidence to illustrate his point. Does this strengthen his case? Explain how it does or does not.

Writing Activity: Friendships and Gender

In a short paper, describe the benefits to you of having close friendships with both men and women. Then, as a group, compile a list of the benefits (or the problems) of same-sex and two-gender relationships.

Friendships between Men and Women

The following reading by David R. Eyler and Andrea P. Baridon explores the relationships between men and women in the workplace. How are personal relationships changing in our current society? Is it possible to have sexual attraction without a sexual relationship when two people spend a great deal of time together? How does one define this type of friendship?

Far More Than Friendship

DAVID R. EYLER, PH.D.,
AND ANDREA P. BARIDON

Our ways of living and loving have changed radically in the   1
last decade. Today men and women are thrust together on the
job, sharing the workplace in equal numbers and, increasingly
often, as professional peers. Work is becoming a major source of
intimate interaction between them as they daily share the physical proximity of working side by side, the stimulation of professional challenge, and the powerful passions of accomplishment
and failure.

Like every other kind of intimacy, the workplace variety   2
brings with it the likelihood of sexual attraction. It is natural. It
is inevitable, hard-wired as we are to respond to certain kinds of
stimuli, although it sometimes comes as a surprise to those it
strikes. But sexual attraction in the office is virtually inevitable
for other reasons as well: The workplace is an ideal pre-screener,
likely to throw us together with others our own age having similar socioeconomic and educational backgrounds, similar sets of
values, and similar aspirations.

It also offers countless opportunities for working friendships   3
to develop. As teams come to dominate the structure of the
business world, the other half of a business team is increasingly
likely to be not only a colleague with complementary skills and
interests, but an attractive member of the opposite sex. As close
as the collaboration between men and women workers can get
at the office, it may be even more so outside it, as workers today
function in an extended workplace of irregular hours and non-
office settings. We are now more likely than ever, for example,
to share the intimate isolation of business travel.

Such opportunity for interaction between the sexes is, in the   4
grand scheme of things, really rather new. Only in the last 20
years, particularly the last 10, have women worked in equal
numbers with men, and as equals rather than subordinates.
Traditionally, society limits the opportunities for relationships
between the sexes—how it does so is typically one of the dis-
tinguishing features of a culture. Until recently, unmarried men
and women who were attracted to each other could date, court,

or marry without raising eyebrows. For attracted couples who were already committed to others, the only option was to avoid each other or give in to an affair that consumed great energy just to be kept secret. So new is our sharing of the workplace that we have not yet created rules or social structures for dealing with today's unfamiliar intermixture of men and women working together.

5   The problem is not that sexual attraction inhabits the workplace, but that the options we traditionally give ourselves for recognizing that passion are far too limited. Conventional thinking tells us there is only one place to take our sexual feelings—to bed together. The modern American mind equates sexual attraction with sexual intercourse—the word "sex" serves as a synonym for physical contact. But intercourse is only one possible outcome among many.

6   Sexual attraction can be managed. It is not only possible to acknowledge sexual attraction, but also to enjoy the energy generated by it—and without acting on it sexually. The positive energy of sexual attraction is instead focused on work as it pulls men and women into a process of discovery, creativity and productivity. This thinking is part of a broader ethic emerging in this country: It's possible to have a lot without having it all.

7   We propose a new, psychologically unique relationship for which no models currently exist in American culture. It is a positive way for men and women to share intimate feelings outside of marriage or an illicit affair. It rejects altogether the saint-or-sinner model of colleague relations as too simplistic for modern life. In our own work as management consultants, we see the new relationship slowly unfolding in the American workplace. Confused coworkers, lacking guidance of any kind but responding to today's workplace realities, are stumbling toward new ways of relating to each other as they find the old alternatives too confining or otherwise unacceptable. The relationship they are inventing is not quite romantic—but it's not Platonic, either. It adds a dimension of increased intimacy to friendship and removes the sexual aspect from love. We call this relationship More than Friends, Less than Lovers.

8   The new sexually energized but strictly working relationship has already been officially documented. In a study conducted recently by researchers at the University of Michigan, 22

percent of managers reported involvement in such a relationship. Moreover, the relationship, unleashing as it does a great deal of creative energy, was shown to benefit both "couple" and company. And a study at the University of North Dakota found that work teams composed of men and women were more productive than those of same-sex colleagues.

Whatever else, of this we are sure: The new nonsexual love 9 lacks a place among people's traditional expectations. We find that women seem to intuitively understand this new relationship when they learn of it. They are often the ones who move to forge it, often out of the wreckage of a colleague's awkward attempts at something sexual. But men often have a hard time with the idea . . . at first. The conventional models for sexual behavior prescribe a course of sexual conquest for men (seduction for women) and, moreover, they have a large ego-investment in it. Men find it harder to give up the deeply ingrained macho model. They deny that they can be anything other than a successful lover. Nevertheless, we have often observed two people approach this new relationship with unmatched expectations and move to mutually acceptable middle ground—and both benefit. To men we say: Count to 10 and hear us through.

We believe that sexual attraction among certain coworkers is 10 inevitable. The laws of probability alone guarantee that the new gender parity will create a lot of sexual attraction at work that will need an outlet. The new commonplace of shared assignments provides natural opportunities for intimate communication between men and women and nurtures attractions that might have languished for lack of proximity or initiative. As always, some people will pursue sexual attraction to love and/or marriage. Others will become involved in affairs that have potential costs to careers and to other, established relationships outside. But the vast majority will not want or need a romantic relationship at work. We think it is time to bring sexual attraction out of the office closet and let it find its motivational and creative application in people's professional lives.

Left with the old thinking alone, however, in which the only 11 outlet for sexual attraction is physical sex, frustrated attraction has an unwelcome way of turning up as sexual harassment. We all need a way of thinking about sexual attraction that offers us more of a choice than consummation or harassment.

12   There is another incentive for welcoming this new, intimate relationship. Traditional thinking assumes there is only one appropriate place for sexual attraction—between lovers or spouses. But that leads to an untenable burden on our primary relationships—the spouses or lovers with whom we share it all romantically and sexually. As seasoned observers, we believe that it is naive to assume that a single intimate relationship will fulfill us in every way. As busy people leading complex lives outside the home, we cannot expect our primary relationships to also bear the burden of providing total personal and professional satisfaction. We need to grow comfortable loving one person romantically and deeply valuing another intellectually, artistically, or in any of a variety of ways that do not diminish our commitment to a primary partner.

13   The term "consenting adults" needs broadening to include not just those who willingly share physical sex, but those who are open to the possibility of acknowledging their sexual attraction, communicating openly about their feelings, and enjoying their sexuality within mutually agreed-upon boundaries. Above all, the new relationship is a limited relationship. You may share moments of great personal revelation and intimacy, but you do not expect to share your bodies and souls. That leaves only one question: How do you get there?

14   Don and Alicia are attorneys with complementary specialties who work for the same firm and have for years crisscrossed the country taking depositions and building cases together. They share grueling work schedules, meals, hours of strapped-in airliner conversation, and even exercise regimens that overlap away from home. When they put away the briefcases, they look like a couple, and at times they act like one.

15   As is commonly the case, neither can cite any lightning bolts that signalled the beginning of an irresistible attraction between them. Because events dictated their time together, the attraction developed slowly and naturally: they didn't deliberately cultivate it. The fact that they found each other interesting was almost incidental—at the beginning. Now, either will admit the other is good company, attractive, and worthy of a fantasy from time to time. An affair is the last thing they need as partnership looms for each, Don awaits the birth of a child in a happy marriage, and Alicia knows in her heart that he isn't the right guy for her.

In the course of their relationship they talked about affairs,   16
but consciously decided not to have one. At the same time, neither of them wanted a relationship that had been neutered, and
both acknowledged a desire to enjoy the sexual spark between
them, keep it within their chosen boundaries, and continue
working together without falling in love or having sex. Instead,
they deliberately cultivated an intimacy that everyone came to
recognize as special but not romantic.

Neither partner had to overcome the clumsy advances of the   17
other, yet this successful resolution of a modern-workplace attraction came about as the result of an emerging sexual etiquette.
It says we can talk about sex without inviting advances or harassing one another. It offers mutual respect and open communication as alternatives to playing out the old stereotypes of
seduction and conquest. It offers the interpersonal sophistication
to deal with sexual feelings in other than a romance-novel mode.

Since 1983, we have been working together as management   18
trainers. As we traveled around the country, gathering experience with the problems people were having, meeting workers of
all kinds, we learned some things about the new gender-mixed
work force. Alicia and Don's experience is becoming increasingly common. Women like Alicia tell us, "With Don, it didn't
happen overnight. We've spent enough time together to develop
the kind of trust and mutual respect that will let us talk about it.
I know how to say no, and he would never force himself on me.
I trust him completely, and there's no reason we can't enjoy an
attraction that's fun and energizing without ending up in bed."

And men like Don acknowledge that "part of me says it's all   19
or nothing when I have sexual feelings about a woman. But another part of me says it's more complicated than that with someone like Alicia. Somehow it has to be possible to play safely with
sexy feelings, enjoy them, and still not have to sleep together."

A New Sexual Etiquette

On the basis of our experience, we have developed a practical,   20
two-person model of sexual etiquette for those who wish to ex-
ploit the energy of workplace attraction without physical sex or
falling in love, or avoiding each other altogether and pretending
that the workplace is genderless. At its heart is a consciously

managed relationship founded on mutual trust, respect, and acceptable boundaries that are openly agreed on, communicated, and monitored by both parties. Unlike friends, these partners share moments of great personal revelation. But unlike lovers, they do not expect to share bodies and souls. They divulge only what they choose to.

21   Natural human desire is something any two people should be able to feel without guilt or awkwardness. Where we set our boundaries is what distinguishes committed, romantic relationships from the near loving feeling of those who come to know each other intimately through work. These are the five keys to pulling off the new relationship:

22   *Setting boundaries.* Our personal boundaries are the psychological barriers that define us as individuals. You need a strong sense of your own values and purpose to risk sharing them intimately with someone else—even more so when you rely on your boundaries to permit tremendous personal intimacy yet prevent its becoming physical. You and your partner openly discuss and decide what is and is not off-limits.

23   You establish boundaries and expectations for the relationship right at the outset, as a means for defining and consciously managing it. You agree that you will not develop a personal life together and that your relationship will not be allowed to become a love affair. Some boundaries, notably the sexual one, are lines you agree never to cross; they remain forever out of bounds. Similarly, neither physical contact nor the language of lovers has a place in the relationship—they will only send misunderstood signals.

24   Other boundaries may be set and changed as you grow safe and comfortable in this new, unfamiliar relationship: defining the kinds of situations in which you allow yourselves to be alone, discussing certain facets of your personal lives, the giving and accepting of compliments, allowing your partner to see you when you are not at your best, and admitting the high value you place on the relationship without fear of being misunderstood.

25   You will also have internal boundaries to contend with—very personal ones you set and maintain without the knowledge of your partner. These are the lines you draw for monitoring your own thoughts and behavior; coping with near-love feelings is a personal matter each partner handles in his/her own way.

Part of the contract between you is an agreement to respect   26
each other's privacy and individual identities. Situations may
arise when you feel you must reinforce a boundary; you can do
it indirectly, by altering the direction of a conversation, or directly, by discussing the unwelcome inquiry openly, as part of
the process of consciously managing your relationship.

Conscious management. There are no sure paths to ideal   27
relationships between mutually attracted men and women
under any circumstances. But without conscious management
of this relationship, personal attraction can lead to destructive
consequences—from ruined marriages to tainted professional
reputations. Consciously managed, the relationship becomes a
series of purposeful, directed events, rather than random ones
that could drift into unplanned physical intimacy. You expect
to have differences that you will resolve openly, instead of
dancing around issues and leaving them open to ambiguity.

Through discussion, you create a voluntary contract in which   28
you both agree that you will divert your sexual energy from
personal attraction between you to the working relationship
supporting it. You agree that your attraction is a positive thing
that makes your working relationship exciting. You define
ways to behave that will help you maintain your mutual
boundaries. You communicate honestly with each other about
your feelings and expectation. You make no attempt to hide
the relationship from your spouse or lover on the one hand, or
your company managers on the other, although you maintain
discretion.

At first, you will probably find it difficult and awkward to   29
discuss the emotional issues involved in creating and managing this relationship. It's new and unfamiliar turf and you're
not sure what constitutes the right measure of trust. Your best
guide is to sense when tension builds—that's when something
needs to be brought into the open for honest discussion.

Monitoring each other. Two people seldom approach a   30
relationship—any relationship—with perfectly matched expectations. You and your partner both know that adjustments in your
behavior will sometimes be necessary to keep things on an even
keel. You share the responsibility for keeping your own behavior,
feelings and expectations in line with the boundaries you establish. Monitoring each other ensures that open communication

takes place when you sense your partner may infringe on a boundary or yield to temptation.

31   Monitoring each other also sets the expectation of open communication. You come to your relationship with respect for each other's intellect, tastes, and competencies. You look to each other to supplement what you individually bring to your work—to stimulate your thinking and enhance your creativity.

32   *Open discussion.* You are making deliberate use of sexual chemistry to become both more personally satisfied and more successful and productive. The overarching technique you use to keep behavior within the boundaries you set is open discussion. It short-circuits problems that tend to build with time. Instead of maintaining the relationship by one-sided internal coping, you raise concerns to the level of two-person reasoning.

33   You clarify areas of misunderstanding where individual interpretations of events or intentions may be wrong. In time, you'll probably be laughing at simple misunderstandings. You vent frustrations to each other as well as understanding and being understood—eliminating the need to reject and the pain of rejection. The secret is not some perfect progression through an ideal set of relationship-building steps, but rather in the openness that says, "Ask me. Let's talk about it. We can work this out."

34   *Cooling-off periods.* Unlike husbands and wives, you have the advantage of regular time-outs from each other, away from a nonphysical but demanding association. In permanent relationships, a large tolerance quotient is both desirable and required. In this relationship, by contrast, you are not obligated to keep each other happy or to take care of each other or to tolerate differences in food or music or television preferences on a daily and nightly basis. You deny yourselves some of the privileges of a fully committed couple while you avoid some of their frictions.

35   On the rare occasions when work isn't going well, or your conscious management techniques are flagging, you can acknowledge this is not going to be the right day to accomplish much together and step back to a comfortable distance.

36   On the good days, this relationship fosters inspired work that is intense, demanding and fulfilling. When it ends, parting involves ambivalence. You enjoy what you do so you are reluctant to stop, but you feel a sense of relief in getting away for a

time to relax and be nourished in different ways with your family and friends. Down time spent apart allows you to keep a view of your work partner as someone special.

The "Business Couple"

Nothing promises to replace the committed love of a primary   37
relationship. But the bottom line is that men and women working closely together find themselves in relationships that in many ways mimic courtship and marriage. They ride the emotional roller coaster of success and failure side by side. They become interdependent. They think alike and share values. Common goals emerge and are met through mutual effort. They have a de facto marriage minus the morning breath, the kids' problems and the mortgage payments. Fresh tailored clothes, a perpetually clean-shaven face, and a crisp clean shirt spare coworkers the gritty reality that personal appearances take on at home.

As pretty as this picture looks, however, a review of life's pri-   38
orities quickly suggests to participants what it lacks. Coworkers who are more than friends come to realize that their work partner is not the one who takes care of them when they are sick, who shares the joys of the children, who wakes them up on Christmas morning. They take part in none of the life activities that make their at-home romantic relationships primary and their work relationships secondary. Above all, the privilege of discarding boundaries that separate individuals, the free merging of two people, is exclusive to the primary relationship.

Loving center-of-our-lives arrangements remain the source   39
of our deepest satisfactions sexually and otherwise, but secondary relationships provide treasured qualities of narrow depth and exclusive experience not found elsewhere, especially since professional interests are dominant factors in our identities. They allow discovery and elaboration of parts of ourselves that remain unexplored in other relationships—passions for art or music or sports, say. One very sober "business couple" we know discovered to their vast amusement that they are both avid Elvis fans. On a business trip to Memphis they decided to use their free time to visit Graceland, simply because it's there—something their mates wouldn't do for money.

Good Work Is Sexy

40   "Business couples" breathe life into their projects together. They find themselves struggling to make them survive. They grieve when they fail. And they revel in the joy of what they've created in their intense interaction. They may travel together closing deals, winning accolades, recounting victorious days together. Good work is sexy!

41   Michelle and Kevin are intimates but not lovers. They are experimental chemists in the new-products division of a pharmaceutical company. They think and plan and dispute ideas together, then defend their ideas in the corporate world with an intensity known only to people who have shared insight. There is a magic between them that transcends chemical formulas and careers, and each of them knows it.

42   Sometimes they look at each other after completing an important thought in unison and, without words, communicate an appreciation for one another that unknowing observers might misconstrue as love. Their lab technique is a symphony of moves developed through countless hours of teamwork—they know each other's professional souls, anticipate their every move, and sometimes it looks and feels very personal. But it isn't, and they know it. When work ends, Michelle is totally absorbed in a life all her own with seldom a thought of her lab partner. In it she shares loving intimacy with another partner who doesn't know a beaker from a Petri dish, but knows her like no one else does, not even Kevin, who has a fulfilling personal life of his own.

Satisfaction

43   We recently talked with Judy and Mark, two industrial trainers who were among the earliest subjects in our investigation of nonloving intimates. We asked them how their arrangement could be so special and sustained and still not have eclipsed their romantic relationships—as many who react to our model suggest it must.

44   "It's terribly unscientific," Mark began, "but anyone who has ever been in love knows what it feels like—and the two of us have just never felt that way about each other. Fascination, respect, some lust from time to time, but never love."

"We care a lot for each other, and we appreciate each other as   45
colleagues, even find each other sexy," Judy added.

"Sexual chemistry was there at the beginning and still is,   46
after a fashion," explains Mark. "It made us special, and it still
does. Things can get complicated when animal attraction occasionally gets mixed in with real caring, but it all amounts to
something less than an irresistible force for us.

"The thoughts of fulfilling an already satisfying relationship   47
come and go, but there's been no real pain in not acting on
them. There has been honest frustration sometimes, but when
work ends and we part company, neither longs for the other or
gets jealous of the people we each go home to."

"The special times have always come when we're putting   48
everything we've got into a project," notes Judy. Over time, the
power of sexual attraction is not diminished, but they gain
more experience and skill in handling it.

Company Benefits

What partners get out of nonloving intimacy is clear. Their   49
relationship is amazingly satisfying psychologically, and very
workable. They pursue their work with an abandon they never
could afford if they were lovers who had to get along both at
work and at home. They do genuinely inspired work together
and honestly love it, their creative energy flowing from a sexual
attraction they've chosen not to indulge physically or force into
love. They have friends and family at home, where they recharge
themselves.

Companies also benefit. They get highly motivated workers   50
who are enthusiastic and happy. The relationship enhances creativity. And partners are not deceiving anyone or stealing work
time. They waste no energy on feeling guilty.

Men and women bring differing and complementary orien-   51
tations to shared work. A tremendous amount of energy can
flow from their sex-based differences when they are allowed to
keep their sexual identities, rather than suppress them in con-
formance with the corporate ideal of a safe, genderless workplace. Nonsexual intimates willingly spend time together to
achieve great results—and avoid behavior that would threaten
the relationship.

52   And so love is much as it's always been. Sexual, romantic love has been and will be the many splendored thing, driven by a desire for fusion and physical intimacy and achieving that blurring of boundaries that takes place only in sex. But our model promises legitimacy for what many men and women have felt but dared not admit or act on—the reality that sexual chemistry can be safely shared with an associate and play a constructive role in their lives.

53   It works because what has changed the workplace has crept onto the domestic scene as well. The days of insecure spouses who waited at home has passed, part of the revolution that has swept women into jobs in large numbers. Simply put, peers understand peers. Newly equal husbands, wives and lovers accept what they know from common experience —colleagues may be sorely tempted to become lovers, but they will settle for being more than friends. The trust that makes it all possible is, after all, the only valid measure of romantic fidelity.

Personal Response

Respond to the idea that a relationship, while not Platonic, may not be romantic either. What are your experiences and thoughts? David Eyler and Andrea Baridon suggest that the sexual aspect makes the work team more productive. Do you think this special intimacy exists in other situations too—for instance, in college life?

Content Focus

1. How do the authors' descriptions compare to conventional assumptions?
2. Why is sexual attraction "inevitable"?
3. What features of today's workplace favor the kind of relationship the authors describe?
4. What are the benefits of these relationships?
5. Describe the emerging sexual etiquette. What is it founded on?

Writer's Craft

What is Eyler and Baridon's thesis, and where is it stated? The opening paragraphs make a strong statement. Taking a stand at the beginning catches readers' interest, especially if people are apt to disagree. How do the illustrations of people's experiences strengthen the authors' thesis?

Writing Activity: Opinion Letter

Write a paper in the form of a letter to Eyler and Baridon. Agree or disagree with their findings and opinions. Use a style similar to theirs.

Definition Pattern of Development

A definition paper entails far more than defining a word by looking it up in a dictionary. To truly define a word or a concept means to explain your personal interpretation and understanding. Writers include their views to bring new understandings to readers. Meanings come from people's interpretations, not from words. Words can mean different things to individuals, even when used in the same context. Misunderstandings about meanings happen frequently when people come from other countries or from different regions of a country. But even if people share the same background, words do not always have identical meanings. For example, what does *cold* mean? Or *family, friendship, relationship, love, hate*—what does each of these terms mean to you? Your interpretation isn't a matter of being right or wrong because meaning comes from our experiences and knowledge.

Definitions are often asked for on exams. "What does _____ mean?" "What is the difference between *x* and *y*?" What is required to answer questions such as these is a definition: what something is and what it is not; how something works or interacts. Defining is a way of explaining what one knows about a subject.

Definitions are important in the workplace. One must have a clear idea of what is meant and must be able to explain clearly to others. Vague explanations and unclear meanings may cause serious problems in job situations as well as in personal relationships.

WRITING ASSIGNMENT: DEFINITION PAPER

Your assignment for this chapter is to write a definition paper. You may wish to define friendship in general, or to define what a good friend is. Your paper does not have to be on the topic of friends, however; it might be on stereotypes, equality between genders, societal pressure, peer pressure, or any topics your instructor suggests.

When you are writing a definition paper, it is important to explain exactly what is being defined and the limitations of your definition—under what circumstances this definition is valid. Your introduction could lead off with the etymology of the word and the dictionary meaning. Examples, comparisons and contrasts, and illustrations help to clarify and expand the meanings.

Using Sources

For this assignment you are required to use outside sources. You can use the readings included in Part Three of this book, or you can draw upon other sources. Read over the selections and your responses for examples that support your views or illustrate a point you are making.

You must give credit to other writers' ideas or words. To fail to do so is to plagiarize, a serious mistake. To give credit to another's work is to document where it came from. Use documentation whether you quote directly, paraphrase, or summarize someone else's words and ideas. A writer must include the name(s) of the author(s) of outside sources and information on where the material came from. There are two places to include documentation:

1. In-text citations within the body of the paper (author names)
2. At the end of the paper in a list of sources (where the material came from)

Styles of Documentation

How you will document depends on which documentation style your class is using. The student papers in this book all use the MLA (Modern Language Association) style of documentation. The Nardi article in this chapter used APA (American Psychological Association) style. Your instructor will select the documentation style for you to use, such as APA, *The Chicago Manual of Style,* or CBE (Council of Biology Editors) style. The required style usually depends on the subject matter. For instance, journals for academic fields use styles appropriate for the subject. The biological sciences use CBE; English and languages use MLA; social sciences use APA. When you write for your college classes, the documentation style will reflect the subject. Always ask your instructor what style to use. Whatever style an instructor requires, use only that one. Do not combine styles.

Because you need to know and use more than one style, it is essential that you own a general handbook, such as *The Allyn & Bacon Handbook* or one your instructor suggests. Documentation has many intricacies, and it is important to know where and how to look up the specifics.

Process of Writing

Begin writing your definition paper by using one or more discovery techniques until you have a clear idea of the direction of the definition. Write a first draft. Looking through your readings and responses, select what you want to include in your paper; choose at least two sources to cite. Write another draft incorporating the sources. Revise once on your own, then bring the paper to your writing group for help in revision. Shown here is an example of a response guide for a definition paper.

Response Guide for Definition Paper

1. How can the writer make the introduction or first paragraph more interesting to readers?
2. Are there ways in which the thesis could be more decisive and/or more precise?
3. How is the definition clarified?
4. Where would additional examples and illustrations strengthen the paper?
5. Do the sources flow well into the text? What suggestions do you have for ways to make the sources more natural and helpful?
6. Discuss with everyone in the group the validity and depth of the definition.
7. Make suggestions for improving the paper.

Four

Families

"Writing our lives" is the theme of this book, and families are very much a part of our lives, regardless of the kind of family one has. The word *family* does not have one definition or meaning. For many years, even when reality informed us otherwise, the common consensus was that a family was two parents (a man and a woman) and two or three children. People now look at what makes a family with a more realistic sense of what the word means.

According to the 1992 Census Bureau report, nearly half of the households in the United States did not include a married couple. About one in five families was headed by a single woman or man. The U.S. government still defines *family* as a household that includes people related to each other by marriage, birth, or adoption. But what was once considered traditional has changed.

Whatever type of family you come from, are a part of now, or plan for the future, all family structures share common attributes: caring, responsibility, and nurturing. The degrees of these attributes vary considerably from one family to another, however. A healthy family relies on the mutual caring of all members regardless of sexual preferences, blood ties, or balance of genders. People are a family when they take care of one another and help family members develop a healthy sense of self-esteem.

In Part Four, we focus first on parents and children, then on relationships in families, and finally on the effect of birth order. Discussions on family relationships explore not only our own families but others' experiences as well; a broad understanding of family will emerge from the readings, responses, discussions, and writings. Part Four includes the writing patterns of process analysis, argumentation–persuasion, and cause and effect. The cause-and-effect paper is a group writing experience.

8

Parents and Children

The relationships between children and parents change radically throughout our lifetime. Those of you who are parents are vividly aware of how dependent children are on their parents. How could it be otherwise when the child is an infant? We probably do not recall the time when we ourselves had to depend on a parent for our basic needs in order to survive. We do remember, though, when that dependency began to chafe and we began to pull away and seek more independence. That change happens at different ages and in various ways, but it is necessary if we are to become self-sufficient adults.

Growing Independence

The first reading is Phyllis McGinley's poem about a girl realizing how difficult it is for a parent to accept the growing independence of children.

First Lesson

PHYLLIS MCGINLEY

The thing to remember about fathers is, they're men.
A girl has to keep it in mind.
They are dragon-seekers, bent on improbable rescues.
Scratch any father, you find
Someone chock-full of qualms and romantic terrors,   5
Believing change is a threat—
Like your first shoes with heels on, like your first bicycle
It took such months to get.

Walk in strange woods, they warn you about the snakes there.

10   Climb, and they fear you'll fall.
Books, angular boys, or swimming in deep water—
Fathers mistrust them all.
Men are the worriers. It is difficult for them
To learn what they must learn:

15   How you have a journey to take and very likely,
For a while, will not return.

Personal Responses

Respond with thoughts or feelings about your relationship with your father or stepfather. Write either from a parent's or a child's viewpoint. One theme you might explore is that of the child's independence versus the parent's fears for the child.

Content Focus

1. What "improbable rescues" might a father think he has to make?
2. Why are they improbable?
3. The poet speaks of "romantic terrors." What do you think she means?
4. What is it the father mistrusts? Go beyond the obvious in your answer.
5. Who is learning the "first lesson" in Phyllis McGinley's poem? Explain your answer.

Writer's Craft

Using the child's viewpoint, McGinley sketches the dependent/independent roles of child and parent in only a few lines and captures the essence of the relationship. One could write a two-page essay to accomplish the same result.

Writing Activity: Viewpoint

Write a paragraph or two about an aspect of child/parent relationships. Then choose only the essential ideas and rewrite in a poetic form. For example, you might want to use the same topic as McGinley, but write from the adult's viewpoint.

Across Generations

The next reading is also on the topic of understandings and connections across generations within families.

Like Mother, Like Daughter

SUSAN S. JACOBSON

"When are you coming?"
"On Sunday, why?"
"Because I want to get
some things, make the bed . . ."
"Oh, Mom," she said.   5
I felt an echo in me:
I had made the beds
just the week before
on a visit to my mother's,
because of her back.   10
Always before she had,
but now I did, knowing
where everything was:
I had moved her there.

Looking for recipes   15
of dishes my daughter likes,
I found the ones for meals
I had made my mother,
in her new kitchen,
and put them away   20
like an echo in a drawer.
Reviewing their ways,
looking for similarities
in their rhythms
(there were none);   25
I weighed them against
my need to be alone.

I am related to neither now
(their blue eyes are so dissimilar)
30   and yet I am their link.
There are echoes back
and forth through me:
I live alone, as do
my mother and my daughter,
35   none of us in the house
where we were raised or
spent our marriages.
Each of us is careful
of the others, unyielding
40   in small significant ways.

I now mother my mother
when I can no longer
mother my daughter
who is older than I
45   have ever felt myself to be.

Personal Response

Think of relationships you have with older and younger family members and how the relationships have changed over time—perhaps your relationship with your father or mother, a younger sister or brother, or grandparents. Relationships are not static but always changing, especially those involving different generations. Our roles, expectations, responsibilities, and sense of power change over time. Write about your experiences and your thoughts about these relationships.

Content Focus

1. How does Susan Jacobson illustrate the changing roles among the three women?
2. What does the daughter mean when she says, "Oh, Mom"?
3. What links are there between the woman's feelings for her mother and her daughter?
4. What does she mean by "I am related to neither now"?
5. In what way does the final stanza explain how the woman feels?

Writer's Craft

Jacobson uses the word *echo* in three stanzas. How does this affect the meaning and mood? Repeated words and phrases are used for emphasis and with only a few words can create powerful feelings and reactions in readers. How is *echo* used here? The last stanza has no punctuation until the final period. Read the poem aloud to understand how this contributes to the meaning.

Writing Activity: A Shift in Relationships

Write a short piece on the shift of power and responsibility between a parent and child—of any age. You could use a comparison–contrast form or a description pattern. If you would like to try a different pattern or structure, you could write an "I used to—but now" poem. For example,

> I used to wish I was strong like my father,
> But now I can pick him up.

The following student example by Jessa Olien illustrates this form.

STUDENT PAPER

I USED TO . . . , BUT NOW

Jessa Olien

I used to pick dandelions,
>   but now I hope to pull them.

I used to wear mittens,
>   but now I wear makeup.

I used to take pictures with my Fisher-Price camera,
>   but now I take pictures in my mind.

I used to be deaf to others,
>   but now their cries fill my ears like rain.

I used to cry when I stubbed my toe,
>   but now I will not cry for myself.

```
I used to hold on to my mother for security,
    but now the objects and people I know are
    intangible.
I used to want things,
    but now I want contact.
```

Changing Roles

The final reading for this chapter, as story by Leslie Norris, illustrates how roles change for a boy growing into manhood and his father.

Shaving

———

LESLIE NORRIS

1   Earlier, when Barry had left the house to go to the game, an overnight frost had still been thick on the roads, but the brisk April sun had soon dispersed it, and now he could feel the spring warmth on his back through the thick tweed of his coat. His left arm was beginning to stiffen up where he'd jarred it in a tackle, but it was nothing serious. He flexed his shoulders against the tightness of his jacket and was surprised again by the unexpected weight of his muscles, the thickening strength of his body. A few years back, he thought, he had been a small, unimportant boy, one of a swarming gang laughing and jostling to school, hardly aware that he possessed an identity. But time had transformed him. He walked solidly now, and often alone. He was tall, strongly made, his hands and feet were adult and heavy, the rooms in which all his life he'd moved had grown too small for him. Sometimes a devouring restlessness drove him from the house to walk long distances in the dark. He hardly understood how it had happened. Amused and quiet, he walked the High Street among the morning shoppers.

2   He saw Jackie Bevan across the road and remembered how, when they were both six years old, Jackie had swallowed a pin. The flustered teachers had clucked about Jackie as he stood

there, bawling, cheeks awash with tears, his nose wet. But now Jackie was tall and suave, his thick, pale hair sleekly tailored, his gray suit enviable. He was talking to a girl as golden as a daffodil.

"Hey, hey!" called Jackie. "How's the athlete, how's Barry   3
boy?"

He waved a graceful hand at Barry.   4

"Come and talk to Sue," he said.   5

Barry shifted his bag to his left hand and walked over, form-   6
ing in his mind the answers he'd make to Jackie's questions.

"Did we win?" Jackie asked. "Was the old Barry Stanford   7
magic in glittering evidence yet once more this morning? Were the invaders sent hunched and silent back to their hovels in the hills? What was the score? Give us an epic account, Barry, without modesty or delay. This is Sue, by the way."

"I've seen you about," the girl said.   8

"You could hardly miss him," said Jackie. "Four men, roped   9
together, spent a week climbing him—they thought he was Everest. He ought to carry a warning beacon, he's a danger to aircraft."

"Silly," said the girl, smiling at Jackie. "He's not much taller   10
than you are."

She had a nice voice too.   11

"We won," Barry said. "Seventeen points to three, and it was   12
a good game. The ground was hard, though."

He could think of nothing else to say.   13

"Let's all go for a frivolous cup of coffee," Jackie said. "Let's   14
celebrate your safe return from the rough fields of victory. We could pour libations all over the floor for you."

"I don't think so," Barry said. "Thanks. I'll go straight home."   15

"Okay," said Jackie, rocking on his heels so that the sun   16
could shine on his smile. "How's your father?"

"No better," Barry said. "He's not going to get better."   17

"Yes, well," said Jackie, serious and uncomfortable, "tell him   18
my mother and father ask about him."

"I will," Barry promised. "He'll be pleased."   19

Barry dropped the bag in the front hall and moved into the   20
room which had been the dining room until his father's illness. His father lay in the white bed, his long body gaunt, his still

head scarcely denting the pillow. He seemed asleep, thin blue lids covering his eyes, but when Barry turned away he spoke.

21   "Hullo, Son," he said. "Did you win?"

22   His voice was a dry, light rustling, hardly louder than the breath which carried it. Its sound moved Barry to a compassion that almost unmanned him, but he stepped close to the bed and looked down at the dying man.

23   "Yes," he said. "We won fairly easily. It was a good game."

24   His father lay with his eyes closed, inert, his breath irregular and shallow.

25   "Did you score?" he asked.

26   "Twice," Barry said. "I had a try in each half."

27   He thought of the easy certainty with which he'd caught the ball before his second try; casually, almost arrogantly he had taken it on the tips of his fingers, on his full burst for the line, breaking the fullback's tackle. Nobody could have stopped him. But watching his father's weakness he felt humble and ashamed, as if the morning's game, its urgency and effort, was not worth talking about. His father's face, fine-skinned and pallid, carried a dark stubble of beard, almost a week's growth, and his obstinate, strong hair stuck out over his brow.

28   "Good," said his father, after a long pause. "I'm glad it was a good game."

29   Barry's mother bustled about the kitchen, a tempest of orderly energy.

30   "Your father's not well," she said. "He's down today, feels depressed. He's a particular man, your father. He feels dirty with all that beard on him."

31   She slammed shut the stove door.

32   "Mr. Cleaver was supposed to come up and shave him," she said, "and that was three days ago. Little things have always worried your father, every detail must be perfect for him."

33   Barry filled a glass with milk from the refrigerator. He was very thirsty.

34   "I'll shave him," he said.

35   His mother stopped, her head on one side.

36   "Do you think you can?" she asked. "He'd like it if you can."

37   "I can do it," Barry said.

38   He washed his hands as carefully as a surgeon. His father's razor was in a blue leather case, hinged at the broad edge and with one hinge broken. Barry unfastened the clasp and took out

the razor. It had not been properly cleaned after its last use and lather had stiffened into hard yellow rectangles between the teeth of the guard. There were water-shaped rust stains, brown as chocolate, on the surface of the blade. Barry removed it, throwing it in the wastebin. He washed the razor until it glistened, and dried it on a soft towel, polishing the thin handle, rubbing its metal head to a glittering shine. He took a new blade from its waxed envelope, the paper clinging to the thin metal. The blade was smooth and flexible to the touch, the little angles of its cutting clearly defined. Barry slotted it into the grip of the razor, making it snug and tight in the head.

The shaving soap, hard, white, richly aromatic, was kept in a   39
wooden bowl. Its scent was immediately evocative and Barry could almost see his father in the days of his health, standing before his mirror, thick white lather on his face and neck. As a little boy Barry had loved the generous perfume of the soap, had waited for his father to lift the razor to his face, for one careful stroke to take away the white suds in a clean revelation of the skin. Then his father would renew the lather with a few sweeps of his brush, one with an ivory handle and the bristles worn, which he still used.

His father's shaving mug was a thick cup, plain and service-   40
able. A gold line ran outside the rim of the cup, another inside, just below the lip. Its handle was large and sturdy, and the face of the mug carried a portrait of the young Queen Elizabeth II, circled by a wreath of leaves, oak perhaps, or laurel. A lion and unicorn balanced precariously on a scroll above her crowned head, and the Union Jack, the Royal Standard, and other flags were furled each side of the portrait. And beneath it all, in small black letters, ran the legend: "Coronation June 2nd 1953." The cup was much older than Barry. A pattern of faint translucent cracks, fine as a web, had worked itself haphazardly, invisibly almost, through the white glaze. Inside, on the bottom, a few dark bristles were living, loose and dry. Barry shook them out, then held the cup in his hand, feeling its solidness. Then he washed it ferociously, until it was clinically clean.

Methodically he set everything on a tray, razor, soap, brush,   41
towels. Testing the hot water with a finger, he filled the mug and put that, too, on the tray. His care was absorbed, ritualistic. Satisfied that his preparations were complete, he went downstairs, carrying the tray with one hand.

42   His father was waiting for him. Barry set the tray on a bedside table and bent over his father, sliding an arm under the man's thin shoulders, lifting him without effort so that he sat against the high pillows.

43   "By God, you're strong," his father said. He was as breathless as if he'd been running.

44   "So are you," said Barry.

45   "I was," his father said. "I used to be strong once."

46   He sat exhausted against the pillows.

47   "We'll wait a bit," Barry said.

48   "You could have used your electric razor," his father said. "I expected that."

49   "You wouldn't like it." Barry said. "You'll get a closer shave this way."

50   He placed the large towel about his father's shoulders.

51   "Now," he said, smiling down.

52   The water was hot in the thick cup. Barry wet the brush and worked up the lather. Gently he built up a covering of soft foam on the man's chin, on his cheeks and his stark cheekbones.

53   "You're using a lot of soap," his father said.

54   "Not too much," Barry said. "You've got a lot of beard."

55   His father lay there quietly, his wasted arms at his sides.

56   "It's comforting," he said. "You'd be surprised how comforting it is."

57   Barry took up the razor, weighing it in his hand, rehearsing the angle at which he'd use it. He felt confident.

58   "If you have prayers to say . . ." he said.

59   "I've said a lot of prayers," his father answered.

60   Barry leaned over and placed the razor delicately against his father's face, setting the head accurately on the clean line near the ear where the long hair ended. He held the razor in the tips of his fingers and drew the blade sweetly through the lather. The new edge moved light as a touch over the hardness of the upper jaw and down to the angle of the chin, sliding away the bristles so easily that Barry could not feel their release. He sighed as he shook the razor in the hot water, washing away the soap.

61   "How's it going?" his father asked.

62   "No problem," Barry said. "You needn't worry."

63   It was as if he had never known what his father really looked like. He was discovering under his hands the clear bones of the

face and head, they became sharp and recognizable under his fingers. When he moved his father's face a gentle inch to one side, he touched with his fingers the frail temples, the blue veins of his father's life. With infinite and meticulous care he took away the hair from his father's face.

"Now for your neck," he said. "We might as well do the job 64 properly."

"You've got good hands," his father said. "You can trust 65 those hands, they won't let you down."

Barry cradled his father's head in the crook of his left arm, so 66 that the man could tilt back his head, exposing the throat. He brushed fresh lather under the chin and into the hollows alongside the stretched tendons. His father's throat was fleshless and vulnerable, his head was a hard weight on the boy's arm. Barry was filled with unreasoning protective love. He lifted the razor and began to shave.

"You don't have to worry," he said. "Not at all. Not about 67 anything."

He held his father in the bend of his strong arm and they 68 looked at each other. Their heads were very close.

"How old are you?" his father said. 69

"Seventeen," Barry said. "Near enough seventeen." 70

"You're young," his father said, "to have this happen." 71

"Not too young," Barry said. "I'm bigger than most men." 72

"I think you are," his father said. 73

He leaned his head tiredly against the boy's shoulder. He 74 was without strength, his face was cold and smooth. He had let go all his authority, handed it over. He lay back on his pillow, knowing his weakness and his mortality, and looked at his son with wonder, with a curious humble pride.

"I won't worry then," he said. "About anything." 75

"There's no need," Barry said. "Why should you worry?" 76

He wiped his father's face clean of all soap with a damp towel. 77 The smell of illness was everywhere, overpowering even the perfumed lather. Barry settled his father down and took away the shaving tools, putting them by with the same ceremonial precision with which he'd prepared them: the cleaned and glittering razor in its broken case; the soap, its bowl wiped and dried, on the shelf between the brush and the coronation mug; all free of taint. He washed his hands and scrubbed his nails. His hands were firm and broad, pink after their scrubbing. The fingers were short and strong, the little fingers slightly crooked, and soft dark hair grew on the backs of his hands and his fingers just above the knuckles. Not long ago they had been small bare hands, not very long ago.

78   Barry opened wide the bathroom window. Already, although it was not yet two o'clock, the sun was retreating and people were moving briskly, wrapped in their heavy coats against the cold that was to come. But now the window was full in the beam of the dying sunlight, and Barry stood there, illuminated in its golden warmth for a whole minute, knowing it would soon be gone.

Personal Response

Leslie Norris uses the ritual of shaving to describe the changing relationship between father and son. Respond with experiences and feelings you have had about how rituals may be symbols in families and about how your role in regard to parents has changed. If you have grown children, respond with related experiences.

Content Focus

1. Why is the act of shaving the father important—to both Barry and his father?
2. What kind of person is Barry? Use details from the story to illustrate your answer.
3. Barry is described as having a "devouring restlessness." What causes this feeling?
4. Why does Barry feel humbled and ashamed of his own strength when he is with his father?
5. What happens between father and son during the act of shaving?
6. What is the central truth in the story?

Writer's Craft

Norris uses a wealth of detail in describing the preparations for the shaving. The shaving becomes ritualistic. What purpose does this serve? Also, Barry's hands are minutely described. What do these details add to the overall meaning of the story? Norris uses the detail to explain feelings and truths far beyond the act of shaving.

Process Analysis Pattern of Development

The final writing assignment for this chapter will ask you to use the process analysis form. We perform processes every day, and sometimes we have the occasion to share our knowledge with others. Process analysis is a way of teaching and learning. For many tasks, we need to learn step by step, in a sequence. We learned how to tie our shoes step by step and since then have most likely shared that knowledge with young children. Whether the process is simple or complex, the techniques have to be explained clearly. We have all been frustrated by poorly written instructions when trying to assemble furniture or equipment.

Process analysis fulfills two needs. One is providing step-by-step instructions for someone who plans on performing a task. The other is explaining how something happens, although the explanation is not intended as a blueprint to follow. An example of this kind of process analysis is a description of the stages of grieving. It offers a perspective, not instructions. Both types of process analysis are useful, depending on the writer's purpose.

The step-by-step process analysis is appropriate for loan applications, science experiments, recipes, and work-related instructions. Technical writers frequently use this style. When one writes process analysis for these purposes, the use of "you" is often appropriate, because the reader needs to follow each step exactly. The writer is in effect speaking directly to the reader: "Here is what you do to have the desired results." For the second type of process analysis, the use of "you" is not appropriate. Although the information is in sequential form, a reader is not going to follow each step. Both types are chronological in organization.

Writing Activity: "How-To" Directions

Write a process paper explaining how to accomplish something—think of it as a how-to piece. The topic can be quite ordinary, such as how to bake bread; or more technical, such as how to prepare slides of plant tissue. You must be familiar with the process, so you can explain it to someone who has an interest but little knowledge. Assume your audience has some background information—such as, if you are explaining bread making, basic cooking knowledge. But do not assume too much and skip over important steps. If you write "knead the dough" without explaining how to knead, your directions will not be helpful. Share your first draft with your writing group and help one another to look critically at the process analyses. Make revisions based on their suggestions.

College writing often requires process analyses. For example, essays or test questions that ask students to explain a solution to a problem or why something didn't work out require a process answer. A step-by-step explanation clearly shows an understanding of the problem and the solution. Any "what" or "how" question can be answered with a process approach.

When writing process analysis papers, clearly state in the first paragraph what you are explaining. For an instructional approach, you write what the reader will learn from the process you are explaining. For example, if your topic is changing oil in a motorcycle, the first sentence or two should clearly inform the reader about your intentions. The following student process paper illustrates this type of writing.

STUDENT PAPER

MAKING BEEF STEW
Krista Hauenstein

When you live in the Midwest in the winter, few meals can warm you up as much as a hearty beef stew. And a good stew doesn't take that much time to make. For this stew, you will need several ingredients: one pound of beef, four or five carrots, three or four medium-sized potatoes, half of an onion, a can of mushrooms, one package of brown gravy mix, two tablespoons of flour (or whatever your gravy mix requires), and salt and pepper to taste. You will also need a roasting pan with cover, a vegetable peeler, a knife, a measuring cup, a spoon, a saucepan, a colander (or strainer), and a bowl. Before you begin preparing the stew, preheat the oven to about 300 degrees.

The first step in making the stew is preparing the ingredients. Cut the beef into inch strips or cubes. Peel and cut the carrots and potatoes; the carrots should be sliced in half lengthwise, and the potatoes should be cut into quarters. (If you have less cooking time, cut your vegetables into smaller pieces.) Slice the onion into small pieces. Drain the mushrooms, and put them in a saucepan for later use.

The second step is to put the beef, carrots, potatoes, and onion in a roasting pan. Add water until it reaches the halfway mark in the pan. Sprinkle everything with salt and pepper. Cover. Put the stew in the oven to roast for approximately one and a half hours or until the ingredients are cooked and tender.

The third step is to make the gravy. When the stew ingredients are tender, separate the ingredients from the water using a colander. Add the gravy mix and flour to the saucepan with the mushrooms. Measure the juice from the cooked stew into the saucepan (you may need to add water depending on your gravy mix). Stir the gravy until it is thickened. When the gravy is ready, put the stew ingredients back into the roasting pan, and pour the gravy over everything. Re-cover the pan, and cook in the oven for another fifteen minutes.

The fourth and final step is to eat the stew. Serve the stew on a large plate with a glass of milk. The stew serves two to four people. If you

follow these simple steps, you are guaranteed a
delicious winter meal that will warm your guests
from the inside.

The second type of process analysis, written for the purpose of helping readers understand how something happens or the significance of the happening, requires a strong thesis that states not only what the paper is about but also your attitude or feelings about the process.

In "Shaving" the ritual of shaving carries meaning far beyond the act itself. Although many details are included, the purpose of the process description is not to inform a reader about how to shave with a straight-edge razor. In the story, the ritual of shaving becomes the vehicle for a transfer of authority—more a ceremony than a process. The writing assignment that follows is of this second type of process analysis.

WRITING ASSIGNMENT: PROCESS ANALYSIS PAPER

Family rituals often occur once a year; for instance, the annual preparations for deer hunting or annual religious celebrations. The rituals become a tradition and carry meanings far beyond the actual activities.

Your assignment is to write a process analysis paper about such an occurrence in your family. The purpose is to show readers how this process carries meaning for the participants. You could write about Thanksgiving, leaving home for college, birthday celebrations—any event that affects you and/or family members. The first paragraph must include your purpose, point of view, and thesis. The tone may be serious or humorous. Readers must understand how the ritual carries the meanings and how you feel about it. The paper is to go through the entire writing process. A good way to begin, because you will be describing related sequences, is to brainstorm through mapping or outlining. A suggested response guide for use in writing groups follows.

Response Guide for Process Analysis Paper

1. In the beginning paragraph, how can the writer make his or her attitude more clear?
2. How could the paper support the thesis more strongly?
3. Look for illustrations and examples that reinforce the thesis. Where could more be added?
4. What are the meanings behind the ritual?
5. What feelings are expressed?
6. Look for strong word choice and help the writer avoid vague expressions.
7. In what ways could the writer improve the paper? Remember your goal is to be helpful, not critical.

9

Relationships with Family Members

Relationships with family members, especially brothers and sisters, can be the most difficult and yet the most rewarding relationships we experience. A person who is an only child, too, can become aware through friends of the give and take that goes on between brothers and sisters—and perhaps simulate a "sibling" relationship with a friend or relative.

Siblings

In this chapter we read four selections in which authors write about how they and their siblings related to one another. The first reading is a newspaper essay by Teryl Zarnow, "Sibling Revelry." Zarnow describes a relationship with her sister that has always been strong and supportive.

Sibling Revelry

TERYL ZARNOW

1   She has only just arrived and already we are deep in conversation. With agility, grace and speed we leap from topic to topic. For now, we are just a headline news service hitting the high points of the news since we last saw each other. Later, we will switch to in-depth reporting and thoughtful analysis.

2   We have no formal agenda, but we know exactly the business before us. There are those we will praise, those we will dis and those we totally will trash.

We are in agreement on these items, and that's the way it's supposed to be. She is my sister. 3

My son, whose constant torment of his siblings acquires the status of recreational sport, watches our performance in amazement. His head swivels like a spectator at a pingpong tournament. He has never seen me gorge myself before on a sit-down conversation. 4

I try to explain to him this is part of being a sister. I try to explain to him what it is like. We had two younger brothers. We were all in the produce section, but they were the vegetables and we were the fruits. 5

We were grouped together in separate bins. My sister and I shared a bedroom, we shared our clothes, we shared a phone line and we shared an alliance against our brothers and our parents. 6

We shared endless conversations in the darkness of our bedroom, trading common complaints across the nightstand that separated our beds. We shared the household chores. When I had to vacuum, she had to iron. When our mother made my sister cut her hair too short, I understood the awfulness. When I got stuck wearing an awful outfit, she understood the embarrassment. 7

As the younger sister, of course, I was lucky. My sister, three years older, was the taster who had to go first. She saved me a lot of misery. Once I made a list of all the things for which she had gotten into trouble so I could avoid them. My sister did not hate me for this; she recognized my need for self-preservation. 8

And we both understood she was the sacrificial lamb, fighting on behalf of both of us against early curfews, short hair, geeky saddle shoes and other forms of tyranny. She softened our parents for me. 9

We kept each other's secrets then, and we still do now. We overheard each other's phone conversations. I knew which boy she really liked. She knew if he had a younger brother. If my sister was late, I was the one who unlocked the front door. I never told. 10

So when my sister comes to visit, where we go is secondary to what we do. We talk. 11

12   My sister and I are leaving for the day, I announce to my family. "Can't I come?" asks my daughter, who figures that, as the only other female in residence, she has automatic membership in the club. "Not today," I answer.

13   My daughter is shocked. Rarely do I hoard my friends so selfishly. My son stares. He doesn't get it. What's the big deal?

14   "She's my sister. I haven't seen her for a while, and we want some time alone," I explain. "When you're grown up, you'll want to spend time alone with each other. Your brother and sister could turn out to be your best friends."

15   My kids smirk in disbelief. I don't know which is harder for them to imagine: that they ever will grow up or that they ever will be best friends. Some days I am not sure about the growing up, but I am sure about their becoming friends.

Personal Response

Respond with your own experiences and those of others in your family. Write about what Teryl Zarnow's children thought about her relationship with her sister. Why do you think some siblings are close while others do not share these feelings? If you are an only child, write about your observations of friends who have siblings and about your own experiences as an only child.

Content Focus

1. What picture comes to mind as you think of Zarnow's brothers as vegetables and the two girls as fruits? Try describing your family members by means of a similar metaphor.
2. How do the author's children respond to the behavior of the sisters?
3. How does the author make it clear how very close she and her sister are?
4. How did Zarnow benefit from being the youngest?

Writer's Craft

Zarnow's almost breathless beginning draws in the reader to share the experience with her. Not until the end of the second paragraph does the writer identify her sister. This style of beginning is well suited to Zarnow's topic; and it is one you might consider, as an alternative to the thesis statement in the first line or two, especially if the tone of a piece is light and breezy.

Zarnow gives a lot of information without much detail and uses short sentences to convey the exuberance of her sister's visit. In your writing, try using different sentence lengths to see how that changes the style and mood.

The second reading, Lucille Clifton's "Sisters," shares a similar experience, although the style is quite different.

Sisters

LUCILLE CLIFTON

me and you be sisters.
we be the same.
me and you
coming from the same place.
me and you   5
be greasing our legs
touching up our edges.
me and you
be scared of rats
be stepping on roaches.   10
me and you
come running high down purdy street one time
and mama laugh and shake her head at
me and you.
me and you   15
got babies
got thirty-five
got black
let our hair go back
be loving ourselves   20
be loving ourselves
be sisters.
only where you sing
i poet.

Personal Response

Think about your present relationships with other members of your family. How have they changed? What did you once share, and what do you share now?

Content Focus

1. What did the sisters in Lucille Clifton's poem share?
2. How does a reader know they were close when they were children?
3. In what ways are they close now?
4. How does Clifton view her past life?
5. What is the mood of the poem?

Writer's Craft

Read the poem aloud to have the repetition and rhythm come alive. In a few words, Clifton relates her experience of a joyous life. Consider the way repeated words give meaning to the poem as a whole.

Writing Activity: Describing a Close Family Member

In the previous two selections, the authors used different styles and forms but created many of the same feelings. Write a short description of a similar joy and closeness with a member of your family or a friend. Consider your words and sentence lengths carefully so that the style as well as the words carry meanings.

The next two readings portray a different side to siblings' relationships. There are times when children have difficulty acting fairly and kindly to others in the family. Jim Tolley's "Climbing the Daymarker" is about one of those times.

Climbing the Daymarker

JIM TOLLEY

1   Looking back, most things grow small with years. On the island where I spent my summers as a child, the wharves no

longer reach far over the sea, and the saltbox cottage where my family lived appears to me gray and simple.

Alone among the objects of my memory, the daymarker 2
stands as tall as ever. Built long before the lighthouse, it stood at the crest of the dunes to guide the lobster boats into the harbor. The marker rose as high as our house. It was built of four thick poles slanted together at the top, like a pyramid. Nailed across on the sides were wooden slats that led up like the rungs on a ladder.

Until I was ten years old, our last summer on the island, I had 3
never climbed the daymarker. The poles, worn smooth by blowing sands, had no handholds, and I was too small to reach the lowest slat. Up to then, the top of the daymarker belonged to my brother Mike. When that changed we both changed with it.

Mike had always been a sort of mentor to me. I would 4
awaken in the early morning, peek from the bunk bed at my brother below, and gently shake the bed until he woke, too. Then I would ask, "What will we do today?" Whatever he said, we would do. Most days we spent catching crabs with squid bait at the marina, or pulling sea urchins from the boat ramp. My favorite game was to take a handful of hermit crabs and set them out on the sand and wait for them to crawl from their borrowed shells. We always ended the day by heading, after dinner, to the dunes, following our private trail through the sawgrass. There Mike would climb the daymarker. While I sat in the cooling sand, he would tell me what he could see from the top. Each evening there would be something new to report, a different trawler in the harbor or a freighter pressing the cape. From his spot at the top of the daymarker, Mike always spoke in a distant, wonderful way, a way in which I had never spoken.

When I turned ten, I stopped waking Mike in the morning. I 5
felt a need to be out alone. One morning I found a dead ray on the beach, and another time I picked up the brittle black egg of a mermaid's purse. When I told my parents of these things at dinner, Mike would pretend not to listen. Then he would head out, as always, to the daymarker. I didn't want to follow.

Near the end of the season an old woman who painted wa- 6
tercolors on an easel in front of her cottage saw me carrying a horseshoe crab and asked me to pose. I held the crab out like a trophy. As she painted, the old woman asked me where my

brother was; she had seen us on the beach together early that summer. I told her that I didn't know. When she finished, I ran home late for dinner. Mother had kept my food warm. I gulped it down, then ran out to tell Mike about the portrait. Mike was atop the pyramid, but didn't look at me when I told the story. He didn't say a thing, and would not say what he saw from the peak. What was he seeing? I kicked around in the sand for a while, then left him alone.

7   The next day I was down at the marina when I saw something bigger than a crab moving beneath a moored sailboat. I walked across the dock for a closer look. It was a lobster. I stripped off my shirt and sneakers, dove in, grabbed the lobster, and pulled it out. I took it home, and we boiled it for dinner. Since I had brought home the main course, Mother had Mike wash the dishes even though it was my turn. I ran out to the dunes, happy and not really thinking of Mike back in the house.

8   The daymarker looked very tall, without anyone on top. There was no one around, and I decided to climb it if I could. I had never really tried, not that year; and when I jumped up I was surprised to grab the first slat with ease. I swung a leg over and pulled myself up. The whitewash on the wood rubbed off onto my legs and arms. I was new to this, not like my brother who climbed it cleanly. The height made me feel euphoric, even though the wood slivered my hands. When I reached the peak, I steadied myself and sat. The sun was setting behind me. The sea and sky were fading, but as sharp and clear as anything I had ever seen. I looked over the water at the last sailboats heading in, and at the lighthouse as the turning beam switched on.

9   "What—" I heard Mike below. I looked down and saw him climbing up, climbing after me. For an instant I was startled, not understanding his anger. I started to say, "I would've asked!" but I could see that it didn't matter. Mike was still bigger than I was. I tried to keep him away with my feet, but he grabbed my ankle and twisted until I began to lose my grip. I kicked, but he was too strong. He pulled on my leg, prying me from the top slat, until I fell.

10   I tumbled face down and couldn't breathe until I cleared the sand from my face. I spit the sand from my mouth and felt where I had cut my lip. I wiped the blood with my arm as I knelt,

then stood up and looked at my brother. He was seated at the top, looking east over the water as if nothing had happened between us.

I could've climbed back up and fought him, but the top of the daymarker wasn't so important anymore. When I think about it, I remember the way the cut on my lip healed very slowly. The taste of blood, like rust, seeped for weeks into my mouth. When I remember the day, I realize I had seen more from the daymarker's base, thrown down, than I could ever have seen from its top.

11

Personal Response

Jim Tolley's story concerns the changing relationship between two brothers. What made it change? Respond with your own memories of changing relationships with siblings, other family members, or friends.

Content Focus

1. What is the purpose of the daymarker?
2. Explain the relationship between the narrator and his brother, Mike.
3. What does it mean to be a mentor to someone?
4. Why do you think the narrator stopped waking Mike up in the morning?
5. How does Mike feel about his brother's success?
6. Why wasn't the top of the daymarker important anymore?

Writer's Craft

Tolley gives only the information needed to tell the story of the change between the two brothers. Inexperienced writers often go off on tangents, describing and explaining what is not necessary to the story. Notice that Tolley relates very little about the house the boys lived in or their parents. His point of view is consistent; he never switches to what the older brother is thinking. The result is a strong, tightly knit, effective story. When revising earlier stories and memories you have written, you may want to compare your writing with Tolley's.

The last of these four "siblings" readings is about wishing you could undo an action. The author, David Huddle, describes a situation that occurred for no apparent reason—an action the speaker in the poem still anguishes over.

Icicle

DAVID HUDDLE

I smacked you in the mouth for no good reason
except that the icicle had broken off
so easily and that it felt like a club
in my hand, and so I swung it, the soft
5   pad of your lower lip sprouting a drop,
then gushing a trail onto the snow even
though we both squeezed the place with our fingers.
I'd give a lot not to be the swinger
of that icicle. I'd like another
10   morning just like that, cold, windy, and bright
as Russia, your glasses fogging up, your face
turning to me again. I tell you I might
help both our lives by changing that act to this,
by handing you the ice, a gift, my brother.

Personal Response

If only we could go back and do things differently—when have you had similar feelings?

Content Focus

1. How do you know that the narrator in Huddle's poem was sorry for his action right away?
2. How do you think the brother felt about the incident?
3. What do you think the narrator meant about helping both their lives?

Writer's Craft

In fourteen lines we understand and share a history. Notice what David Huddle chooses to describe in detail and what he ignores. He shapes our response by clear focus on parts of the incident. What does he explain and why? What images come to your mind as you read? As in the previous reading, Huddle demonstrates here the importance of choosing what to tell and what to leave out.

Writing Activity: Narration on Relationships

In the two readings about brothers, one recounts the change in the relationship between two brothers; the other, an action a brother wishes he could take back. Using one of these themes, write a narrative piece about your relationship with a member of your own family (although not necessarily with a sibling). Your account does not have to be from your childhood, as the two readings are, but can come from any time in your life. It should be a personal story, but you can fictionalize if you wish. Following the example of Tolley and Huddle, select only the parts of the incident or narration that are necessary to enable readers to grasp your intended meaning or feeling. Use detail to expand on the moments you want to stand out, as Huddle does when he describes the morning, or as Tolley does in describing the daymarker.

Argumentation–Persuasion Pattern of Development

Argumentation and persuasion are different in tone and approach; both, however, are designed to convince. In a sense, almost every writing involves an element of persuasion. For example, when you wrote about your favorite place, back in Chapter 1, one of your goals was to convince your readers that you had good reasons for choosing this particular place as your favorite. The more convincingly you wrote, using sensory details and examples, the more readers would agree with your premise.

Requests are persuasive; for example, writing home for money, or asking a relative to come and baby-sit, or inviting a friend to fix your car—all use persuasive techniques.

Trying to convince someone of something requires both persuasion and argumentation. The difference between persuasion and argument is that persuasive writing uses emotional language, appeals to the reader, and aims at getting acceptance of the writer's point of view. Argumentation, on the other hand, assumes there is a controversy and uses logic in an effort to convince, while maintaining an ostensibly objective viewpoint. In writing an argument, one uses statistics and reports to strengthen the argument, not emotional appeals. However, readers respond to both—the logical and the emotional; and writers often include both, although they emphasize one approach over the other depending on the topic and the audience.

For example, if you are endeavoring to persuade parents to buy a car for you, the emotional and personal approach will predominate; but you might use figures to plot out a pay-back schedule based on your earnings. These figures may be more convincing than a statement that "you will pay them back—honest!" When you are writing an argumentation using evidence, facts, and statistics, an emotional example illustrating the point you are making may tip the scales for your point of view. An example of this approach: If you were writing to oppose road construction through a previously protected area, you might marshal all the facts and arguments in a logical way, then include an emotional appeal to save a species of butterflies. For some readers, the facts clearly laid out would underscore your argument. For others, the destruction of the butterfly habitat would be the deciding factor. Writers can use both styles to their advantage in argumentation–persuasion papers.

Writing Activity: Convincing an Audience

Write an essay on a topic you have strong opinions or feelings about. Decide on the audience for your essay, then decide if you will employ mainly argumentation or mainly persuasion to present your ideas. Remember that you are writing to convince and/or inform, not only to show your side of the issue. Whichever style you choose, add at least one usage of the other style to further your stand and help sway the readers' response.

Rogerian Arguments

A Rogerian argument, a pattern developed by the psychologist Carl Rogers, seeks to find a common ground between opposing viewpoints. The advantage of this approach is that to convince people you must understand their viewpoint and respond to it. Often in oral arguments we say, "But you don't understand!"— and we won't listen further until the other side demonstrates that they do understand. In written arguments, we lack these spoken reminders telling us to acknowledge others' viewpoints or opposing arguments. But your argument will be much stronger if it is obvious that you have considered other positions.

To write a Rogerian argument, first explain the issue and follow with your position, clearly stated. In the next paragraph summarize the opposing views, and describe the points you agree with. Then go on to state your views, reinforcing them with information, facts, and appeals. The Rogerian format can be used for both argumentation and persuasion.

Rich Swanson, using the Rogerian approach, wrote the following letter to his wife.

Dear Jo,

It has been eight years since Tasha died. I have wanted another dog ever since then, but my life has been too busy with work, raising children, and other demands upon my time. I am currently in a position to seriously consider having a dog again, and would like to have you understand my reasons why.

I consider myself to be a very fortunate guy because I am surrounded by people with whom I have wonderful loving relationships. Having said this, I want to express my desire to bring another relationship into our lives. Dogs are not human, but they are joyful and steadfast companions in a way different from any of our friendships. Now I realize that we have a small house, two kids, a cat, active lives, and grouchy neighbors, but I think that as responsible pet owners we can overcome these small obstacles and our lives will be enriched as a result.

Introducing a puppy into a household is much like bringing a newborn infant home from the hospital. There is bound to be some disruption and adjustments that need to be made, but this shall soon pass as the puppy matures, and we all settle into our routines. I look forward to getting outside for daily walks, the children will have a new playmate, the house will have a low-cost low-maintenance alarm system, and we will have a member of the family who is never moody, a great listener, and always glad to see us. I am experienced in training dogs, so will take most of the responsibility for raising a new pet. We will learn about unconditional love and companionship, while a dog expects so little in return. This sounds like a pretty good deal to me. What do you think?

Love, Rich

WRITING ASSIGNMENT: PERSUASION LETTER

The final assignment for this chapter is to write a Rogerian persuasive piece in letter form. The letter can be addressed to a family member, relative, or friend—someone you have a close relationship with. Or, if you wish, you may write a letter to someone outside your personal circle of friends and family. The purpose of the letter is persuasion. You may choose any topic or style. A list of suggested topics follows.

❑ Ask forgiveness for a transgression you committed
❑ Ask someone to lend you a car or any object
❑ Convince someone to go on a trip with you—one they wouldn't normally be interested in
❑ Seek agreement on a plan of action, perhaps involving your parents or an elderly relation
❑ Convince a local board to follow a particular plan of action
❑ Persuade neighbors to change their behavior

Or you may write on any topic you choose, or on ones your instructor suggests. The topic can be anything that fits the parameters of the assignment—Rogerian structure, persuasive, and a letter. You may even choose a fictional topic, but do write to a real person. The word count should be about 500, or approximately two pages. The following response guide may be helpful in a writing group.

Response Guide for Rogerian Argument

1. Make sure the issue is clear. How can the writer strengthen the opening paragraph?
2. How effectively does the writer explain the opposing side?
3. How could the common ground be more convincing?
4. Where could the language be more precise?
5. Do transitions move the reader easily through the letter?
6. How could the last line sum up the point more clearly?

10

Family Perspectives

Have you ever wondered if your position in the birth order of offspring in your family, or your status as an only child, has shaped your personality? Have you noticed a pattern in your friends' birth-order positions in their families?

Birth Order

The question of the effect of birth order interests many people. Does it matter if one is a firstborn? Will a firstborn generally achieve more than a last-born child? Will a last-born have more fun in life? Is an only child more independent? In spite of numerous studies, there are no definite answers. Some psychologists consider the whole idea of the impact of birth order ridiculous because of little supportive data; others claim that studies show enough connections between birth order and personalities to allow researchers to draw some conclusions.

The two readings in this chapter provide some background on birth order so that you can discuss the issue and reflect on more than one view. You are not asked to come to a conclusion about the issue. The point is to open up discussion on the effect birth order or single birth may have on personality. Because the readings are articles, not essays or stories, the required responses are different from those you have had in previous chapters. The readings call for analysis, note-taking, and summaries; content questions following each reading will require you to use these skills.

In the first reading Judy Dunn cites several studies and carefully presents contradictory findings, giving the reader a well-balanced overview of recent opinions and research.

Birth Order, Age Gap, Gender, and Large Families

JUDY DUNN

1   In some families the children constantly fight with and irritate each other; in others they offer each other affectionate support that is moving to see. Compare the following comments by two mothers, each with a three-year-old and a fourteen-month-old:

> He gets into everything of hers. It drives her crazy. They fight such a lot—screaming quarrels. And it's not just screaming—they really go at each other.

> He [the younger sibling] loves being with her and her friends. . . . He trails after Laura . . . they play in the sand a lot . . . making pies. She organizes it and whisks away things that are dangerous and gives him something else. They go upstairs and bounce on the bed. Then he'll lie there while she sings to him and reads books to him. And he'll go off in a trance with his hankie [comfort object]. The important thing is they're becoming games that they'll play together. He'll start something by laughing and running toward some toy, turning round to see if she's following. He'll go upstairs and race into the bedroom and shriek, and she joins him.

What could explain these differences in how the children get along together and in what they feel for each other? Books for parents frequently imply that jealousy and quarrels between siblings are largely the fault of the parents. But it is also often said that a child's birth order, the age difference between her and her siblings, and their sexes all influence how well they get along. How much evidence is there to support these views?

Firstborns and Laterborns

2   It certainly seems plausible that firstborn children should feel more hostility toward siblings than is felt by laterborns. The first-

born children are, after all, the ones who have been displaced. As one mother said of her two-year-old's feelings about her younger brother, the secondborn: "She was queen of the world . . . no wonder she minds and seems to resent him." And as a precocious four-year-old put it quite explicitly to his mother on the birth of his brother: "Why have you ruined my life?"

It will not surprise any parent who has more than one child to hear that firstborn children tend to express more ambivalence and hostility about their siblings than vice versa. Both firstborns and laterborns believe that the parents align themselves with the younger siblings rather than with the eldest. This remark by a five-year-old girl in Helen Koch's study is not an unusual comment from a firstborn child: "Yes, I would like to change places with my baby brother. Then I could yell my head off and my mommy would take care of nobody but me." 3

Firstborns are less likely to say that they prefer to play with their siblings than with other children. They are seen by both first- and laterborn children as bossier and more dominant than laterborn children, and studies of five- and six-year-olds show that their power tactics in dealing with their siblings tend to differ. Here is a firstborn boy describing how he gets his sister to do what he wants: "I told her to get out of my room. And I kept shouting at her and she wouldn't go. And I started hitting her, and she still wouldn't go. So I just picked her up and threw her out." 4

According to a study of siblings' power tactics by Brian Sutton-Smith, firstborn children attack, use status more, and bribe. Laterborns tend to sulk, pout, plead, cry, and appeal to parents for help. The more polite techniques of explaining, taking turns, and asking are perceived by most children as the strategies only of firstborn girls. Sutton-Smith and his colleagues offer the following interpretation of these differences. The status tactics, bossiness, and dominance of firstborns are typical of the powerful members of any social system—those who are larger and have greater ability; the appeals of laterborn children to their parents for support are typical of the weak members of social groups and are encouraged by the greater indulgence and comfort offered to laterborn children by their parents. The tendency of firstborn girls to explain and give reasons reflects the way in which 5 the girls model themselves on their mother, with whom (it is assumed) they have closer relations than do the secondborn girls. Sutton-Smith's account sounds plausible, but it is probably far too simple, and we simply don't have evidence to support some of the arguments. For instance, there's no good evidence that secondborn girls have a less close relationship with their mothers than firstborn girls.

6   During their early years, laterborn children are frequently more directly aggressive than their older siblings, according to the interview studies. They may not be any more hostile—but they do express their aggression very directly and physically. Firstborns tend to be more verbally aggressive, criticizing and disparaging their younger brothers and sisters mercilessly. This "child's-eye" view of firstborns as bossy and dominant is supported by experiments in which siblings are asked to play or carry out tasks together. Seven- and eight-year-old firstborns are in these situations more likely to dominate, to praise, and to teach their siblings than vice versa.

7   Of course, it is not always the eldest who is the dominating one. When competition or domination comes from a younger sibling it can be particularly devastating for the older sibling. Here are the comments of a Nottingham mother, in the Newsons' study, describing her seven-year-old's reaction to a very bright younger sibling:

> He's not afraid of anything physical—his fears are attached to not being able to understand. He's said once or twice something that rather horrified me: "I don't understand; there must be something the matter with me." This is the business of his relationship with Katherine [aged five-and-a-half]. It's just simply that James is not so intelligent as Katherine, and he's cottoning on to this fact very quickly, and I don't know what to do about it. [Has he been conscious of it for some time?] I think so—since Katherine started going to school and came home with reports of what she'd done, what book they were reading. His initial response was "You couldn't have done"; and she said "We did" and proceeded to show him. He was absolutely devastated.

What is so poignant here is the awareness of both child and mother that this is not a problem that will disappear, but one that will have to be lived with, for a lifetime.

Firstborn children from large families, especially, often have   8
a particular role as disciplinarians, caregivers, and leaders. The
study by James Bossard and Eleanor Boll includes many vivid
examples of the responsibilities placed on firstborn children.
The adults recalling these experiences felt that they had important consequences for their development. These are the recollections of the oldest daughter in a family with nine children:

> For as long as I can remember, I helped with the dishes and then
> was given the responsibility of other tasks as I grew older. . . .
> There were eleven of us eating every day. Life seemed to be one
> eternity of dirty dishes after another. . . . It was my job to make
> the chocolate cupcakes for five school lunches that were carried,
> pack the lunches, and set the table for breakfast. I was in dis-
> grace with my brothers and sisters if I failed to get up in time to
> make the cakes and I was too poor a baker to make them good
> enough to be edible the next day. I learned to bake bread and to
> iron before I was in high school. I have a faint recollection of
> washing, feeding, and caring for the baby when I was seven
> years old. I was "mother's little helper" in so many ways for
> years. Mother certainly needed me. When we went visiting, it
> was my responsibility to see that the younger children did no
> damage or did not get hurt. My household tasks gradually in-
> creased until I was doing more of it than mother was. Her last
> baby was born at the beginning of Christmas vacation of my last
> year in high school, and I was put into complete charge, includ-
> ing mother and the baby. Being the oldest girl in a large family
> meant that many of my own desires remained unfulfilled.

And here are the comments of the oldest of eight:

> From the time that I was five, I can remember taking care of the
> children. I used to lie on my mother's bed and push my little
> brother back and forth in his carriage until he fell asleep. Mother
> kept on having babies. Many problems beset us. By the time I
> was in third grade, I was always helping mother while the others
> played with the neighboring children. This made me old beyond
> my years, serious, and quite responsible for all that went on in
> the household. . . . Each Saturday, my mother went in to the city
> six miles away for the groceries and stayed for the day. In the
> evening she and dad visited friends and came home at about
> midnight. From age fifteen to nineteen, I found myself responsi-
> ble for seeing that the housework was finished, cooking lunch

and dinner for the children, and caring for the newest baby. At night, I bathed six children, washed their heads, and tucked them into bed. Saturday nights continued like this until I rebelled. I wanted to have time for dates like other girls had.

9   In contrast, if we look at siblings in smaller families and take account of individual differences in affection, warmth, aggression, and conflict between siblings, it is surprising how unimportant birth order per se turns out to be. Although power and dominance between siblings are closely related to birth order, these other features of the relationship are *not.* The closeness, intimacy, support, and affection a child feels for his brother or sister is not clearly linked to whether he is a firstborn or laterborn, and it is these features of the sibling relationship that are likely to be of particular importance in the influence of siblings upon one another.

10   The interview and questionnaire studies of children between the ages of six and twelve suggest that the sex and personality of the firstborn child are more likely to influence the secondborn than vice versa, at least in terms of gender role, interests, and activities. Firstborns, in comparison, are more likely to be influenced by their parents. In families with very young children, laterborn children imitate their older siblings far more than their older siblings imitate them—at least after the first year of life. It is likely, then, that laterborn children model themselves on their older siblings much more than the other way around. But we should not jump to the simple conclusion that whereas laterborns are influenced by their older siblings, firstborns are not influenced by their younger siblings. This is an oversimplification that masks a very complex pattern of mutual influences between siblings and their parents. However, the first child's feelings about the sibling, and his or her behavior toward the sibling in the first years, are of quite special significance as an influence on the way their relationship develops. In one Cambridge study, firstborn children were observed over many months, beginning before the birth of the second child. In families where the first child showed marked affectionate interest in the newborn, the younger child was likely to be particularly friendly to the elder one year later. In these families the firstborns, by their initial in-

terest in the baby sibling, set up a relationship of affection that continued for several years to be very friendly. The differences in the firstborn children's response to the birth were, then, very important in accounting for differences in the relationship which developed between the first two children in the family.

What could explain these differences between firstborn children in their behavior toward the new sibling? One key factor was the nature of the parents' relationship with the first child before and immediately after the sibling's birth. Another was the firstborn's temperament. Children who were anxious, "withdrawing" individuals before the birth usually had little interest in or affection for the new sibling. However, the age gap between the children was *not* related to their interest in the baby. Among the most affectionately interested were some very young children —only eighteen to nineteen months old—and some three- to four-year-olds. And there were no differences between the boys and girls in the sample in how interested they were in the baby sibling. 11

Follow-up observations of these siblings showed just how important the first child's feelings about the baby were as an influence on their developing relationship. However, it is also likely that differences in the secondborn's behavior toward the first, even in the first eighteen months of life, affect how the older child feels about the second. Michael Lamb studied pairs of siblings when the secondborn was twelve months old, and then again six months later. He found that the behavior of the first children toward their siblings was predicted *better* by the behavior of the secondborn infants at the first visits than it was by the firstborn children's own behavior at those first visits. The more sociable the babies were at the first session, the more sociable their older siblings were toward them at the second visit. 12

We just do not know, with children older than preschoolers, whether differences in the behavior of the first- and laterborn siblings influence the way in which the relationship between the children develops. This is partly because most studies have looked only at the sex of and age gap between the siblings and not at the individual differences in affection or hostility. It has been assumed that it is the sex of the children and the age gap 13 between them that are of the most significance. But do boys and girls differ in the way they behave toward their siblings?

Sex Differences

14   It's often said that a boy growing up with several sisters will be "feminine" in his interests and a girl with brothers will be a "tomboy." In the 1950s and 1960s several psychologists looked at the relation between the extent to which children and adolescents were "masculine" or "feminine" in their interests, occupations, and games, and whether they had grown up with brothers or sisters. The results were complicated, and in some ways contradictory. Laterborn children with an older sibling of the same sex did tend to be the most "stereotypically sex typed." A second-born boy with an older brother was likely to be very "masculine" in his interests, and girls with older sisters were likely to be particularly "feminine" in theirs.

15   But the picture is not a simple or a consistent one. For instance, some studies suggested that boys with *two* older sisters showed *less* interest in "feminine" games and occupations, and interacted less with girls in the classroom than did boys with brothers. In explaining these results it was argued that whereas some children "identified" with their siblings, imitated them, and modeled their behavior on them, other children reacted against their siblings by developing very different interests and opposing styles.

16   It is clear that we could "explain" any particular combination of personalities and interests among the brothers and sisters within a family by referring to these two processes of "identification" and its opposite, "deidentification." Certainly we cannot predict with any confidence the personality or behavior of a child simply on the basis of knowing his or her sex and the sex of the other children in the family.

17   There are no clear or consistent differences between very young boys and girls in the ways that they behave toward their siblings. For instance, it is sometimes assumed that older sisters are more likely to be nurturant—"little mothers"—than older brothers. But in the cross-cultural studies of John and Beatrice Whiting, in which sibling caregiving by both girls and boys was very common, no sex differences were found in the behavior of the older siblings, although the younger siblings asked for help,

comfort, and security from older sisters more frequently than from older brothers.

Sisters are sometimes said to be better teachers than brothers. 18 Boys and girls do have rather different teaching styles. Rob Stewart asked a number of children between the ages of four and five to teach their two-year-old siblings how to use a camera. The best teachers were boys with younger brothers, especially those who were relatively advanced in understanding how to take the perspective of another person. In contrast, Victor Cicirelli found that sisters were more effective teachers than brothers: they used a deductive method more than boys, they offered help more often, and their help was more likely to be accepted.

However, children with an older brother appeared to do better 19 when working alone than children with an older sister. Cicirelli suggests that this may be because a child with an older brother is stimulated by the competition and rivalry of an older brother to learn more than from an older sister, but that in a more formal teaching situation the younger child will learn more from an older sister because she expects to give help and the younger expects to receive it.

In contrast to these results from experimental studies, no sex 20 differences in frequency of teaching by older siblings, or in acceptance of teaching by their younger siblings, have yet been found in studies of children at home.

The same contradictions appear when same-sex and different- 21 sex pairs are compared. With very young siblings there is often a greater amount of friendly, helpful interaction and imitation in same-sex pairs. But in Rob Stewart's study, in which sibling pairs were left alone in a laboratory playroom, the older siblings who were *least* likely to comfort and support their younger siblings were brothers in two-boy families. And among older children, aggression and dominance were more often evident in same-sex pairs: mothers of six-year-olds in the Cambridge studies reported more jealousy in same-sex pairs, for instance. Yet in Helen Koch's extensive interviews, more six-year-olds with same-sex siblings than with different-sex siblings said that they would prefer to play with their sibling rather than with a friend, and more said that they liked looking after their sibling. It was very rare, among Koch's six-year-olds, for a child who had a same-sex sibling to say that he or she would be happier without the sibling.

22   Why should there be such contradictory results? The different cultural backgrounds of the families studied, the different ages of the children, differences in the way in which the children were studied—all of these factors could contribute to the inconsistencies. But clearly, sex differences in either younger or older siblings *cannot* be linked in a simple or powerfully predictive way to differences in the way the children relate to one another.

Age Differences

23   People often hold even stronger views on the importance of the age gap between siblings than on the significance of the sex of siblings. Some parents attribute the intimacy and friendliness of their children to their closeness in age. The close matching of interest and effectiveness as partners in play of children who are only two years apart is held to be of real importance. Other parents believe that their children get along well because there is a large age gap between them. The older child, they argue, does not feel so displaced, and since he's more secure is more friendly toward the younger. Both accounts sound plausible, and we can find evidence to support either point of view. With preschool-aged children, the age gap does not appear to be nearly as important as physicians and psychiatrists have supposed. The ways in which firstborns react to the arrival of a sibling do differ with age: fifteen-month-olds tend to react by becoming miserable and clinging, whereas three- to four-year-olds often become very difficult and demanding. But the age difference does not appear to affect the positive interest in the new baby, or the incidence of marked disturbance, or the quality of the relationship between the two children as they grow up. Play, companionship, and affection are as frequently shown whether the age gap is four years or only eleven months; so too are aggression, hostility, and teasing.

24   The more "parent-like" behaviors of teaching and caregiving are more frequently shown by the older children in families in which there is a large age gap. But in many studies the larger the age gap between the children, the greater the age of the older child, and it is hardly surprising that with increasing age children are more effective teachers or caregivers.

With children aged six, seven, and eight, the story is rather dif-   25
ferent. Helen Koch found that if the gap between the children
was between two and four years, all the effects she described—
modeling, rivalry, competition—were heightened. With a larger
age gap the children played less together, but the laterborns accepted teaching from their older siblings more often and more
willingly. In general, the age gap between siblings seems to be
more important with six- to eight-year-olds than it is with little
children, but there are still many inconsistencies in the findings
of different studies. For instance, one study compared seven-
and eight-year-olds as they played with their siblings in a competitive game, and as they wrapped a very large box together. If
the seven- and eight-year-olds had a sibling close in age (with
only one to two years between them), they were more aggressive and less likely to be friendly than if the age gap was three
to four years. In contrast, Helen Koch found that siblings who
were more than two years apart in age had more competitive and
stressful relationships. These contradictions show that we clearly
should not draw simple conclusions about the significance (or
the insignificance) of the age gap between sisters and brothers.

Growing Up in a Large Family

Until now, I have talked about the relationship between brothers   26
and sisters mostly in terms of *pairs* of siblings. How different is
the experience of growing up with lots of brothers and sisters?
The focus on two-children families reflects both the kind of
studies that have been done by psychologists and the typical
families of Western Europe and the United States. The study of
large families conducted by Bossard and Boll in the 1950s gives
a different picture of family life. They interviewed and collected
written life histories from over 150 people from families with
more than six children. It was a retrospective study, drawing on
people's recollections and reflections on their childhood experiences, rather than a direct study of the children themselves. It
was also not a formal, systematic study. But the insights it gives
us are interesting, and balance the picture of brothers and sisters
given by studies of smaller families.

First, for many of the children in those large families there was   27
an important closed world of play with their brothers and sisters:
"We rarely had outside company and did not feel the need of it.

We had good imaginations and played many games, which were joined in by two dogs and a cat. This life continued for some years, and, as far as we children were concerned, it was the closest thing to heaven." Some children felt that this closed family world limited their ability to relate to others. Most children, however, felt that living in a large family had very important and useful consequences: learning to share, to develop self-control, and to show consideration for others were repeatedly mentioned. The following three quotations are typical of the views of people from large families:

> Living in a large family socializes a child to an appreciable extent. . . . In general, living and being reared in a large family teaches one that life is not a "bed of roses" and that there are other people in the world all with "equal rights" to the pursuit of happiness in life . . . a child in a large family has brothers and sisters of contemporary age who understand him as a child and in the "give and take" of their everyday life each learns to control emotions, think in terms of "we" and not "me," "to live and let live," to look out for oneself and yet to consider the rights of others, and a host of similar terms all meaning to live as a real human being should and not as an animal.

> I think that large family life teaches self-control and self-discipline. When you have three or four or more brothers and sisters who aggravate you in various ways at various times, you soon learn that it is not considered good conduct to grab, shake or strike your brothers and sisters. You learn to control those nasty antisocial acts, or carry their problems to the impartial courts of the law, I don't know. You learn to discipline yourself in many ways, and to govern your conduct along acceptable social ways. . . . I think that being part of a large family establishes the desire to belong or to be needed. It makes you like to love and be loved; a large family does not tend to produce cold, aloof, withdrawn people. It teaches respect for private property, and consideration for each other. It produces the desire to help each other or to guide each other.

> Yes, I do honestly believe that living in a large family does have its effect on socialization because consideration must be given to each other during the course of living together. A form of unity develops and with it a sense of attachment for each other. Though pri-

vacy is at a minimum, or rather impossible, one does gain somewhat of a group spirit which implies thinking through things together and arriving at decisions that are reasonably acceptable to all. I am convinced that a much more charitable consideration for "the other person" is engendered by a person who derives from a large family than one who is a product of a small family.

A second point is that siblings in large families often have   28
special roles as disciplinarians of their younger siblings; this rarely happens in two-child or three-child families. Earlier I quoted the words of one firstborn who had to assume many responsibilities. How do younger siblings feel about the discipline meted out by their older siblings? The quotations show that in many ways sibling discipline can work very well, from the children's point of view. First, the siblings in the study did feel that they understood each other and each other's problems—often better than the parents. Second, they felt that they often had better judgment than the parents as to what should be considered misbehavior. According to them, this meant that discipline imposed by siblings was often more reasonable, and had more meaning, than discipline by parents. Third, and most important, they suggested that sibling discipline was more effective than adult discipline because the disapproval of siblings mattered so much more than the disapproval of adults. And as Bossard and Boll comment: "Siblings know what kinds of discipline are effective. They know that a sound spanking, while it may hurt for the time being, may have far less meaning than not being allowed to go fishing with the others. It may be argued here that children are often very cruel to each other, and this certainly is true. Perhaps the real reason for this is not what adults assume it to be, but because children are realists. They know what matters, and what hurts."

The security provided by siblings was stressed by a sur-   29
prisingly large number of the people from large families—surprisingly, because according to conventional psychiatric wisdom, security for a child is based on the parent–child (and usually the mother–child) relationship. I have commented on the security that even preschool-aged and infant siblings apparently provide for each other. Here is a parallel emphasis on the security that siblings can provide much later in childhood.

30   Why should living with a large number of siblings lead to a sense of emotional security? Several reasons were given. One was that within the large family, dependability was highly appreciated, even fostered, in the face of the many hardships with which the family had to cope.

> We did feel a sense of security that must be lacking in small families, because we were required to work together and to the well-being of all of us. This feeling remains—even in our adult years.

> We have the philosophy that if we stick together we can get through any crisis. If we stand alone, it makes a hardship on the family. . . . Fear with us was unknown, probably because we never stood completely alone.

> Emotionally there was strength in being a member of a large family. A crisis was met by everyone and to back up an individual there was a whole clan.

It was also stressed that within the group of siblings there was likely to be at least one person with whom a child could pair up, and who would provide support: "We always had at least one other family member to play with. In smaller families, if you are feuding with your only brother or sister, you would be quite lonely. One very seldom feuds with seven or eight other people, though, so in a large family there is always someone left to turn to for consolation and love."

31   The point that siblings *know* each other so well was believed by many to be the key to the emotional security provided by a large family. According to Bossard and Boll, some informants felt that their own siblings had a better understanding of the problems that younger children faced than did their parents. They not only realized when and why their young siblings felt insecure, but also helped them through such difficult situations.

> My oldest brother took my youngest brother to his first Scout meeting. I took him to his first day at school. When a child is faced with a new experience it must be a great comfort to know that someone is there who has been through it all before.

> Mother spanked my third brother. Sister cried as hard as if she had been spanked and as soon as Mother left the room, she ran

to his side, put her arm around him, and said through her tears, "You'll be all right, don't cry."

Three of us had mumps at the same time. We could console one another as we lay sick in bed.

The boys down the street and my second brother would get into a fight. The minute my eldest brother and I discovered it we were also in it, beating the other kid up or helping our little brother to hold his own. Surely it is a good feeling for a child to know there are others to help fight his battles, whether he be right or wrong.

For some children in the study, the security of the relationship 32 with the brothers and sisters was closely related to the problem that the children all faced together. Often the children helped each other through the difficulties of coping with an inadequate mother or father, or difficult social circumstances. And some siblings felt that their security together came from the very fact that there was no opportunity for emotional "coddling" of any of them by the parents, with the exception perhaps of the youngest.

The picture of a childhood spent with several brothers and 33 sisters as one of security, strength, and a rich shared world of play is of course only a partial one. Rivalry and competition were described too. Often the large families split into factions and cliques, or shifting alliances against particular children or subgroups of children. But they stressed rivalry less than did individuals from smaller families. It could well be that this was because these informants were recalling their childhood experiences, and tended to remember the better moments rather than the irritations of living with so many siblings. The children who were interviewed while still living at home did in fact stress conflict and rivalry more than the other informants.

We have looked at the issue of why children differ so dramat- 34 ically in the affection and hostility that they show toward their siblings, and specifically at the question of how the age gap, birth order, and gender of the siblings contribute to these differences. It is clear that if we want to explain the individual differences in how well brothers and sisters get along, and the ways in which they influence one another, we must move away from asking simply: Is it the age gap that matters? Is it the sex of the siblings that is crucial? We must realize first what a complicated equation we are dealing with when we ask what influences the relationship between the children in a family. Not only age and sex, but the personalities of the children, the size of the family, the social circumstances, and especially the children's relations with their parents must be taken into account. A great many factors affect the relationship between siblings. It is hardly surprising that we do not find simple clear connections between a child's position in the family, the sex of his siblings, and the way children get along or the way in which their personalities develop.

35   However, the studies of birth order and gender do help answer the questions raised by the book's first theme, which concerns the ways in which siblings influence one another's development. The sex and personality of the firstborn are, for instance, more likely to influence the laterborn children in a direct way than vice versa. How a first child feels about his or her sibling appears to influence the way in which their relationship develops from the earliest weeks. Firstborns are more likely to express ambivalence or hostility than laterborns. But the extent of intimacy and affection that a child feels and shows toward a sibling—which is probably of prime importance in *how* he or she influences the sibling—is not simply related to birth order, age gap, or gender.

36   We still know very little about the way in which the personalities of the individual children affect the quality of the relationship or vice versa. But it is clear that each child's relationship with the parents is closely implicated in many of the differences between siblings.

Content Questions

Because of the wealth of material presented in Judy Dunn's article, it is essential that you take notes as you read. At specific points along the way, share your notes in writing group to facilitate discussion. Begin by reading the first section, "Firstborns and Laterborns."

1. How would you yourself describe firstborns? In what ways do your descriptions fit the findings of the various studies?

2. Discuss the Brian Sutton-Smith study. What conclusions does he come to? What precautions does Dunn suggest readers consider?

3. What are the connections between birth order and dominance?

4. The relationship between first- and second-born children seems to depend on several factors. What are they?

Read the next section, "Sex Differences."

1. What were the results of the studies done in the 1950s and 1960s?

2. What does Dunn conclude from the studies?

3. How are gender roles connected to children's mothering and teaching of younger siblings?

4. Dunn reports on two studies, Stewart's and Koch's, that have quite different results. What may account for the contradictions?

Read the section "Age Differences."

1. What were the findings of Helen Koch's study?

2. What contradictions were found?

3. Dunn states that ". . . we clearly should not draw simple conclusions about the significance (or the insignificance) of the age gap between sisters and brothers." Respond to this statement.

Read the remainder of the article, beginning with the section "Growing Up in a Large Family."

1. What were the insights from the Bossard and Boll study?

2. How do younger siblings feel about their older siblings as disciplinarians?

3. What were the findings concerning emotional security?

4. What does Dunn suggest as the best way to design further studies, and why?

5. What is her final conclusion?

Using your notes and answers to the questions, write a response to the entire article.

The second article, "Places Everyone" by Stephen Harrigan, takes a more lighthearted view of birth order but agrees in many ways with Judy Dunn. Answer the following questions as you read the article:

Content Questions

1. In what ways does Stephen Harrigan compare himself to the classic younger brother?

2. Summarize the traits Harrigan associates with each birth place: oldest, middle, youngest. In what ways do you agree/disagree?

3. What statement does psychologist Kevin Leman make that Judy Dunn would heartily agree with?

4. What is your opinion of Leman based on Harrigan's description of him?

5. What does Alfred Adler believe about the importance of birth order?

6. Describe Adler's life and work.

7. Why have many researchers stopped looking at birth order, according to Toni Falbo?

8. In what ways do you agree/disagree with Falbo's interpretation?

9. Harrigan believes the birth order theory lives on because—why?

Places Everyone

STEPHEN HARRIGAN

1   A few months ago, when I was in Los Angeles, I paid a call on my older brother at the gleaming new downtown office building where he works. I gave my name at the reception booth in the lobby, and then ascended the many floors to his corner office in an elevator that glided upward as silently as a spider on a thread.

He was standing there to greet me, dressed in a gray suit, when the doors opened on the 56th floor. As ever, he was three inches taller, and quicker on the draw with his handshake. My older brother's name is Jim, though I have noticed that professionally he goes by the commanding initials J. P. As he led me on a tour of his building, past works of corporate art, through conference rooms and executive dining rooms while I trailed along with my untied shoelace flapping on the marble floor, it occurred to me that even in childhood—when he was Jimmy and I was Stevie–somehow I had already perceived him as J. P.

Decades of adulthood, I realized, had not bred the younger brother out of me. Nor could I expect it to. There is a school of thought—and a cottage industry to go with it—that decrees that birth order is destiny. We are who we are because of who was there ahead of us when we were born, and who came behind. In my own case, one might argue, the scenario was so predictable it could have been plotted on a graph. "The younger brother of a brother," wrote psychologist Walter Toman, "has lived with an older, taller, smarter, stronger, more perfect boy than himself as far back as he can remember." In order to avoid the hopeless task of competing against Jim, I became in many ways his opposite—a process that is known in psycho-jargon as sibling deidentification. Where he was authoritative, I was cunningly acquiescent. Where he was athletic, I was bookish. Without either of us consciously knowing it, I conceded him the title of standard-bearer, conservator, defender of the realm—then scouted out the terrain and found my own dreamy path.

It is intoxicatingly simple, this idea that our place in the family is the fount of our strengths and failings, our drives and our fears. If we know our place in the family, the birth order gurus suggest in their hyper-friendly self-help books, we know ourselves. If you're one of the 44 percent of the population who's first or only born, you were the early recipient of the brunt of your parents' attention and expectations. That means you're likely to be hard driving, demanding, doggedly responsible. Oldest children tend to spend more time with adults, so it's natural that they grow up faster, eager to invest themselves with leadership and grave responsibility. (All seven Mercury astronauts were firstborns.) If you are an only child, you are supposed to be just as much a perfectionist as a firstborn, but intransigent and finicky as well, since you never experienced the tempering trauma of dethronement by a younger sibling.

5   Middle children, like me, are the hardest to nail down, but in general we are seen as the victims of benign neglect, the ones with the fewest pictures in the family photo album. To cope with that lack of attention, we became rebellious and secretive, relying on friends for the companionship that somehow eluded us within the family. And because we never got our parents all to ourselves, we learned to compromise. By the time we were out of childhood, we were already seasoned diplomats.

6   Youngest children may smolder with thwarted ambition (like Joseph in the Old Testament, who dreamed of himself as a sheaf of wheat that suddenly stood upright in a field, commanding obeisance from the lesser sheaves representing his ten brothers), but typically by the time they were born their parents had exhausted their expectations on all the siblings ahead of them, and were content to pamper the youngest without condition. Last borns are described variously as clowns, cutups, and mascots.

7   Birth order experts are full of breezy observations and prescriptions. They tell us we should marry into relationships that roughly duplicate our old sibling connections. So if we are the youngest brother of sisters we should marry the oldest sister of brothers, or if we are the youngest sister of brothers we should marry the oldest brother of sisters. We are advised that the secret to good parenting is to use birth order to understand the behavior of our own children—the supercharged firstborn, the mediating middle child, the restless last born.

8   When viewed through the birth order lens, human nature all at once seems marvelously comprehendable. Of *course* Hillary Clinton and Henry Kissinger are firstborns! Of *course* Katie Couric and Richard Simmons are youngest children! Firstborn, second born, last born—thinking of ourselves in these terms, we seem to snap immediately into place.

9   But is it true? Are the insights we receive from pondering birth order any more authentic than those we find in a daily horoscope, or in the lugubrious responses from a Ouija board?

10   "What could make more sense?" psychologist Kevin Leman asked one bright morning as we left his Tucson office to go out in search of breakfast. "A theory based on the dynamics between parents and children and between children and their siblings. It's

not just that you're number one or number two. It's more complex than that. You have to take the whole family into account. But you *can* use birth order to get a quick handle on people."

Leman is the reigning pooh-bah of birth order, the author of 11
The Birth Order Book, which bears the confident subtitle *Why You Are the Way You Are,* as well as *Growing Up Firstborn: The Pressure and Privilege of Being Number One.* His books are found in that vast self-help section of the nineties bookstore devoted to co-dependency, addiction, miscarriage, Cinderella complexes, and books by both sexes on what's wrong with men.

Needless to say, Leman's office is not a dark Freudian lair, but 12
a sunny enclave on the second floor of an office strip. Leman himself is as uncomplicated as his book titles suggest. Sandy-haired and clean-shaven, he was wearing jeans the day I met him. (As a last born, he can't stand to wear a suit.)

Leman told me he first heard about birth order when he was 13
a graduate student at the University of Arizona, and the theory had the force of an epiphany. "All I could think about was my family—my firstborn sister who has clear vinyl runners on the carpet and whose children are always color coordinated; my older brother, who bears my father's name; and then me, the baby of the family."

As we approached his car, Leman pointed to his personal- 14
ized licence plates, which bore the message ZAP ASU. "Now that's a typical thing for a baby of the family to do," he said. "Out here in Tucson, we hate ASU because they're the University of Arizona's rivals. To me it's worth it to pay twenty-five dollars a year to have people pull up and honk.

"Have you ever seen me on TV?" Leman asked as we drove 15
off to the restaurant. "I'm funny. You'll find that most comedians—Steve Martin, Eddie Murphy, Goldie Hawn—are last borns."

Leman has promoted his ideas on most of the major talk 16
shows and in various business seminars, where he advises executives on how to use birth order information as a strategic tool. If you own a car dealership, for example, you'd want to know that a last born might very well be the star of the sales force, but would be a disaster in the general-manager slot, which should go to a firstborn.

"I was on 'Jenny Jones' last week," he said. "Producers love 17
to do this kind of thing: They bring out three siblings and make

me guess which one is which. I was in good form that day. I nailed them, which made me feel like Mickey Mantle in 1956. I felt so confident I took a stab at Jenny herself. I guessed that she was a baby girl, since she was overflowing with affection, and I was right."

18   He turned to me, sized me up for a moment, and said, "I'd say you're the firstborn son with an older sister."

19   "Actually," I confessed, "second-born son with a younger sister."

20   "Hmmmm," Leman said.

21   "Most of this stuff on birth order," complains Harold Mosak, a clinical psychologist who teaches a course on the subject at the Adler School of Professional Psychology in Chicago, "is just psychological pap that depends on popular notions and misconceptions. People who want to understand themselves rush to this stuff just like they rush to astrology."

22   Even Alfred Adler, the founding father of birth order theory, believed that the idea could be carried too far.

23   "There has been some misunderstanding," he wrote in 1918, "of my custom of classification according to position in the family. It is not, of course, the child's number in the order of successive births which influences his character, but the situation into which he is born and the way he interprets it." Adler recognized that classifying people by birth order was overly simplistic. But, in retrospect, his basic observations on the subject still have the sort of ringing self-evidence that is often associated with ideas of genius. He pointed out, for instance, that second-born children often have dreams in which they picture themselves running after trains and riding in bicycle races. "Sometimes this hurry in his dreams is sufficient by itself to allow us to guess that the individual is a second child."

24   Adler was convinced that his own life was shaped by his birth order. Born in 1870 in Penzing, a suburb of Vienna, he was the second of six children. He was a sickly boy who felt hopelessly overshadowed by his older brother. "One of my earliest recollections," he wrote, "is of sitting on a bench, bandaged up on account of rickets, with my healthy elder brother sitting opposite me. He could run, jump, and move about quite effortlessly, while for me movement of any sort was a strain and an

effort." Even when he was an old man, Adler was haunted by the robust power of his older brother. "He is *still* ahead of me!" he lamented near the end of his life.

Adler's resentment of his older brother's authority invested   25
him with a rebellious streak that would leave its stamp on the burgeoning science of psychology. He began his career as a physician, and was keenly interested in the influence of environment on physical and mental health. In 1902, his brilliance brought him to the attention of Sigmund Freud, who was then refining his theories of the unconscious mind and consolidating his position as the high priest of psychoanalysis. Freud was 13 years older than Adler, and in his authoritarian cast of mind a classic firstborn who was used to ruling his younger siblings. ("I am by temperament nothing but a conquistador," he once admitted to a friend.)

Adler was asked to join Freud's famous weekly discussion   26
group that later became known as the Vienna Psychological Society. Over the course of ten years Adler contributed greatly to the insights and even the terminology of Freud's work (the term *inferiority complex,* for instance, was first coined by Adler).

But the firstborn Freud, sensing a rival, began to hound and   27
berate his colleague. Adler, still suffering from his lifelong resentment at being number two, bristled and left the sanctum. "Why should I always do my work under your shadow?" he asked Freud in a parting shot.

Adler took a small group of followers with him and started   28
his own rival mental health dynasty. His ideas were simpler and more pragmatic than Freud's. The hallmark of what he called individual psychology was a conviction that people do not live in a gloomy, deterministic universe, subject to unconscious drives they cannot control. Adler's focus was on getting his patients up and running, showing them what was wrong with their lives and then allowing them to make a choice to either sink into despair or become productive members of society.

Today, Adlerians—such as Kevin Leman—are a distinct mi-   29
nority in a mental health industry still largely influenced by Freudian thought, but it is they who have kept the concept of birth order alive.

Even the Adlerians have found, however, that it's tricky to   30
prove that birth order counts for much. Since Adler's death,

various studies *have* turned up some interesting observations. Last borns are more likely to write their autobiographies (what better way to be noticed?). They also are statistically more inclined to alcoholism. It turns out that more firstborns seek psychological counseling. Renowned baseball players have tended to be middle and youngest children (by conditioning, perhaps, they're more drawn to team sports). And firstborn girls are over-represented among striptease artists.

31   By and large, though, the idea that birth order is directly related to personality has proven to be as ungraspable as it is enticing. "Birth order influence is a disappointment," says Jules Angst, a psychologist from Zurich. "It doesn't explain a lot."

32   Angst arrived at this conclusion after surveying, with his colleague Cecile Ernst, 34 years of birth order research, from 1946 to 1980. Ernst and Angst came away unimpressed. In short, birth order didn't consistently predict which sibling is most likely to be an extrovert, feel pain, take risks, lack self-esteem, select certain marriage partners, feel guilt, adopt conservative political views, get frustrated easily, need autonomy, or suffer psychological problems. Only a few of the studies they considered gave even marginal support to the idea that birth order influence is a factor in shaping personality, and most of these, Angst says, were fraught with "methodological fallacies."

33   "Most serious researchers have stopped talking about birth order," says Toni Falbo, an educational psychologist at the University of Texas in Austin. "If you look at all the factors that lead to a particular outcome in shaping someone's personality, on a good day, birth order might account for one percent."

34   The big problem with assessing birth order is the almost impossible task of getting a clear focus on what it is that's being studied. A family is a densely woven fabric made up of innumerable threads, some of which are apparent and some of which are not. Even if you could extract that one birth order thread out of the carpet—leaving in place a background of other powerful influences like socioeconomic status, race, class, values, aspirations, disease, death, ancestral history—you would still have a great deal of untangling to do.

35   Take, as an example, a family with four siblings. The children might have been born one after another at regular intervals, in which case their birth order positions would be fairly clear. But

what if they came along in sets of two that were separated by a wide gap of years? Wouldn't the third child be likely to develop the characteristics of a firstborn, and might not the second child share the same last born traits of the fourth child? What if the firstborn was a boy, and all the rest were girls? Wouldn't the oldest girl develop a firstborn personality in relation to her sisters? How would an oldest son turn out if he were haunted by the knowledge of a "phantom" older brother lost to an early death?

The permutations of gender, spacing, and circumstance are so endless and complicating that it hardly seems worthwhile trying to sort through them. For Kevin Leman, however, they're just more spice for the stew. 36

"Every time another child is born," he says, "the entire environment changes. How parents interact with each child as it enters the family circle determines in great part that child's final destiny. 37

"Now the reason I guessed that you're a firstborn son with an older sister," he explained to me on the way to the restaurant that morning, "is because you seem to have a nice, easygoing demeanor. Which tells me one of two things: You have sisters above you in the family, or you have a good relationship with your mother. Now one of those things has to be true or you can get out of the car and walk. 38

"Also," he went on, "you're a reporter. Reporters are almost always firstborns. On my last tour I was interviewed by ninety-two people. Out of the ninety-two, eighty-seven were firstborns. Same thing with pilots. If you want to have fun on the flight home, stick your head into the cockpit and ask, 'How are the firstborns today?' Eighty-eight percent of them are. And librarians! Firstborns are voracious readers. I challenge you to call thirty librarians and find out their birth orders." 39

Over breakfast, Leman sketched his own history as a last born goofball. He was a poor student and behavior problem in high school, he said, and when he managed to find a college that would take him, he was more or less kicked out in his third semester. Leman was working as a janitor when he met his wife, Sande, who as fate would have it was a firstborn and therefore ideally suited to the task of shaping him up. Leman also credits his wife with helping him find a sustaining belief in God, the ultimate firstborn. 40

41 Leman related all this with good humor and a certain commonsense gravity, which made him seem less superficial than I had expected. But it was clear that his last born traits had prepared him well for the role of pop psychologist. Not only was he gleeful in his disregard for the academics who might consider him a lightweight ("Academia! You want to talk about an unreal world?"), he was also still enough of a showboat to put his birth order knowledge to use as a kind of parlor game.

42 Just then, for instance, he was trying to guess the birth order of our waiter.

43 "Okay, Eric," Leman said, glancing at the waiter's name tag. "Give me a description of your mom or dad. Either one."

44 "Well," Eric said, "my dad is very shy."

45 "How about little boy Eric? Age five to twelve?"

46 "Well, I guess some people would have said I was a mama's boy."

47 "Hmmmm. And when you grew up, did you marry a firstborn, middle child, or baby?"

48 "Baby. She's the last of four kids."

49 "So," Leman said. "I bet you're a firstborn son."

50 Eric smiled. "You got it," he said, and went back to the kitchen.

51 "What tipped you off?" I asked Leman.

52 "Two things. First, did you notice the way he came out and wanted our order right away? He was impatient, he didn't want to fool with us. The other thing was *very*. He described his father as 'very shy.' So he probably sees things in black or white—not much gray. That's definitely a firstborn trait."

53 I went home impressed, willing to overlook Leman's misreading of my own birth order. If the Great Birth Order Theory did not quite bear up under the weight of evidence, it was still tantalizing enough to my imagination to *seem* true. That, surely, is what keeps it alive. Scientific scrutiny may erode the birth order stereotype, but we tend to shore it up again whenever we meet a supercharged eldest child or a last born who is lost in the ozone.

54 I called 30 librarians. It turned out that only 18 of them were firstborns or only children. As I had come to expect when dealing with the notion that birth order rules our lives, I was neither

convinced nor resoundingly disabused. As a middle child, I could see only shades of gray.

Cause-and-Effect Pattern of Development

The two articles you read examined the effects of birth order. To put it another way, they examined the theory that birth order *causes* certain *effects* to result. The final paper for this chapter will use a cause-and-effect pattern.

The cause-and-effect pattern of development is a way of solving problems by finding connections among occurrences. We look for connections between causes and outcomes, and these connections provide us with new knowledge. We can solve problems when we discover the causes for an effect that happened or prevent possible unwanted effects of some occurrence.

The cause-and-effect pattern is useful when you are writing essays for college classes. An essay assignment might ask you to explore the causes of a particular situation, such as a dramatic change in weather patterns; or to analyze the possible effects of a bill or law; or to explain the effects of using a new drug or the causes of an outbreak of a disease. Anytime one discusses why something happened or explains the results of an event, a cause-and-effect pattern is useful.

Looking beyond the obvious is important when you work on determining causes and effects. There may be a temptation to accept a simple answer; however, a cause can have many effects and an effect many causes. Be sure to consider your subject carefully in depth so as not to jump to hasty conclusions. Most relationships between causes and effects are complex and need to be questioned with care. Ask yourself what other reasons might cause an effect. Quick answers often lead to confusion and faulty conclusions.

One way to organize a cause-and-effect essay is chronological: You list results in the order they occurred. In some situations, a cause creates an effect, which in turn is the cause of another effect. A chronological approach works best for this type of situation. Other situations may involve several effects and no clear time pattern. In cases such as this, it is best to explain the causes or effects in order of importance, usually leaving the most important or powerful one for last to make a strong impact.

Cause and effect can be used in conjunction with the other patterns of development you have already studied. In fact, combining patterns is often the best strategy. This textbook presents each pattern individually to give you opportunities to learn that style well, but many times a combination of patterns produces a stronger result. Even when using more than one pattern, though, make certain you adhere to the specific guidelines for each pattern in order to create the most effective paper. For narration, for example, the focus was on detailed examples, active verbs, and specific adjectives and adverbs. The use of these elements will enhance almost any type of writing, and a writer needs to look consciously for them when revising. Process analysis relies heavily on sequence—again, an element important in many kind of writing. When deciding what pattern to use, you must consider the best way to present the material for the intended audience.

WRITING ASSIGNMENT:
COLLABORATIVE CAUSE-AND-EFFECT PAPER

Your assignment is to write a collaborative cause-and-effect paper based on birth placement. This assignment is a group project, with three to five authors to a group. Form the groups by birth placement: In one group all the members should be the oldest sibling; in another, the middle child; in another, the youngest; and in another, the only child. To keep the groups fairly uniform in size, the class may need two or more groups for one or more birth placements. The "cause" you will write about is your position in relation to parents and/or siblings; the "effects" are how that position shaped your life. Each group should decide on the possible effects of being born in a certain birth order position or being an only child and choose subtopics of those effects to explore. For example, one group might decide to look at children's responsibilities, relationship with parents, self-esteem, and peer interaction. Using the chosen topics, the group members then contribute their experiences related to each topic.

Writing a Collaborative Paper

A difficulty students have in composing a multiauthored paper is deciding on an organization scheme that allows for each voice to be distinct and yet for the paper to flow with coherency. Students have discovered that it is generally best to have each person write in response to each subtopic. For example, if the subtopic is discipline, then each member writes about how he or she was disciplined. After each author responds, the group reads all the contributions and writes a collective summary. What effects are similar and what ones are different? What conclusions can you draw about the "effect" of discipline based on the "cause" of birth order? Remember, you are not trying to generalize to the population as a whole, only to draw conclusions based on the data or experiences of your group. Follow this procedure for each of the subtopics or questions you have chosen.

Transitions are especially important in a collaborative paper as you move from one author to the next. A group of middle-child students used the conclusion of one paragraph to lead into the next. For example, on the topic of relationships with parents, a student wrote at the end of her paragraph: "My parents will always be an important part of my life, and by being a middle child I have received the perfect combination of their parenting. Although Emmy's parents were divorced, she also feels that she and her parents have a special relationship." The next writer, Emmy, then wrote her paragraph about her relationship with her parents. She ended the paragraph with "Jennifer's relationship with her parents also differed from that of her two siblings." Jennifer was the writer who followed. The students continued this pattern throughout the paper, giving the reader clues not only to who was writing but also to the connections between the experiences.

The conclusion of your collaborative paper should discuss the connections between the findings explained in the Dunn and Harrigan articles and your group's experiences. Group members may find that their collective experiences relate closely to one another's, and therefore may discover patterns that connect to several of the findings in the articles. Members of other groups may find few similarities among their experiences; and for many groups, the results will lie somewhere in between.

Some students do not like to write collaborative papers; however, many careers require people to work on writing projects together. Grant writing, reports, explanations, and other job-related kinds of writing are seldom done by one person. For this reason, it is important that you have the experience of working with others on a writing project. Students often are concerned with the work distribution and the final grade. But with careful planning and advance discussion of expectations, many problems do not occur. Also, while some of the tasks need to be done by the group as a group, others are done individually. The following guidelines help promote good working relations:

1. Brainstorm as a group to decide what subtopics are pertinent to the group's experiences and interests.
2. Work on one topic at a time. Each person writes a paragraph or two about his or her experience relative to this one topic and brings the paragraph to class.
3. In your group, read and respond to everyone's paragraphs. Revision should be done topic by topic; otherwise the task becomes overwhelming.
4. Before leaving class, decide as a group which topic you will all write on next and when members must bring it to class. Follow this procedure for every subtopic.
5. After everyone has written on every subtopic, work as a group to write the transitions to ensure a smooth flow from writer to writer. Also write the subtopic summaries as a group.
6. It is important that everyone keep a copy of all the notes and completed writing he or she does as well as of all the writing done by the group. This way, the group can always continue the work even if someone is absent.

Student Reactions to Collaborative Writing

Student comments bear out the usefulness of collaborative writing, even though many of these students were dubious about the project before they began.

❑ "It seemed to me that the collaboration paper was extremely beneficial and rewarding. The group work allowed me to understand different aspects of team work that I regard as a very important part of educational process."

❏ "I really enjoyed doing a paper with my group because we all put our thoughts and feelings into the whole paper. My group was a true team in which everybody was as important as anyone else."

❏ "I learned a lot about myself and the people in my group. I like to think of them as my friends because we got a chance to know each other. I really learned how to work with other people and meet the expectations of others."

❏ "I believe the group project went well, but at the beginning I was leery. I'm not a people person so I didn't want to share my life with a bunch of strangers. It didn't turn out that bad though. I like the fact that we as a group disagreed about research findings. This was a great experience for me. Past experiences made me fret doing this, but now I'm glad we did."

The following student paper was written by a group of seven members. Six of them were eldest children, and one was an only child. The group members decided on four topics to explore: relationship with parents, relationships with other family members, responsibilities each had in the family, and the issue of material distribution. Each member wrote on each topic, and that resulted in a fairly long paper—approximately thirty-two pages. Because of space limitations only portions of the paper are included here; however, sections will illustrate how the writers used transitions for an easy-to-follow format and how the various voices complement one another with different points of view and experiences. The group wrote the introduction and conclusion in the third person, which gives the paper an objective group voice. The introduction explains each person's background, so readers know something about the authors before hearing each personal account. Then each person discusses his or her views and experiences in the first person. Transitions provide smooth connections between the different voices.

STUDENT PAPER

BIRTH ORDER

A Collaborative Essay

The student authors of these excerpts are Sara Koerper, Renee Schmidt, Tona Sollee Mullen, Todd Salisbury, and Beth Harding. Sara Koerper began the introduction.

Sara is a sophomore at UWEC. Her situation is unique because there is a large age difference between her and her sisters. One sister, Emily, is eleven years old; her other sister, Amanda, is eight years old. Sara's position in the family is characterized by a large amount of responsibility. In general, the relationships that Sara has with her family members are positive ones. Being the oldest child has given Sara helpful experience in care giving and has encouraged her to be a positive role model. Although she often wishes that her siblings were closer to her in age, she has never desired an older sibling. She treasures her position as the oldest child in the family.

Tona was adopted from South Korea at the age of six months. She has two younger sisters, Trisha, sixteen, and Tyann, eleven. Her dad, Terry, graduated from U of MN with a degree in marketing. Because he is a hard worker he has moved up in the company he works for, thus money never seemed to be a problem. Her mom, Teryl, graduated from the university as a dental hygienist. When Tona was adopted, Teryl quit her job and became a stay-at-home mom. Tona's relationship with her family has varied greatly despite their closeness. Because of the unreliable and unstable relationship among the family members, responsibility within the family was minimal.

Section one of the paper is "Relationship with Parents." The authors used first-person when responding to each of the four topics but third-person transitions between authors to identify the next writer, connect the paragraphs, and create a flow that is easy for a reader to follow. The following excerpt begins with the transition at the end of Justin's part (excluded here), which introduces Renee.

Renee's experience is similar to Justin's because it is a negative relationship gradually turning positive.

My relationship with my parents has undergone extensive changes from my childhood to the present. The oldest of three girls, I was expected to do my share of the work around the house and set an example for my siblings. Sometimes I resented my parents for this responsibility.

When I was a young child, my parents and I got along rather well. I was close to my mother especially, though my father and I did not have any real problems at that early age. My sisters and I were with my mother constantly, and I feel that we had a close stable relationship. My mother and I talked about everything, shopped together, cleaned the house together, fixed meals beside one another, and relaxed in front of the television.

As I grew older, the relationship with my parents changed. When I entered high school, my interests, ideas, and attitude altered a great deal. Although my mother and I could still share numerous times together, we began to fight as well. My father and I drifted apart quickly. He was constantly working and did not spend much time with his children. Although I respected him for his hard work and provisions, I missed him as my dad and felt uncomfortable when he was around.

I began to have a great deal of personal problems that affected the entire family. Our relationship basically deteriorated altogether. During my final year of high school, my parents and I fought with vehemence and intensity. I hated to be at home, and the three of us were unhappy together. About two weeks before Christmas, during my senior year, my parents and I engaged in a huge blowout that resulted in my leaving the house for good. I moved in with another family, and that is where I stayed.

In the many months that followed, my parents and I were forced to deal with issues that challenged us to forgive and go on. Piece by piece, we are again building our relationship, although the progress is slow. I hope to once again be close to my mom and dad, but the effort has to come from both sides.

Tona's relationship has gone through a series of changes.

My parents and I have had every kind of relationship possible. We have been the best of friends, enemies and everything in between. When I was young, my father and I were best friends; it seemed like we were always together. We went to football games together, went hiking, skating, and camping. We were very close.

Then came junior high. I wanted to spend more time with my friends. Surprisingly, I also found myself wanting to date boys instead of beating them up. So as a result, spending time with my dad became less frequent, and long talks with my mom became more frequent. Talks about boys, clothes, and makeup became a daily thing. She played a big part in my life. As most families do, though, because I was the oldest they had a hard time seeing their "little girl" grow up.

Being the only adopted child in the family, I felt they were overprotective of me. They always tried to protect me. This made independence nearly impossible. In junior high I also started to understand what adoption really meant. Up until that time it never seemed like a big deal. Kids asked questions, but I replied, "Well, I have two birthdays, my original one and my adoption one." They thought it was great.

However, I began to wonder why my biological mother gave me up for adoption. As usual, I thought the worst. Did my mother not love me? Was I a bad baby? I felt that it was my fault. After all, if my mother, my own flesh and blood, did not love me, who could? As far-fetched as these ideas sound, it is how I felt. Being adopted made me feel worthless. I had a lot of trouble dealing with it. I use to get depressed or angry towards anyone who mentioned it. Finally I got sick of blaming myself because my self-esteem was in the gutter. I needed someone to blame: I blamed my parents for adopting me and taking me away from my homeland and any chance to find my biological parents. Resentment turned to rebellion. They reprimanded me and made more rules, but I started to break them, trying to break free. Throughout the rest of junior high and high school, my parents and I fought like cats and dogs. This made any form of communication impossible. It never failed; after being in the same room for more than half an hour, we would be at each other's throats.

As high school progressed, my behavior was more rebellious. As each day went on, I became more and more out of control. During my junior year, I decided to go to Japan to find out something about my Oriental background. My parents agreed because they were sick of me, and they wanted me out of the house. The trip was planned for the summer, and when I left my parents and I were in a huge fight because they did not approve of my boyfriend. There I was on a plane to a foreign country with a different culture that spoke a language different from my own, and I was all by myself. Needless to say, the trip was hell. I never realized how different the Oriental culture was. I never realized how great my parents were. All of their reprimanding was because they were worried, and they were just trying to do their best to raise me well. Even though I knew that my parents and I were not on good terms, I called them sobbing. My parents immediately told me how much they loved me. Even though we had our differences, they were and are still there for me. This strengthened our relationship for the time being. When I came back, our relationship was great for awhile. Then I lost my patience with them and fighting was once again part of our daily routine.

College is the best thing I have done for our relationship. They are finally realizing that I am not a child anymore and am old enough to make my own decisions. It is easier to talk with them about life in general, and fighting is now at a minimum. My mom even calls me for advice about my two youngest sisters. Being older now, I realize how great my parents are and how much they love me. We are slowly building our relationship; there is no doubt that we will be close once again.

The second topic the group investigated was "Relationships with Siblings." The following excerpt was written by Todd.

Like Beth's sibling relationships, Todd's also vary from sibling to sibling.

I had a different relationship with each of my two brothers. Travis, three years younger than I, and I never really got along. On the other hand, Troy, ten years my junior, and I get along really well.

Growing up, Travis and I were always fighting with each other. Sometimes we would hit each other for what seemed like hours before Mom and Dad returned home and stopped it. My parents blamed me of course, because I was older. Perhaps because we were so close in age, everything Travis did seemed to irritate me. I remember one time when Travis had just returned home from the hospital after having his appendix removed. He was singing an irritating song, and I did not like it. I slugged him in the stomach where he had just undergone surgery. He cried for hours from the pain, and I cried for hours from the pain I felt when my father paddled my bare butt.

Troy and I, on the other hand, have always gotten on well. Whenever Troy wanted someone to play catch or to throw the ball around, I was always available. He looked up to me and wanted to do whatever I did. The sports that I played, he wanted to play. If I wore my hat backward, he wore his hat backward as well.

Even though I do not always get along with my brothers, it is nice having them around to take some of the burden off myself.

The third topic was "Material Distribution." Beth's and Sara's work is excerpted here.

Beth was the only girl in the family; there-fore, she feels that the materials were evenly distributed among siblings.

Being the oldest child and the only girl, I received many of my own things. I rarely had to share any of my toys because most of them were dolls and Barbies, and my brothers did not want to play with them. My youngest brother did receive some of my other brother's clothes, but he usually had his own toys. It seemed as though my youngest brother had a lot more than Kyle or I ever did, but he bought a lot of it himself. Since I am the only girl, I received many more clothes than my brothers, but it all evened out as my parents purchased my brothers one-hundred-dollar pairs of tennis shoes for sports every year.

Sara feels that the unfair distribution of materials in her family was due to different times and different financial situations.

When I was younger and living at home, I was often angered by the seemingly unfair distribution of material possessions among my sisters and me. Although, perhaps due to my maturity, the subject does not cross my mind today, at one time it created a significant barrier in my relationships with my sisters.

When I was born, my parents were in their early twenties and both were working to pay off college loans. My mother handmade much of my clothing to save money. When my sisters were born, my parents were in a more favorable financial situation. They were both in their thirties and had been working full time for a number of years. Many of my friends who had older siblings wore hand-me-downs; I expected Emily and Amanda would wear my old clothes. This was not the case. I knew that my polyester plaid bellbottoms were somewhat out of style, but I expected to see my old tee shirts on new family members. That didn't happen. Emily and Amanda received not only new clothes, but store-bought ones.

Nice clothing was not the only material good that I felt I had been cheated out of. When I was a baby, I slept in an old crib that my mother had picked up at a garage sale. When Emily was born, Mom and Dad bought a beautiful solid oak crib. My high chair had been plastic and metal; Emily and Amanda used a new wooden one.

As ridiculous as this may sound, I once thought that the uneven distribution inferred that Emily and Amanda were more worthy of rewards than I was-- that they were favored over me. I now realize that the differences were simply caused by the different financial situations that were present at the respective times of our births.

The fourth section is "Responsibility in the Family." Renee's and Todd's work is excerpted here.

Renee was responsible for various chores at home; however, she was not burdened with more responsibility than any of her family members.

Although I was the oldest child, I never felt required to do a larger portion of the work in our household. Heidi and I were separated by one year, and my parents treated the two of us equally the majority of the time. Responsibility in the family was distributed among my sisters accordingly. Teresa, the baby, was not expected to do a great deal. She did not have major responsibilities, such as chores, that Heidi and I had. My parents were hard working and routinely stressed the importance of chores in their child rearing. Heidi and I shared responsibilities and chores together, while Teresa often helped on her own.

I never felt overburdened by the work that my sisters and I were responsible for. My parents were careful to divide the chores as evenly as possible, with Teresa doing the least and Heidi and I carrying a heavier work load. Although at times I resented my parents for insisting that we do our share, I now realize how important it was for who we were to become. By insisting that I take responsibility at home, my parents taught me its importance.

Todd's responsibility in his family was of a form different from household chores: he was expected to be a positive role model.

Growing up, I did not have much responsibility delegated to me. I was not expected to do dishes or cook supper--my mother did that. Basically my mother took care of the household. I would just come home from school, eat, and then go to bed. I was, however, expected to set a good example for my younger brothers.

Throughout school, my parents always stressed that good grades were important. They told me that if I received good grades, my younger brothers would want to get good grades also. My brothers looked up to me and wanted to be like me.

In addition to being expected to get good grades, I was also expected to stay out of trouble

and to act responsibly. I feel that I did a good
job of this growing up--all the way through high
school. If my younger brothers now stay out of
trouble and get good grades, then I did my job.

The members wrote the conclusion together as a group, comparing and contrasting their experiences and views. Even though they shared a common place in the family, their experiences depended on many other factors: number and age of siblings, economics, parents' expectations, and personalities.

PART

Five

Knowing Oneself

What factors determine who we are and, consequently, why we act the way we do? Our beliefs and behavior are shaped by many influences. However, our values are fundamental in influencing who we are. People have different worldviews about what is important and how we should behave. What music is appropriate, what books children should read—in all facets of life people have attitudes based on their underlying beliefs or values. Values are reflected in behavior, possessions, personality, and likes and dislikes. If a person says he or she values honesty, then we might expect that person to be honest in their dealings with others. A person may like modern art; what then could you say she values in an artistic sense? Another person loves American primitives; what values might this preference reflect? Our taste in music can reveal our values as well.

Many of our values are traditional and timeless. We accept them because they have been the foundation of our lives. But accepting values as truths may not be the same thing as living our lives as if we truly believe them. In the following chapter, we will look at personal values—not to judge them, but to consider what values we believe in and how these values shape our lives.

Values could be described as ways of knowing right from wrong. We behave in a particular way because we think it is the right way. Problems can arise, however, when people's values collide. In fact, sometimes a person complains that another person has no values. The reality may be that while the other person does have values, they may be different ones; two sets of values may be in opposition.

Values determine how we make choices—they constitute a belief system. For this reason, thinking about our values helps us make decisions and plan our future. This and the next two chapters focus on understanding and defining ourselves and making career decisions. A close look at one's own values aids that progression.

11

Values

Identifying Values

How does one begin to identify personal and societal values? It may be difficult to think of values you have. One way to begin is to create a group list, because once you hear what others consider as their values, it is easier to think of ones you believe in. In a group, brainstorm all the values the members believe they and other people may have. The list is not only a personal one; it should also include values that others may have but that are not important to you. Each group shares with the whole class; the end result is a list that represents a range of individual choices.

As an example, the following is what one class decided on:

friends	self-esteem	happiness
love	ability	trust
faith	honesty	approval
money	morality	health
success	appearance	justice

The lists will vary, but everyone should be able to recognize values on the class list that they believe are important.

Writing Activity: Identifying Your Own Values

Choose the top five values that matter the most to you as an individual, and write a short paragraph for each of these top five values explaining why it is important. Ask yourself if you have believed in a given value for a long time, if it is shared by family and/or friends, if an experience helped form this value, if your family instilled this value in you, and if your behavior illustrates this value.

Society's Values

Societies and cultures have collective values as well as the individual values of their members. We agree with some societal value systems and disagree with others. When we have difficulty understanding people's behavior and choices, it is often because of a difference in values. How can one know what values a society has? What do you think are your society's top values, and how do you know?

Russell Baker wrote the following essay, discussing how music represents societal values, shortly after Bing Crosby died. Baker, a Pulitzer Prize–winning political satirist, is well known for his humorous newspaper columns on political issues. He has written several books and numerous magazine articles.

From Song to Sound: Bing and Elvis

RUSSELL BAKER

1   The grieving for Elvis Presley and the commercial exploitation of his death were still not ended when we heard of Bing Crosby's death the other day. Here is a generational puzzle. Those of an age to mourn Elvis must marvel that their elders could really have cared about Bing, just as the Crosby generation a few weeks ago wondered what all the to-do was about when Elvis died.

2   Each man was a mass culture hero to his generation, but it tells us something of the difference between generations that each man's admirers would be hard-pressed to understand why the other could mean very much to his devotees.

3   There were similarities that ought to tell us something. Both came from obscurity to national recognition while quite young and became very rich. Both lacked formal music education and went on to movie careers despite lack of acting skills. Both developed distinctive musical styles which were originally scorned by critics and subsequently studied as pioneer developments in the art of popular song.

4   In short, each man's career followed the mythic rags-to-triumph pattern in which adversity is conquered, detractors are

given their comeuppance, and estates, fancy cars and world tours become the reward of perseverance. Traditionally this was supposed to be the history of the American business striver, but in our era of committee capitalism it occurs most often in the mass entertainment field, and so we look less and less to the board room for our heroes and more and more to the microphone.

Both Crosby and Presley were creations of the microphone. 5 It made it possible for people with frail voices not only to be heard beyond the third row but also to caress millions. Crosby was among the first to understand that the microphone made it possible to sing to multitudes by singing to a single person in a small room.

Presley cuddled his microphone like a lover. With Crosby 6 the microphone was usually concealed, but Presley brought it out on stage, detached it from its fitting, stroked it, pressed it to his mouth. It was a surrogate for his listener, and he made love to it unashamedly.

The difference between Presley and Crosby, however, reflected 7 generational differences which spoke of changing values in American life. Crosby's music was soothing; Presley's was disturbing. It is too easy to be glib about this, to say that Crosby was singing to, first, Depression America, and, then, to wartime America, and that his audiences had all the disturbance they could handle in their daily lives without buying more at the record shop and movie theater.

Crosby's fans talk about how "relaxed" he was, how "nat- 8 ural," how "casual and easy going." By the time Presley began causing sensations, the entire country had become relaxed, casual and easy going, and its younger people seemed to be tired of it, for Elvis's act was anything but soothing and scarcely what a parent of that placid age would have called "natural" for a young man.

Elvis was unseemly, loud, gaudy, sexual—that gyrating 9 pelvis!—in short, disturbing. He not only disturbed parents who thought music by Crosby was soothing but also reminded their young that they were full of the turmoil of youth and an appetite for excitement. At a time when the country had a population coming of age with no memory of troubled times, Presley spoke to a yearning for disturbance.

10   It probably helped that Elvis's music made Mom and Dad climb the wall. In any case, people who admired Elvis never talk about how relaxed and easy going he made them feel. They are more likely to tell you he introduced them to something new and exciting.

11   To explain each man in terms of changes in economic and political life probably oversimplifies the matter. Something in the culture was also changing. Crosby's music, for example, paid great attention to the importance of lyrics. The "message" of the song was as essential to the audience as the tune. The words were usually inane and witless, but Crosby—like Sinatra a little later—made them vital. People remembered them, sang them. Words still had meaning.

12   Although many of Presley's songs were highly lyrical, in most it wasn't the words that moved audiences; it was the "sound." Rock 'n' roll, of which he was the great popularizer, was a "sound" event. Song stopped being song and turned into "sound," at least until the Beatles came along and solved the problem of making words sing to the new beat.

13   Thus a group like the Rolling Stones, whose lyrics are often elaborate, seems to the Crosby-tuned ear to be shouting only gibberish, a sort of accompanying background noise in a "sound" experience. The Crosby generation has trouble hearing rock because it makes the mistake of trying to understand the words. The Presley generation has trouble with Crosby because it finds the sound unstimulating and cannot be touched by the inanity of the words. The mutual deafness may be a measure of how far we have come from really troubled times and of how deeply we have come to mistrust the value of words.

Personal Response

Respond with your thoughts about music and entertainers. Whom do you like and why?

Content Focus

1. How did Elvis and Bing represent society's values?
2. Why do values change?
3. What do you think of the Russell Baker's comment that "Words still had meaning" in Bing Crosby's lyrics?
4. Baker writes that people have come to "distrust the value of words." Comment on your opinion of that statement.

Writer's Craft

1. What pattern of development does Baker use to make his point?
2. What is his thesis? How does he support the thesis?
3. Why does Baker discuss similarities at the beginning of the essay?

Writing Activity: Changing Values

Write a short essay on your experiences with changing values. Perhaps you are aware of values that have changed across generations, or perhaps your own personal values have changed over time.

Values and Creeds

Values are often expressed in a creed (statement of beliefs) or plan for life. The following reading, "Desiderata," was discovered in Old Saint Paul's Church in Baltimore, Maryland, and dated 1692. The author is unknown. The piece describes a plan for living.

Desiderata

ANONYMOUS

Go placidly amid the noise and Haste, and remember what peace there may be in silence. As far as possible without surrender be on good terms with all persons. Speak your truth quietly and clearly; and listen to others, even the dull and ignorant; they too have their story. Avoid loud and aggressive persons, they are vexations to the spirit. If you compare yourself with others, you may become vain and bitter; for always there will be greater and lesser persons than yourself. Enjoy your achievements as well as your plans. Keep interested in your own career, however humble; it is a real possession in the changing fortunes of time. Exercise caution in your business affairs; for the world is full of trickery. But let this not blind you to what virtue there is; many persons strive for high ideals; and everywhere life is full of heroism. Be yourself. Especially, do not feign affection. Neither be cynical about love; for in the face of all aridity and disenchantment it is perennial as the grass. Take kindly the counsel of the years, gracefully surrendering the things of youth. Nurture strength of spirit to shield you in sudden misfortune. But do not distress yourself with imaginings. Many fears are born of fatigue and loneliness. Beyond a wholesome discipline, be gentle with yourself. You are a child of the universe, no less than the trees and the stars; you have a right to be here. And whether or not it is clear to you, no doubt the universe is unfolding as it should. Therefore be at peace with God, whatever you conceive Him to be, and whatever your labors and aspirations, in the noisy confusion of life keep peace with your soul. With all its sham, drudgery and broken dreams, it is still a beautiful world. Be careful. Strive to be happy.

Response Questions

After reading "Desiderata" answer the following questions and discuss in a group.

1. What do you believe are the values expressed?
2. In what ways are they appropriate in today's society?
3. Where might you disagree or change the ideas somewhat?
4. What sections fit into your own life?
5. What line speaks most eloquently to you?
6. What line is of the least use or importance to you?

Writing Activity: Advice for a Happy Life

Write a paragraph giving advice for a happy life. Outline the personal traits that promote happiness; then explain how people can develop these traits—much the way the author of "Desiderata" did, but incorporating your own ideas and advice.

Values and Behaviors

If people truly believe in a particular value, then their behavior will represent that belief. For example, if a person claims to value a healthy body but does little to achieve a healthy lifestyle, the value is of little true consequence. At times it is important not only to consciously state your values but to look closely at how your behavior demonstrates those values. In the following reading, Ellen Goodman describes a man whose top value was work. Goodman writes a syndicated column and has won the Pulitzer Prize for commentary.

The Company Man

ELLEN GOODMAN

He worked himself to death, finally and precisely, at 3:00 A.M. Sunday morning.   1

The obituary didn't say that, of course. It said that he died of a   2
coronary thrombosis—I think that was it—but everyone among his friends and acquaintances knew it instantly. He was a perfect Type A, a workaholic, a classic, they said to each other, and shook their heads—and thought for five or ten minutes about the way they lived.

This man who worked himself to death finally and precisely   3
at 3:00 A.M. Sunday morning—on his day off—was fifty-one years old and a vice-president. He was, however, one of six vice-presidents, and one of three who might conceivably—if the president died or retired soon enough—have moved to the top spot. Phil knew that.

He worked six days a week, five of them until eight or nine at   4
night, during a time when his own company had begun the four-day week for everyone but the executives. He worked like the Important People. He had no outside "extracurricular interests," unless, of course, you think about a monthly golf game that way. To Phil, it was work. He always ate egg salad sandwiches at his desk. He was, of course, overweight, by 20 or 25 pounds. He thought it was okay, though, because he didn't smoke.

On Saturdays, Phil wore a sports jacket to the office instead   5
of a suit, because it was the weekend.

He had a lot of people working for him, maybe sixty, and most   6
of them liked him most of the time. Three of them will be seriously considered for his job. The obituary didn't mention that.

But it did list his "survivors" quite accurately. He is survived   7
by his wife, Helen, forty-eight years old, a good woman of no

particular marketable skills, who worked in an office before marrying and mothering. She had, according to her daughter, given up trying to compete with his work years ago, when the children were small. A company friend said, "I know how much you will miss him." And she answered, "I already have."

8   "Missing him all these years," she must have given up part of herself which had cared too much for the man. She would be "well taken care of."

9   His "dearly beloved" eldest of the "dearly beloved" children is a hard-working executive in a manufacturing firm down South. In the day and a half before the funeral, he went around the neighborhood researching his father, asking the neighbors what he was like. They were embarrassed.

10   His second child is a girl, who is twenty-four and newly married. She lives near her mother and they are close, but whenever she was alone with her father, in a car driving somewhere, they had nothing to say to each other.

11   The youngest is twenty, a boy, a high-school graduate who has spent the last couple of years, like a lot of his friends, doing enough odd jobs to stay in grass and food. He was the one who tried to grab at his father, and tried to mean enough to him to keep the man at home. He was his father's favorite. Over the last two years, Phil stayed up nights worrying about the boy.

12   The boy once said, "My father and I only board here."

13   At the funeral, the sixty-year-old company president told the forty-eight-year-old widow that the fifty-one-year-old deceased had meant much to the company and would be missed and would be hard to replace. The widow didn't look him in the eye. She was afraid he would read her bitterness and, after all, she would need him to straighten out the finances—the stock options and all that.

14   Phil was overweight and nervous and worked too hard. If he wasn't at the office, he was worried about it. Phil was a Type A, a heart-attack natural. You could have picked him out in a minute from a lineup.

15   So when he finally worked himself to death, at precisely 3:00 A.M. Sunday morning, no one was really surprised.

16   By 5:00 P.M. the afternoon of the funeral, the company president had begun, discreetly of course, with care and taste, to make inquiries about his replacement. One of three men. He asked around: "Who's been working the hardest?"

Personal Response

Respond with thoughts and experiences—firsthand stories or stories you've heard from others, films you've seen, books you've read, your own views on the work ethic—whatever comes to mind.

Content Focus

1. What clues do you have about how Phil's wife felt?
2. Why did Phil's eldest son ask neighbors about his own father?
3. Although Ellen Goodman does not explicitly state her thesis, what is implied?
4. What was Phil's job like? In what ways could it be satisfying?
5. Why did Phil work such long hours? What do you think his core values were?

Writer's Craft

Goodman gives no information about how Phil felt. What effect does this have on readers? Why does she repeat the time of death at the end? What style does Goodman use? Think of how and when a similar style would be appropriate for you in your writing.

Values in Conflict

At times our own values are in conflict. For example, a person may value saving money but may also value fashionable clothes. The two values could be at odds, causing internal conflict and unhappiness—or at least an uncomfortable feeling. Hugh Pentecost, in the next reading, experiences a difficult situation because of his own conflicting values.

A Kind of Murder

HUGH PENTECOST

You might say this is the story of a murder—although nobody was killed. I don't know what has become of Mr. Silas Warren, but I have lived for many years with the burden on my conscience of having been responsible for the existence of a walking dead man.

1

2   I was fifteen years old during the brief span of days that I knew Mr. Silas Warren. It was toward the end of the winter term at Morgan Military Academy. Mr. Etsweiler, the chemistry and physics teacher at Morgan, had died of a heart attack one afternoon while he was helping to coach the hockey team on the lake. Mr. Henry Huntingdon Hadley, the headmaster, had gone to New York to find a replacement. That replacement was Mr. Silas Warren.

3   I may have been one of the first people to see Mr. Warren at the Academy. I had been excused from afternoon study period because of a heavy cold, and allowed to take my books to my room to work there. I saw Mr. Warren come walking across the quadrangle toward Mr. Hadley's office, which was located on the ground floor under the hall where my room was.

4   Mr. Warren didn't look like a man who was coming to stay long. He carried one small, flimsy suitcase spattered with travel labels. Although it was a bitter March day he wore a thin, summer-weight topcoat. He stopped beside a kind of brown lump in the snow. That brown lump was Teddy, the school dog.

5   Teddy was an ancient collie. They said that in the old days you could throw a stick for Teddy to retrieve until you, not he, dropped from exhaustion. Now the old, gray-muzzled dog was pretty much ignored by everyone except the chef, who fed him scraps from the dining room after the noon meal. Teddy would be at the kitchen door, promptly on time, and then find a comfortable spot to lie down. He'd stay there until someone forced him to move.

6   Mr. Warren stopped by Teddy, bent down, and scratched the dog's head. The old, burr-clotted tail thumped wearily in the snow. Mr. Warren straightened up and looked around. He had narrow, stooped shoulders. His eyes were pale blue, and they had a kind of frightened look in them. *He's scared,* I thought; *coming to a new place in the middle of a term, he's scared.*

7   I guess most of the other fellows didn't see Mr. Warren until he turned up at supper time at the head of one of the tables in the dining room. We marched into the dining room and stood behind our chairs waiting for the cadet major to give the order to be seated. The order was delayed. Mr. Henry Huntingdon Hadley, known as Old Beaver because of his snowy white beard, made an announcement.

"Mr. Warren has joined our teaching staff to fill the vacancy   8
created by the unfortunate demise of Mr. Etsweiler." Old Beaver
had false teeth and his s's whistled musically. "I trust you will
give him a cordial welcome."

"Be seated," the cadet major snapped.   9

We sat. Old Beaver said grace. Then we all began to talk. I   10
was at Mr. Warren's right. He had a genial, want-to-be-liked
smile.

"And your name is?" he asked me in a pleasant but flat voice.   11

"Pentecost, sir."   12

He leaned toward me. "How's that?" he asked.   13

"Pentecost, sir."   14

Sammy Callahan sat across from me on Mr. Warren's left.   15
Sammy was a fine athlete and a terrible practical joker. I saw a
gleam of interest in his eyes. As Mr. Warren turned toward him
Sammy spoke in an ordinary conversational tone. "Why don't
you go take a jump in the lake, sir?"

Mr. Warren smiled. "Yes, I guess you're right," he said.   16

Sammy grinned at me. There was no doubt about it—Mr.   17
Warren was quite deaf!

It was a strange kind of secret Sammy and I had. We didn't   18
really know what to do with it, but we found out that night. Old
Beaver was not a man to start anyone in gradually. It would
have been Mr. Etsweiler's turn to take the night study hour, so
that hour was passed on to Mr. Warren.

He sat on the little platform at the head of the study hall—   19
smiling and smiling. I think there must have been terror in his
heart then. I think he may even have been praying.

Everyone seemed unusually busy studying, but we were all   20
waiting for the test. The test always came for a new master the
first time he had night study hour. There would be a minor disturbance and we'd find out promptly whether this man could
maintain discipline, or not. It came after about five minutes—
a loud, artificial belch.

Mr. Warren smiled and smiled. He hadn't heard it.   21

Belches sprang up all over the room. Then somebody threw   22
a handful of torn paper in the air. Mr. Warren's smile froze.

"Now, now boys," he said.   23

More belches. More torn paper.   24

"Boys!" Mr. Warren cried out, like someone in pain.   25

26   Then Old Beaver appeared, his eyes glittering behind rimless spectacles. There was something I never understood about Old Beaver. Ordinarily his shoes squeaked. You could hear him coming from quite a distance away—squeak–squeak, squeak–squeak. But somehow, when he chose, he could approach as noiselessly as a cat, without any squeak at all. And there he was.

27   The study hall was quiet as a tomb. But the silence was frighteningly loud, and the place was littered with paper.

28   "There will be ten demerit marks against every student in this room," Old Beaver said in his icy voice. "I want every scrap of paper picked up instantly."

29   Several of us scrambled down on our hands and knees. Mr. Warren smiled at the headmaster.

30   "Consider the lilies of the field," Mr. Warren said. "They toil not, neither do they spin. Yet I tell you that Solomon in all his glory—"

31   "Silence!" Old Beaver hissed, with all the menace of a poised cobra. He turned to Mr. Warren. "I'll take the balance of this period, Mr. Warren. I suggest you go to your room and prepare yourself for tomorrow's curriculum."

32   I didn't have any classes with Mr. Warren the next day, but all you heard as you passed in the corridors from one class period to the next were tales of the jokes and disorders in the physics and chemistry courses. Somehow nobody thought it was wrong to take advantage of Mr. Warren.

33   The climax came very quickly. In the winter, if you weren't out for the hockey or winter sports teams, you had to exercise in the gym. There were the parallel bars, and the rings, and the tumbling mats. And there was boxing.

34   The boxing teacher was Major Durand, the military commandant. I know now that he was a sadist. Major Durand was filled with contempt for everyone but Major Durand. I saw the look on his face when Mr. Warren appeared.

35   Mr. Warren had been assigned to help in the gym. He was something to see—just skin and bones. He had on a pair of ordinary black socks and, I suspect, the only pair of shoes he owned—black oxfords. He'd borrowed a pair of shorts that could have been wrapped twice around his skinny waist. Above that was a much mended short-sleeved undershirt. He looked around, hopeless, amiable.

"Mr. Warren!" Major Durand said. "I'd like you to help me 36
demonstrate. Put on these gloves if you will." He tossed a pair
of boxing gloves at Mr. Warren, who stared at them stupidly.
One of the boys helped him tie the laces.

"Now, Mr. Warren," Durand said. The Major danced and 37
bobbed and weaved, and shot out his gloves in short vicious
jabs at the air. "You will hold your gloves up to your face, sir.
When you're ready you'll say 'Hit!'—and I shall hit you."

I'd seen Major Durand do this with a boy he didn't like. You 38
held up the gloves and you covered your face and then, with
your throat dry and aching, you said "Hit!"—and Major Durand's left or right would smash through your guard and pul-
verize your nose or mouth. It was sheer strength I know now,
not skill.

Mr. Warren held up his gloves, and he looked like an actor 39
in an old Mack Sennett comedy—the absurd clothes, the sickly
smile.

Durand danced in front of him. "Whenever you say, Mr. 40
Warren. Now watch this, boys. The feint—and the jab."

"Hit!" said Mr. Warren, his voice suddenly falsetto. 41

Pow! Major Durand's left jab smashed through the guard of 42
Mr. Warren's nose. There was a sudden geyser of blood.

"Again, Mr. Warren!" the Major commanded, his eyes glit- 43
tering.

"I think I'd better retire to repair the damage," Mr. Warren 44
said. His undershirt was spattered with blood and he had pro-
duced a soiled handkerchief which he held to his nose. He hurried out of the gym at a sort of shambling gallop.

That night the payoff came in study hall. Mr. Warren was 45
called on this time to substitute for Old Beaver, who had taken
over for him the night before. Sammy Callahan staged it. Suddenly handkerchiefs were waved from all parts of the room—
handkerchiefs stained red. Red ink, of course.

"Hit!" somebody shouted. "Hit, hit!" Nearly all the boys 46
were bobbing, weaving, jabbing.

Mr. Warren, pale as a ghost, cotton visibly stuffed in one nos- 47
tril, stared at us like a dead man.

Then there was Old Beaver again. 48

Somehow the word was out at breakfast the next morning. 49
Mr. Warren was leaving. He didn't show at the breakfast table.

I felt a little squeamish about it. He hadn't been given a chance. Maybe he wasn't such a bad guy.

50   It was during the morning classroom period that we heard it. It was a warm day for March and the ice was breaking up on the lake. The scream was piercing and terrified. Somebody went to the window. The scream came again.

51   "Somebody's fallen through the ice!"

52   The whole school—a hundred and fifty boys and masters—hurried down to the shore of the lake. The sun was so bright that all we could see was a dark shape flopping out there, pulling itself up on the ice and then disappearing under water as the ice broke. Each time the figure rose there was a wailing scream.

53   Then the identification. "It's Teddy!" someone shouted.

54   The school dog. He'd walked out there and the ice had caved in on him. The screams were growing weaker. A couple of us made for the edge of the ice. Old Beaver and Major Durand confronted us.

55   "I'm sorry, boys," Old Beaver said. "It's a tragic thing to have to stand here and watch the old dog drown. But no one—no one connected with the school—is to try to get to him. I'm responsible for your safety. That's an order."

56   We stood there, sick with it. Old Teddy must have seen us because for a moment there seemed to be new hope in his strangled wailing.

57   Then I saw Mr. Warren. He was by the boathouse, his old suitcase in his hand. He looked out at the dog, and so help me there were tears in Mr. Warren's eyes. Then, very calmly, he put down his bag, took off his thin topcoat and suit jacket. He righted one of the overturned boats on the shore and pulled it to the edge of the lake.

58   "Mr. Warren! You heard my order!" Old Beaver shouted at him.

59   Mr. Warren turned to the headmaster, smiling. "You seem to forget, sir, I am no longer connected with Morgan Military Academy, and therefore not subject to your orders."

60   "Stop him!" Major Durand ordered.

61   But before anyone could reach him, Mr. Warren had slid the flat-bottomed rowboat out onto the ice. He crept along on the

ice himself, clinging to the boat, pushing it across the shiny surface toward Teddy. I heard Mr. Warren's thin, flat voice.

"Hold on, old man! I'm coming." 62

The ice gave way under him, but he clung to the boat and 63
scrambled up—and on.

"Hold on, old man!" 64

It seemed to take forever. Just before what must have been 65
the last, despairing shriek from the half-frozen dog, Mr. Warren reached him. How he found the strength to lift the watersoaked collie into the boat, I don't know; but he managed, and then he came back toward us, creeping along the cracking ice, pushing the boat to shore.

The chef wrapped Teddy in blankets, put him behind the 66
stove in the kitchen, and gave him a dose of warm milk and cooking brandy. Mr. Warren was hustled to the infirmary. Did I say that when he reached the shore with Teddy the whole school cheered him?

Old Beaver, for all his tyranny, must have been a pretty de- 67
cent guy. He announced that night that Mr. Warren was not leaving after all. He trusted that, after Mr. Warren's display of valor, the boys would show him the respect he deserved.

I went to see Mr. Warren in the infirmary that first evening. 68
He looked pretty done in, but he also looked happier than I'd ever seen him.

"What you did took an awful lot of courage," I told him. 69
"Everybody thinks it was really a swell thing to do."

Mr. Warren smiled at me—a thoughtful kind of a smile. 70
"Courage is a matter of definition," he said. "It doesn't take courage to stand up and let yourself get punched in the nose, boy. It takes courage to walk away. As for Teddy—somebody had to go after him. There wasn't anyone who could but me, so courage or not, I went. You'd have gone if Mr. Hadley hadn't issued orders." He sighed. "I'm glad to get a second chance here. Very glad."

Somehow I got the notion it was a last chance—the very last 71
chance he'd ever have.

It was a week before Mr. Warren had the night study hall 72
again. It was a kind of test. For perhaps fifteen minutes nothing happened and then I heard Sammy give his fine, artificial belch.

I looked up at Mr. Warren. He was smiling happily. He hadn't heard. A delighted giggle ran around the room.

73   I was on my feet. "If there's one more sound in this room I'm going after Old Beaver," I said. "And after that I'll personally take on every guy in this school if necessary, to knock sense into him!"

74   The room quieted. I was on the student council and I was also captain of the boxing team. The rest of the study period was continued in an orderly fashion. When it was over and we were headed for our rooms, Mr. Warren flagged me down.

75   "I don't know quite what was going on, Pentecost," he said, "but I gather you saved the day for me. Thank you. Thank you very much. Perhaps when the boys get to know me a little better they'll come to realize—" He made a helpless little gesture with his bony hands.

76   "I'm sure they will, sir," I said. "I'm sure of it."

77   "They're not cruel," Mr. Warren said. "It's just high spirits, I know."

78   Sammy Callahan was waiting for me in my room. "What are you, some kind of a do-gooder?" he said.

79   "Give the guy a chance," I said. "He proved he has guts when it's needed. But he's helpless there in the study hall."

80   Sammy gave me a sour grin. "You and he should get along fine," he said. "And you'll need to. The guys aren't going to be chummy with a do-gooder like you."

81   It was a week before Mr. Warren's turn to run the study hour came around again. In that time I'd found that Sammy was right. I was being given the cold shoulder. Major Durand, who must have hated Mr. Warren for stealing the heroic spotlight from him, was giving me a hard time. One of the guys I knew well came to me.

82   "You're making a mistake," he told me. "He's a grown man and you're just a kid. If he can't take care of himself it's not your headache."

83   I don't like telling the next part of it, but it happened.

84   When Mr. Warren's night came again, the study hall was quiet enough for a while. Then came a belch. I looked up at Mr. Warren. He was smiling. Then someone waved one of those fake bloody handkerchiefs. Then, so help me, somebody let out a baying howl—like Teddy in the lake.

Mr. Warren knew what was happening now. He looked down 85
at me, and there was an agonizing, wordless plea for help in his
eyes. I—well, I looked away. I was fifteen. I didn't want to be
called a do-gooder. I didn't want to be snubbed. Mr. Warren *was*
a grown man and he should have been able to take care of himself. The boys weren't cruel: they were just high spirited—hadn't
Mr. Warren himself said so?

I looked up from behind a book. Mr. Warren was standing, 86
looking out over the room. His stooped, skinny shoulders were
squared away. Two great tears ran down his pale cheeks. His
last chance was played out.

Then he turned and walked out of the study hall. 87

No one ever saw him again. He must have gone straight to 88
his room, thrown his meager belongings into the battered old
suitcase, and taken off on foot into the night.

You see what I mean when I say it was a kind of murder? 89
And I was the murderer. 90

Response Questions

Answer the following questions during and after your reading of "A
Kind of Murder."

1. What was your first impression of Mr. Warren? In what ways does
   he remind you of someone you know?
2. What was the narrator's first impression of him?
3. Why did the boys test Mr. Warren? Give several reasons.
4. Why did Mr. Warren say, "Consider the lilies of the field"? What
   does that phrase from the New Testament mean in general?
5. Respond to Pentecost's statement that "Somehow nobody thought
   it was wrong to take advantage of Mr. Warren."
6. Describe Major Durand. What kind of person was he?
7. What do you think Durand's values were?
8. What was important to the boys in the school?
9. Why did the narrator have second thoughts about Mr. Warren?
10. What was the effect of Mr. Warren's saving Teddy?
11. What was Mr. Warren hoping the boys would realize?
12. Why did the narrator not help Mr. Warren a second time? How
    might you react in a similar situation?
13. Who was to blame for Mr. Warren's failure at the school?

Writing Activity: Comparing Values

Compare and contrast two or more of your values. How and when might they be in conflict? How can you resolve such conflicts?

Changing Values

Age, experiences, and knowledge all have an impact on our values. We wouldn't expect our personal values to remain the same for our entire lifetime; some values are timeless, but others more situational. In what ways do you think your values may change over the years? Which values will remain consistent? A student, Amy Matlock, wrote the following essay about her present values and how they may change in the future.

STUDENT PAPER

VALUES

Amy Matlock

Currently I am an eighteen-year-old college student who has had little experience in the "real world." The values that are important to me right now are not necessarily the values that will be important to me in the future. Sooner or later, these new values will take a higher priority over the ones that I thought were important to me now. My values will change to fit the life I will be leading and will continue to change as I mature and experience the real world. For now, I know what values are important to me and why I think those values will change as I become more experienced.

Right now I would have to say that friendship is the value I hold dearest. I began to realize this when I left for school and was separated from my best friend, Lora, for the first time. I thought I'd be fine without her; I was wrong. I suddenly found myself alone with no one to talk to, not having enough will power to go out and make new friends. Lora is someone I can tell anything to. We did everything together, and it was hard to realize that I once thought it would be easy living without her. Being away from her hit me hard. I slowly got over it and learned that it was possible for me to exist without her by my side. It was strange really because it was like we were living in the same skin for so long and a layer of it was stripped away; it left me cold. It is important for me to have someone to talk to, one person who won't judge me no matter what I've done. Her friendship is one of the most important things in my life right now. I can always count on her to tell me the truth and be honest.

Honesty is also an important value to me. I always find it necessary for people to tell me the truth. I am a gullible person because I try to believe much of what people tell me; within reason, of course. When I discover that someone has lied to me, I take it quite hard. I begin criticizing myself for having believed them in the first place. I never tend to blame the individual, but look at my believing the lie as a fault in myself. That is why it is extremely important that people are honest with me. When I am lied to, it lowers my self-respect, and self-respect is another value that is of great significance to me.

No matter what we do or what may happen, we should always try to maintain our self-respect. Self-respect is the one thing people can't strip you of as long as you are confident in yourself. Sometimes I find it difficult to keep my self-respect because there are many times I feel like I have nothing. In those times, I try to think that I still have myself. I always try to be positive, no matter what the circumstances. My personal struggle with self-respect is on an emotional level. I have trouble, as many individuals do, with having faith in myself. Sometimes I misplace my self-respect, but eventually find it with the help of friends.

The three values I have covered are only a few that are important to me. Will those values change in the future? Perhaps the values themselves won't change, but the meaning behind them will. Other values will come into play more often during different phases of my life. The values I treasure now will end up taking a back seat to new ones. Events will take place as I begin to experience the real world, such as graduating from college, getting a job, being in love, getting married, and, possibly, having kids. All of these events will bring into play different values depending on my current situation. Until then I have the values that are important to me right now, at this time, in my experience.

Which values of yours are similar to Amy's? What do you think she means when she says that perhaps her values themselves won't change, but the meaning behind them will?

WRITING ASSIGNMENT: VALUES

The paper for this chapter is an in-depth explanation of your values. Describe them, discuss how your behavior does and does not reflect the values, and predict how and why your values may change in the future. Finally, explain how your values will affect your choice of career. You may use whatever pattern or patterns fit the points you are making and will best present the information. Use the readings in this chapter to support and explain the points you make. Revise the paper with the help of your writing group, edit, and proofread.

12

Defining Oneself

We may feel that we know ourselves well; but, surprisingly, we may not realize our talents and skills. A sense of self comes not only from what others say and think about us but from what we know to be true. The better we know our strengths, the more we learn about ourselves, and the more skills we develop, the stronger our self-esteem becomes.

Hopes, Dreams, and Expectations

You have learned more about yourself by examining your values, an important place to begin. In this chapter, you have opportunities to focus on your hopes, dreams, and expectations.

You need to decide for yourself what you are like and what you want in life. Your understanding of your personality increases when you seriously consider what you are capable of, what you enjoy doing, how you want to spend your time, and what your strengths are. Understanding your talents increases your self-confidence. The following writing activity helps clarify what is important to you.

Writing Activity: Three Wishes

If time and money did not have to be considered, what three things would you like to do? Take into account your values, talents, and personality. Your wishes don't have to take a lot of money; you might want to sit on a beach or a mountain, away from everyone for a few days, to have time to think. Or you might want to take time to develop your talent as a painter or writer. When you think, "If only," what comes to mind? Write your three wishes and elaborate by adding some details; you don't need to share the wishes with your writing group unless you want to. Now consider how you might attain them. Write your ideas of what you could do, and how, to make the wishes a reality—if not now, then in the future. How central are these wishes to your happiness? A person can always dream, but some dreams are more important than others. What dreams are really life goals for you?

How Others See Us

People who are close to us—family and friends—often have ideas about what our goals should be. These ideas may not be in conflict with our own hopes; still, it is important that while we consider what others think, we make sure it fits in with our self-knowledge.

Writing Activity: Describing Yourself from Someone Else's Viewpoint

People who know us well have their own images of who we are and what we are like. We let down our defenses when we are around people we trust, but we still may not reveal all we think and do. How accurate are your friends' and family's opinions of you? Write a paragraph or two describing yourself from someone else's viewpoint. Choose a person who knows you quite well. As a conclusion, compare the other person's image with your sense of self.

The following paper, "Who am I?," was written by a student, Dawn Rucker, for an assignment in which she was asked to describe herself through others' eyes.

STUDENT PAPER

WHO AM I?

Dawn Rucker

Dawn is a unique individual. As she goes through life, people perceive her in different ways. Parents, teachers, and friends all see different sides of Dawn.

To begin, Dawn's friends see her as an outgoing, trustworthy, friendly, and honest person. Dawn is the type of person that her friends can go to when they have a problem. Her friends know that she will be there for them when they need someone to talk to or to cheer them up. The reason they feel so comfortable telling her their problems is that she respects and honors their privacy.

When she is not listening to their problems, she loves to go out and have a good time. A lot of times Dawn is indecisive about what the group of friends should do because she doesn't want to make people angry. Most of her friends see her as a happy-go-lucky type of person because she only shows her feelings to her close friends.

On the other hand, her professors see Dawn as a quiet, courteous, and respectful person. Dawn's professors don't see her as regularly as her friends do, so they see Dawn in a different light. Dawn is the type who gets embarrassed easily in front of people who she does not know too well, so she tries not to draw too much attention towards her direction.

An employer perceives Dawn as hard working, perceptive, and well presented. Dawn tries her best to get the job done correctly so the employer won't get mad at her. She also knows that if she picks up bad habits early in life, they will be hard to get rid of when she gets older.

Dawn's parents see her as a person who likes to be on the road all the time, someone who takes control because of her good leadership qualities, and who is the rebel of the family. Dawn is old enough to be out on her own, but her parents do worry about her. Dawn knows she can do whatever she wants, and her parents trust her enough to give her the freedom she needs.

Everyone sees Dawn a little differently. However, that doesn't mean that one side of her is the way she should always be. These people have helped her become a part of who she is today. Dawn is very thankful for these people for helping her become who she is.

Writing Activity: Roles We Play

People who do not know us well still make judgments about the kind of person we are. They judge us by the image we project, and that depends on the role we play when we are with them. What are the life roles you fulfill? Like Dawn, you may be a friend, student, employee, and daughter; or you may play any of countless other roles. Choose the four or five roles that are dominant in your life, and describe what kind of person you are in each one. Describe how you see yourself and how others understand you. Discuss the similarities and differences among your roles and between your own and others' views of you.

People who hardly know you make judgments about you based on what you wear. How much does your appearance reflect who you really are? The following article, "The Language of Clothes" by author Alison Lurie, explores the connection between appearance and identity.

The Language of Clothes

ALISON LURIE

1   For thousands of years human beings have communicated with one another first in the language of dress. Long before I am near enough to talk to you on the street, in a meeting or at a party, you announce your sex, age and class to me through what you are wearing—and very possibly give me important information (or misinformation) as to your occupation, origin, personality, opinions, tastes, sexual desires and current mood. I may not be able to put what I observe into words, but I register the information unconsciously; and you simultaneously do the same for me. By the time we meet and converse we have already spoken to each other in an older and more universal tongue.

2   If clothing is a language, it must have a vocabulary and a grammar like other languages. Of course, as with human speech, there is not a single language of dress, but many: some (like Dutch and German) closely related and others (like Basque) almost unique. And within every language of clothes there are many different dialects and accents, some almost unintelligible to members of the mainstream culture. Moreover, as with speech, each individual has his own stock of words and employs personal variations of tone and meaning.

The Vocabulary of Fashion

3   The vocabulary of dress includes not only items of clothing but also hairstyles, accessories, jewelry, makeup and body decoration. Theoretically, at least, this vocabulary is as large as or larger than that of any spoken tongue, since it includes every garment, hairstyle and type of body decoration ever invented.

In practice, of course, the sartorial resources of an individual may be very restricted. Those of a sharecropper, for instance, may be limited to five or ten "words" from which it is possible to create only a few "sentences" almost bare of decoration and expressing only the most basic concepts. A so-called fashion leader, on the other hand, may have several hundred "words" at his or her disposal, and thus be able to form thousands of different "sentences" that will express a wide range of meanings. Just as the average English-speaking person knows many more words than he or she will ever use in conversation, so all of us are able to understand the meaning of styles we will never wear.

To choose clothes, either in a store or at home, is to define   4 and describe ourselves. Occasionally, of course, practical considerations enter into these choices: considerations of comfort, durability, availability and price. Especially in the case of persons of limited wardrobe, an article may be worn because it is warm or rainproof or handy to cover up a wet bathing suit—in the same way that persons of limited vocabulary use the phrase "you know" or adjectives such as "great" or "fantastic." Yet, just as with spoken language, such choices usually give us some information, even if it is only equivalent to the statement "I don't give a damn what I look like today."

Archaic Words

Besides containing "words" that are taboo, the language of   5 clothes, like speech, also includes modern and ancient words, words of native and foreign origin, dialect words, colloquialisms, slang and vulgarities. Genuine articles of clothing from the past (or skillful imitations) are used in the same way a writer or speaker might use archaisms: to give an air of culture, erudition or wit. Just as in educated discourse, such "words" are usually employed sparingly, most often one at a time—a single Victorian cameo or a pair of 1940s platform shoes or an Edwardian velvet waistcoat, never a complete costume. A whole outfit composed of archaic items from a single period, rather than projecting elegance and sophistication, will imply that one is on one's way to a masquerade, acting in a play or film or putting oneself on display for advertising purposes. Mixing garments from several different periods of the past, on the other hand, suggests a confused but intriguingly "original" theatrical personality. It is therefore often fashionable in those sections of the art and entertainment industry in which instant celebrities are manufactured and sold.

6   When using archaic words, it is essential to choose ones that are decently old. The sight of a white plastic Courrèges mini-raincoat and boots (in 1963 the height of fashion) at a gallery opening or theater today would produce the same shiver of ridicule and revulsion as the use of words such as "groovy," "Negro" or "self-actualizing."

7   In *Taste and Fashion,* one of the best books ever written on costume, the late James Laver proposed a timetable to explain such reactions; this has come to be known as Laver's Law. According to him, the same costume will be:

Indecent	10 years before its time
Shameless	5 years before its time
Daring	1 year before its time
Smart	
Dowdy	1 year after its time
Hideous	10 years after its time
Ridiculous	20 years after its time
Amusing	30 years after its time
Quaint	50 years after its time
Charming	70 years after its time
Romantic	100 years after its time
Beautiful	150 years after its time

Laver possibly overemphasizes the shock value of incoming fashion, which today may be seen merely as weird or ugly. And, of course, he is speaking of the complete outfit, or "sentence." The speed with which a single "word" passes in and out of fashion can vary, just as in spoken and written languages.

Foreign Words

8   The appearance of foreign garments in an otherwise indigenous costume is similar in function to the use of foreign words or phrases in standard English speech. This phenomenon, which is common in certain circles, may have several different meanings.

9   First, of course, it can be a deliberate sign of national origin in someone who otherwise, sartorially or linguistically speaking, has no accent. Often this message is expressed through headgear. The Oxford-educated Arab who tops his Savile Row suit with a turban is telling us graphically that he has not been

psychologically assimilated, that his ideas and opinions remain those of an Asian. As a result, we tend to see the non-European in Western dress with native headgear or hairdo as dignified, even formidable, while the reverse outfit—the Oriental lady in a kimono and a plastic rain hat or the sheikh in native robes and a black bowler—appears comic. Such costumes seem to announce that their wearers, though not physically at ease in our country, have their heads full of half-baked Western ideas.

More often the wearing of a single foreign garment, like the   10
dropping of a foreign word or phrase in conversation, is meant not to advertise foreign origin or allegiance but to indicate sophistication. It can also be a means of advertising wealth. When we see a fancy Swiss watch, we know that its owner either bought it at home for three times the price of a good English or American watch or else he or she spent even more money traveling to Switzerland.

Slang and Vulgar Words

Casual dress, like casual speech, tends to be loose, relaxed and   11
colorful. It often contains what might be called "slang words": blue jeans, sneakers, baseball caps, aprons, flowered cotton housedresses and the like. These garments could not be worn on a formal occasion without causing disapproval, but in ordinary circumstances they pass without remark. "Vulgar words" in dress, on the other hand, give emphasis and get immediate attention in almost any circumstances, just as they do in speech. Only the skillful can employ them without some loss of face, and even then they must be used in the right way. A torn, unbuttoned shirt, or wildly uncombed hair, can signify strong emotions: passion, grief, rage, despair. They are most effective if people already think of you as being neatly dressed, just as the curses of well-spoken persons count for more than those of the customarily foulmouthed.

Items of dress that are the sartorial equivalent of forbidden   12
words have more impact when they appear seldom and as if by accident. The Edwardian lady, lifting her heavy floor-length skirt to board a tram, appeared unaware that she was revealing a froth of lacy petticoats and embroidered black stockings. Similarly, today's braless executive woman, leaning over her

desk at a conference, may affect not to know that her nipples show through her silk blouse. Perhaps she does not know it consciously; we are here in the ambiguous region of intention versus interpretation which has given so much trouble to linguists.

Personal Fashion: Situation and Self

13   As with speech, the meaning of any costume depends on circumstances. It is not "spoken" in a vacuum but at a specific place and time, any change in which may alter its meaning. Like the remark "Let's get on with this damn business," the two-piece tan business suit and boldly striped shirt and tie that signify energy and determination in the office will have quite another resonance at a funeral or picnic.

14   In language we distinguish between someone who speaks a sentence well—clearly, and with confidence and dignity—and someone who speaks it badly. In dress, too, manner is as important as matter, and in judging the meaning of any garment we will automatically consider whether it fits well or is too large or too small, whether it is old or new and especially whether it is in good condition, slightly rumpled and soiled or crushed and filthy. Cleanliness may not always be next to godliness, but it is usually regarded as a sign of respectability or at least of self-respect. It is also a sign of status, since to be clean and neat involves the expense of time and money.

15   In a few circles, of course, disregard for cleanliness has been considered a virtue. Saint Jerome's remark that "the purity of the body and its garments means the impurity of the soul" inspired generations of unwashed and smelly hermits. In the '60s some hippies and mystics scorned overly clean and tidy dress as a sign of compromise with the establishment and too great an attachment to the things of this world. There is also a more widespread rural and small-town dislike of the person whose clothes are too clean, slick and smooth. He—or she—is suspected of being untrustworthy, a smoothy or a city slicker.

16   In general, however, to wear dirty, rumpled or torn clothing is to invite scorn and condescension. This reaction is ancient; indeed, it goes back beyond the dawn of humanity. In most species, a strange animal in poor condition—mangy, or with matted and muddy fur—is more likely to be attacked by other animals. In the same way, shabbily dressed people are more apt to be treated shabbily. A man in a clean, well-pressed suit who

falls down in a central London or Manhattan street is likely to be helped up sooner than one in filthy tatters.

Eccentric and Conventional Speech

In dress as in language, there is a possible range of expression 17 from the most eccentric statement to the most conventional. At one end of the spectrum is the outfit of which the individual parts or "words" are highly incongruent, marking its wearer (if not on stage or involved in some natural disaster) as very peculiar or possibly deranged. Imagine, for instance, a transparent sequined evening blouse over a dirty Victorian cotton petticoat and black rubber galoshes. (I have observed this getup in real life; it was worn to a lunch party at a famous Irish country house.) If the same costume were worn by a man, or if the usual grammatical order of the sentence were altered—one of the galoshes placed upside down on the head, for example—the effect of insanity would be even greater.

At the opposite end of the spectrum is the costume that is the 18 equivalent of a cliché; it follows some established style in every particular and instantly establishes its wearer as a doctor, a debutante, a hippie or a whore. Such outfits are not uncommon, for as two British sociologists have remarked, "Identification with and active participation in a social group always involves the human body and its adornment and clothing." The more significant any social role is for an individual, the more likely he or she is to dress for it. When two roles conflict, the costume will either reflect the more important one or it will combine them, sometimes with incongruous effects, as in the case of the secretary whose sober, efficient-looking dark suit only partly conceals a tight, bright low-cut blouse.

The cliché outfit may in some cases become so standardized 19 that it is spoken of as a "uniform": the pin-striped suit, bowler and black umbrella of the London City man, for instance, or the blue jeans and T-shirts of high school students. Usually, however, these costumes only look like uniforms to outsiders; peers will be aware of significant differences. The London businessman's tie will tell his associates where he went to school; the cut and fabric of his suit will allow them to guess at his income. High school students, in a single glance, can distinguish new jeans from those that are fashionably worn, functionally or decoratively patched or carelessly ragged; they grasp the fine distinctions of meaning conveyed by straight-leg, flared, boot-cut and peg-top. When two pairs of jeans are identical to the naked eye, a label handily affixed to the back pocket gives useful information, identifying the garment as expensive (so-called designer jeans) or discount-department-store. And even within the latter category there are distinctions: In our local junior high school, according to a native informant, "freaks always wear Lees, greasers wear Wranglers and everyone else wears Levis."

20   Of course, all these students are identical only below the waist; above it they may wear anything from a lumberjack shirt to a lace blouse. Grammatically, this costume seems to be a sign that in their lower or physical natures these persons are alike, however dissimilar they may be socially, intellectually or esthetically. If this is so, the opposite statement can be imagined—and was actually made by my own college classmates 30 years ago. During the daytime we wore identical baggy sweaters over a wide variety of slacks, plaid kilts, full cotton or straight tweed or slinky jersey skirts, ski pants and Bermuda shorts. "We're all nice coeds from the waist up; we think and talk alike," this costume proclaimed, "but as women we are infinitely various."

Dressing for "Success"

21   For over 100 years books and magazines have been busy translating the correct language of fashion, telling men and women what they should wear to seem genteel, rich, sophisticated and attractive to the other sex. Journals addressed to what used to be called "the career girl" advised her how to dress to attract "the right kind of man"—successful, marriage-minded. Regardless of the current fashion, a discreet femininity was always recommended: soft fabrics and colors, flowers and ruffles in modest profusion, hair slightly longer and curlier than that of the other girls in the office. The costume must be neither too stylish (suggesting expense to the future husband) nor dowdy (suggesting boredom). Above all, a delicate balance must be struck between the prim and the seductive, one tending not to attract men and the other to attract the wrong kind. Times have changed somewhat, and the fashion pages of magazines such as *Cosmopolitan* now seem to specialize in telling the career girl what to wear to charm the particular wrong type of man who reads *Playboy*, while the editorial pages tell her how to cope with the resulting psychic damage.

Two recent paperbacks, *Dress for Success* and *The Woman's*   22
Dress for Success Book, by John T. Molloy, instruct businessmen
and businesswomen how to select their clothes so that they will
look efficient, authoritative and reliable even when they are in-
competent, weak and shifty. Molloy, who is by no means unin-
telligent, claims that his "wardrobe engineering" is based on
scientific research and opinion polls. Also, in a departure from
tradition, he is interested in telling women how to get promoted,
not how to get married. The secret, apparently, is to wear an expensive but conventional "skirted suit" in medium-gray or navy
wool with a modestly cut blouse. No sweaters, no pants, no very
bright colors, no cleavage, no long or excessively curly hair.

Anyone interested in scenic variety must hope that Molloy is   23
mistaken; but my own opinion polling, unfortunately, backs him
up. A fast-rising lady executive in a local bank reports to me—
reluctantly—that "suits do help separate the women from the
girls—provided the women can tolerate the separation, which is
another question altogether."

Malevolent Clothing

At the other extreme from clothing which brings good luck   24
and success is the garment of ill-omen. The most common and
harmless version of this is the dress, suit or shirt which (like
some children) seems to attract or even to seek out dirt, grease,
protruding nails, failing ketchup and other hazards. Enid Nemy,
who has written perceptively about such clothes for *The New York
Times,* suggests that they may be lazy: "They'd just as soon rest
on a hanger, or in a box—and they revolt when they're hauled
into action." Or, she adds, they may be snobs, unwilling to associate with ordinary people. Whatever the cause, such accident-
prone garments rarely if ever reform, and once one has been
identified it is best to break off relations with it immediately.
Otherwise, like accident-prone persons, it is apt to involve you
in much inconvenience and possibly actual disaster, turning
some important interview or romantic tryst into a scene of farce
or humiliation. More sinister, and fortunately more rare, is the
garment which seems to attract disasters to you rather than to itself. Ms. Nemy mentions an orange linen dress that apparently
took a dislike to its owner, Margaret Turner of Dover Publica-
tions. Orange clothes, as it happens, do occasionally arouse hostility in our culture, but this dress seems to have been a special

case. "Women friends seemed cattier, men seemed more aloof and I'd get into bad situations with my boss," Ms. Turner reported. "And that wasn't all. I'd spill coffee, miss train connections and the car would break down."

25   For some people the daily task of choosing a costume is tedious, oppressive or even frightening. Occasionally such people tell us that fashion is unnecessary; that in the ideal world of the future we will all wear some sort of identical jump suit—washable, waterproof, stretchable, temperature-controlled, timeless, ageless and sexless. What a convenience, what a relief it will be, they say, never to worry about how to dress for a job interview, a romantic tryst or a funeral!

26   Convenient, perhaps, but not exactly a relief. Such a utopia would give most of us the same kind of chill we feel when a stadium full of Communist-bloc athletes in identical sports outfits, shouting slogans in unison, appears on TV. Most people do not want to be told what to wear any more than they want to be told what to say. In Belfast recently, 400 Irish Republican prisoners "refused to wear any clothes at all, draping themselves day and night in blankets," rather than put on prison uniforms. Even the offer of civilian-style dress did not satisfy them; they insisted on wearing their own clothes brought from home or nothing. Fashion is free speech, and one of the privileges, if not always one of the pleasures, of a free world.

Response Questions

1. Write a personal response comparing yourself and others to Alison Lurie's classifications. What elements of Lurie's discussion do you agree and disagree with?
2. Lurie writes, "To choose clothes, either in a store or at home, is to define and describe ourselves." In what ways is this true?
3. How do clothes affect the way you feel and the way people treat you?
4. What are your favorite clothes? Why do you like them?
5. Describe your most uncomfortable clothes.
6. What kind of clothes make you feel especially good about yourself?

Our Dreams

Part of who we are is what we want to accomplish during our lifetime. On the practical side is our choice of an occupation, but what about our dreams? What do we really want to work toward

or realize in our lives? The following two poems were written by
Langston Hughes. He wrote them describing the anguish of the
unfulfilled dreams of people working and hoping for civil rights.

Dreams

LANGSTON HUGHES

Hold fast to dreams
For if dreams die
Life is a broken-winged bird
That cannot fly.

Hold fast to dreams   5
For when dreams go
Life is a barren field
Frozen with snow.

Dream Deferred

LANGSTON HUGHES

What happens to a dream deferred?

Does it dry up
like a raisin in the sun?
Or fester like a sore—
And then run?   5

Does it stink like rotten meat?
Or crust and sugar over—
like a syrupy sweet?

Maybe it just sags
like a heavy load.   10

Or does it explode?

Response Questions: "Dreams"

1. Langston Hughes uses metaphors to make the images powerful. What is the emotional impact of the poem?
2. What is the message of the poem?
3. Relate the message to your own life, in your own words.

Response Questions: "Dream Deferred"

1. Hughes uses similes to give readers strong images. What dreams of yours fit each of the similes in one way or another?
2. What is the difference between a dream that dries up like a raisin and one that festers like a sore?
3. What is the significance of the title?

When you were a child, you had dreams and wishes about what you expected or hoped life would be like. Our experiences shape the way we view life. The following poem by Naomi Shihab Nye, "Making a Fist," relates a child's perception of herself and then compares the experience to an adult's way of looking at life.

Making a Fist

NAOMI SHIHAB NYE

For the first time, on the road north of Tampico,
I felt the life sliding out of me,
a drum in the desert, harder and harder to hear.
I was seven, I lay in the car
5   watching palm trees swirl a sickening pattern past the glass.
My stomach was a melon split wide inside my skin.

"How do you know if you are going to die?"
I begged my mother.
We had been traveling for days.
10   With strange confidence she answered,
"When you can no longer make a fist."

Years later I smile to think of that journey,
the borders we must cross separately,
stamped with our unanswerable woes.
I who did not die, who am still living,   15
still lying in the backseat behind all my questions,
clenching and opening one small hand.

Response Questions

The child is experiencing a severe case of car sickness. How does the
mother's response to the question shape the way the child views life
now? What might "making a fist" symbolize? What advice or wisdom
from your childhood affects you now?

Defining Ourselves

We define ourselves by our experiences, the views others have
of us, our values, the stories we believe, and the patterns of our
lives. The final paper for this chapter will be an essay on your
view of yourself—but first read the essay by author and teacher
Nancy Mairs that follows.

On Being a Cripple

NANCY MAIRS

To escape is nothing. Not to escape is nothing.

—Louise Bogan

The other day I was thinking of writing an essay on being a   1
cripple. I was thinking hard in one of the stalls of the women's
room in my office building, as I was shoving my shirt into my
jeans and tugging up my zipper. Preoccupied, I flushed, picked
up my book bag, took my cane down from the hook, and un-
latched the door. So many movements unbalanced me, and as I
pulled the door open I fell over backward, landing fully clothed
on the toilet seat with my legs splayed in front of me: the old
beetle-on-its-back routine. Saturday afternoon, the building

deserted, I was free to laugh aloud as I wriggled back to my feet, my voice bouncing off the yellowish tiles from all directions. Had anyone been there with me, I'd have been still and faint and hot with chagrin.

2   I decided that it was high time to write the essay.

3   First, the matter of semantics. I am a cripple. I choose this word to name me. I choose from among several possibilities, the most common of which are *handicapped* and *disabled.* I made the choice a number of years ago, without thinking, unaware of my motives for doing so. Even now, I'm not sure what those motives are, but I recognize that they are complex and not entirely flattering. People—crippled or not—wince at the word *cripple,* as they do not at *handicapped* or *disabled.* Perhaps I want them to wince. I want them to see me as a tough customer, one to whom the fates/gods/viruses have not been kind, but who can face the brutal truth of her existence squarely. As a cripple, I swagger.

4   But, to be fair to myself, a certain amount of honesty underlies my choice. *Cripple* seems to me a clean word, straightforward and precise. It has an honorable history, having made its first appearance in the Lindisfarne Gospel in the tenth century. As a lover of words, I like the accuracy with which it describes my condition: I have lost the full use of my limbs. *Disabled,* by contrast, suggests any incapacity, physical or mental. And I certainly don't like *handicapped,* which implies that I have deliberately been put at a disadvantage, by whom I can't imagine (my God is not a Handicapper General), in order to equalize chances in the great race of life. These words seem to me to be moving away from my condition, to be widening the gap between word and reality. Most remote is the recently coined euphemism *differently abled,* which partakes of the same semantic hopefulness that transformed countries from *undeveloped* to *underdeveloped,* then to *less developed,* and finally to *developing* nations. People have continued to starve in those countries during the shift. Some realities do not obey the dictates of language.

5   Mine is one of them. Whatever you call me, I remain crippled. But I don't care what I am called, as long as it isn't *differently abled,* which strikes me as pure verbal garbage designed, by its ability to describe anyone, to describe no one. I subscribe to George Orwell's thesis that "the sloppiness of our language makes it easier for us to have foolish thoughts." And I refuse to participate in the

degeneration of the language to the extent that I deny that I have lost anything in the course of this calamitous disease; I refuse to pretend that the only differences between you and me are the various ordinary ones that distinguish any one person from another. But call me *disabled* or *handicapped* if you like. I have long since grown accustomed to them; and if they are vague, at least they hint at the truth. Moreover, I use them myself. Society is no readier to accept crippledness than to accept death, war, sex, sweat, or wrinkles. I would never refer to another person as a cripple. It is the word I use to name only myself.

I haven't always been crippled, a fact for which I am soundly   6
grateful. To be whole of limb is, I know from experience, infinitely more pleasant and useful than to be crippled; and if that knowledge leaves me open to bitterness at my loss, the physical soundness I once enjoyed (though I did not enjoy it half enough) is well worth the occasional stab of regret. Though never any good at sports, I was a normally active child and young adult. I climbed trees, played hopscotch, jumped rope, skated, swam, rode my bicycle, sailed. I despised team sports, spending some of the most wretched afternoons of my life, sweaty and humiliated, behind a field-hockey stick and under a basketball hoop. I tramped alone for miles along the bridle paths that webbed the woods behind the house I grew up in. I swayed through countless dim hours in the arms of one man or another under the scattered shot of light from mirrored balls, and gyrated through countless more as Tab Hunter and Johnny Mathis gave way to the Rolling Stones, Creedence Clearwater Revival, Cream. I walked down the aisle. I pushed baby carriages, changed tires in the rain, marched for peace.

When I was twenty-nine, I started to trip and drop things.   7
What at first seemed my natural clumsiness soon became too pronounced to shrug off. I consulted a neurologist, who told me that I had a brain tumor. A battery of tests, increasingly disagreeable, revealed no tumor. About a year and a half later I developed a blurred spot in one eye. I had, at last, the episodes "disseminated in space and time" requisite for a diagnosis: multiple sclerosis. I have never been sorry for the doctor's initial misdiagnosis, however. For almost a week, until the negative results of the tests were in, I thought that I was going to die right away. Every day for the past nearly ten years, then, has been a kind of gift. I accept all gifts.

8   Multiple sclerosis is a chronic degenerative disease of the central nervous system, in which the myelin that sheathes the nerves is somehow eaten away and scar tissue forms in its place, interrupting the nerves' signals. During its course, which is unpredictable and uncontrollable, one may lose vision, hearing, speech, the ability to walk, control of bladder and/or bowels, strength in any or all extremities, sensitivity to touch, vibration, and/or pain, potency, coordination of movements—the list of possibilities is lengthy and horrifying. One may also lose one's sense of humor. That's the easiest to lose and the hardest to survive without.

9   In the past ten years, I have sustained some of these losses. Characteristic of MS are sudden attacks, called exacerbations, followed by remissions, and these I have not had. Instead, my disease has been slowly progressive. My left leg is now so weak that I walk with the aid of a brace and a cane; and for distances I use an Amigo, a variation on the electric wheelchair that looks rather like an electrified kiddie car. I no longer have much use of my left hand. Now my right side is weakening as well. I still have the blurred spot in my right eye. Overall, though, I've been lucky so far. My world has, of necessity, been circumscribed by my losses, but the terrain left me has been ample enough for me to continue many of the activities that absorb me: writing, teaching, raising children and cats and plants and snakes, reading, speaking publicly about MS and depression, even playing bridge with people patient and honorable enough to let me scatter cards every which way without sneaking a peek.

10   Lest I begin to sound like Pollyanna, however, let me say that I don't like having MS. I hate it. My life holds realities—harsh ones, some of them—that no right-minded human being ought to accept without grumbling. One of them is fatigue. I know of no one with MS who does not complain of bone-weariness; in a disease that presents an astonishing variety of symptoms, fatigue seems to be a common factor. I wake up in the morning feeling the way most people do at the end of a bad day, and I take it from there. As a result, I spend a lot of time *in extremis* and, impatient with limitation, I tend to ignore my fatigue until my body breaks down in some way and forces rest. Then I miss picnics, dinner parties, poetry readings, the brief visits of old friends from out of town. The offspring of a puritanical tradition of ex-

ceptional venerability, I cannot view these lapses without shame. My life often seems a series of small failures to do as I ought.

I lead, on the whole, an ordinary life, probably rather like the   11 one I would have led had I not had MS. I am lucky that my predilections were already solitary, sedentary, and bookish— unlike the world-famous French cellist I have read about, or the young woman I talked with one long afternoon who wanted only to be a jockey. I had just begun graduate school when I found out something was wrong with me, and I have remained —interminably—a graduate student. Perhaps I would not have if I'd thought I had the stamina to return to a full-time job as a technical editor; but I've enjoyed my studies.

In addition to studying, I teach writing courses. I also teach   12 medical students how to give neurological examinations. I pick up free-lance editing jobs here and there. I have raised a foster son and sent him into the world, where he has made me two grand-babies, and I am still escorting my daughter and son through ado-lescence. I go to mass every Saturday. I am a superb, if messy, cook. I am also an enthusiastic laundress, capable of sorting a hamper full of clothes into five subtly differentiated piles, but a terrible housekeeper. I can do italic writing and, in an emer-gency, bathe an oil-soaked cat. I play a fiendish game of Scrab-ble. When I have the time and the money, I like to sit on my front steps with my husband, drinking Amaretto and smoking a cigar, as we imagine our counterparts in Leningrad and make sure that the sun gets down once more behind the sharp childish scrawl of the Tucson mountains.

This lively plenty has its bleak complement, of course, in all   13 the things I can no longer do. I will never run again, except in dreams, and one day I may have to write that I will never walk again. I like to go camping, but I can't follow George and the children along the trails that wander out of a campsite through the desert or into the mountains. In fact, even on the level I've learned never to check the weather or try to hold a coherent con-versation: I need all my attention for my wayward feet. Of late, I have begun to catch myself wondering how people can propel themselves without canes. With only one usable hand, I have to select my clothing with care not so much for style as for ease of ingress and egress, and even so, dressing can be laborious. I can no longer do fine stitchery, pick up babies, play the piano, braid my hair. I am immobilized by acute attacks of depression, which may or may not be physiologically related to MS but are certainly its logical concomitant.

14   These two elements, the plenty and the privation, are never pure, nor are the delight and wretchedness that accompany them. Almost every pickle that I get into as a result of my weakness and clumsiness—and I get into plenty—is funny as well as maddening and sometimes painful. I recall one May afternoon when a friend and I were going out for a drink after finishing up at school. As we were climbing into opposite sides of my car, chatting, I tripped and fell, flat and hard, onto the asphalt parking lot, my abrupt departure interrupting him in mid-sentence. "Where'd you go?" he called as he came around the back of the car to find me hauling myself up by the door frame. "Are you all right?" Yes, I told him, I was fine, just a bit rattly, and we drove off to find a shady patio and some beer. When I got home an hour or so later, my daughter greeted me with, "What have you done to yourself?" I looked down. One elbow of my white turtleneck with the green froggies, one knee of my white trousers, one white kneesock were blood-soaked. We peeled off the clothes and inspected the damage, which was nasty enough but not alarming. That part wasn't funny: The abrasions took a long time to heal, and one got a little infected. Even so, when I think of my friend talking earnestly, suddenly, to the hot thin air while I dropped from his view as though through a trap door, I find the image as silly as something from a Marx Brothers movie.

15   I may find it easier than other cripples to amuse myself because I live propped by the acceptance and the assistance and, sometimes, the amusement of those around me. Grocery clerks tear my checks out of my checkbook for me, and sales clerks find chairs to put into dressing rooms when I want to try on clothes. The people I work with make sure I teach at times when I am least likely to be fatigued, in places I can get to, with the materials I need. My students, with one anonymous exception (in an end-of-the-semester evaluation), have been unperturbed by my disability. Some even like it. One was immensely cheered by the information that I paint my own fingernails; she decided, she told me, that if I could go to such trouble over fine details, she could keep on writing essays. I suppose I became some sort of bright-fingered muse. She wrote good essays, too.

The most important struts in the framework of my existence, 16
of course, are my husband and children. Dismayingly few marriages survive the MS test, and why should they? Most twenty-
two- and nineteen-year-olds, like George and me, can vow in
clear conscience, after a childhood of chicken pox and summer
colds, to keep one another in sickness and in health so long as
they both shall live. Not many are equipped for catastrophe: the
dismay, the depression, the extra work, the boredom that a degenerative disease can insinuate into a relationship. And our
society, with its emphasis on fun and its association of fun with
physical performance, offers little encouragement for a whole
spouse to stay with a crippled partner. Children experience
similar stresses when faced with a crippled parent, and they are
more helpless, since parents and children can't usually get divorced. They hate, of course, to be different from their peers,
and the child whose mother is tacking down the aisle of a school
auditorium packed with proud parents like a Cape Cod dinghy
in a stiff breeze jolly well stands out in a crowd. Deprived of
legal divorce, the child can at least deny the mother's disability,
even her existence, forgetting to tell her about recitals and PTA
meetings, refusing to accompany her to stores or church or the
movies, never inviting friends to the house. Many do.

But I've been limping along for ten years now, and so far 17
George and the children are still at my left elbow, holding tight.
Anne and Matthew vacuum floors and dust furniture and haul
trash and rake up dog droppings and button my cuffs and bake
lasagna and Toll House cookies with just enough grumbling so
I know that they don't have brain fever. And far from hiding me,
they're forever dragging me by racks of fancy clothes or through
teeming school corridors, or welcoming gaggles of friends while
I'm wandering through the house in Anne's filmy pink baby-
doll pajamas. George generally calls before he brings someone
home, but he does just as many dumb thankless chores as the
children. And they all yell at me, laugh at some of my jokes,
write me funny letters when we're apart—in short, treat me as
an ordinary human being for whom they have some use. I think
they like me. Unless they're faking. . . .

Faking. There's the rub. Tugging at the fringes of my con- 18
sciousness always is the terror that people are kind to me only
because I'm a cripple. My mother almost shattered me once,

with that instinct mothers have—blind, I think, in this case, but unerring nonetheless—for striking blows along the fault-lines of their children's hearts, by telling me, in an attack on my selfishness, "We all have to make allowances for you, of course, because of the way you are." From the distance of a couple of years, I have to admit that I haven't any idea just what she meant, and I'm not sure that she knew either. She was awfully angry. But at the time, as the words thudded home, I felt my worst fear suddenly realized. I could bear being called selfish: I am. But I couldn't bear the corroboration that those around me were doing in fact what I'd always suspected them of doing; professing fondness while silently they put up with me because of the way I am. A cripple. I've been a little cracked ever since.

19   Along with this fear that people are secretly accepting shoddy goods comes a relentless pressure to please—to prove myself worth the burdens I impose, I guess, or to build a substantial account of good will against which I may write drafts in times of need. Part of the pressure arises from social expectations. In our society, anyone who deviates from the norm had better find some way to compensate. Like fat people, who are expected to be jolly, cripples must bear their lot meekly and cheerfully. A grumpy cripple isn't playing by the rules. And much of the pressure is self-generated. Early on I vowed that, if I had to have MS, by God I was going to do it well. This is a class act, ladies and gentlemen. No tears, no recriminations, no faintheartedness.

20   One way and another, then, I wind up feeling like Tiny Tim, peering over the edge of the table at the Christmas goose, waving my crutch, piping down God's blessing on us all. Only sometimes I don't want to play Tiny Tim. I'd rather be Caliban, a most scurvy monster. Fortunately, at home no one much cares whether I'm a good cripple or a bad cripple so long as I make vichyssoise with fair regularity. One evening several years ago, Anne was at the diningroom table reading while I cooked dinner. As I opened a can of tomatoes, the can slipped in my left hand and juice spattered me and the counter with bloody spots. Fatigued and infuriated, I bellowed, "I'm so sick of being crippled. . . ." Anne glanced at me over the top of her book. "There now," she said, "do you feel better?" "Yes," I said, "yes I do." She went back to her reading. I felt better. That's about all the attention my scurviness ever gets.

Because I hate being crippled, I sometimes hate myself for   21
being a cripple. Over the years I have come to expect—even
accept—attacks of violent self-loathing. Luckily, in general our
society no longer connects deformity and disease directly with
evil (though a charismatic once told me that I have MS because
a devil is in me) and so I am allowed to move largely at will,
even among small children. But I'm not sure that this revision of
attitude has been particularly helpful. Physical imperfection,
even freed of moral disapprobation, still defines and violates the
ideal, especially for women, whose confinement in their bodies
as objects of desire is far from over. Each age, of course, has its
ideal, and I doubt that ours is any better or worse than any other.
Today's ideal woman, who lives on the glossy pages of dozens
of magazines, seems to be between the ages of eighteen and
twenty-five; her hair has body, her teeth flash white, her breath
smells minty, her underarms are dry; she has a career but is still
a fabulous cook, especially of meals that take less than twenty
minutes to prepare; she does not ordinarily appear to have a
husband or children; she is trim and deeply tanned; she jogs,
swims, plays tennis, rides a bicycle, sails, but does not bowl; she
travels widely, even to out-of-the-way places like Finland and
Samoa, always in the company of the ideal man, who possesses
a nearly identical set of characteristics. There are a few exceptions. Though usually white and often blonde, she may be
black, Hispanic, oriental, or native American, so long as she is
unusually sleek. She may be old, provided she is selling a laxa-
tive or is Lauren Bacall. If she is selling a detergent, she may be
married and have a flock of strikingly messy children. But she is
never a cripple.

Like many women I know, I have always had an uneasy re-   22
lationship with my body. I was not a popular child, largely, I
think now, because I was peculiar; intelligent, intense, moody,
shy, given to unexpected actions and inexplicable notions and
emotions. But as I entered adolescence, I believed myself un-
popular because I was homely: my breasts too flat, my mouth
too wide, my hips too narrow, my clothing never quite right in
fit or style. I was not, in fact, particularly ugly, old photographs
inform me, though I was well off the ideal; but I carried this
sense of self-alienation with me into adulthood, where it regen-
erated in response to the depredations of MS. Even with my

brace I walk with a limp so pronounced that, seeing myself on
the videotape of a television program on the disabled, I couldn't
believe that anything but an inchworm could make progress
humping along like that. My shoulders droop and my pelvis
thrusts forward as I try to balance myself upright, throwing my
frame into a bony S. As a result of contractures, one shoulder is
higher than the other and I carry one arm bent in front of me,
the fingers curled into a claw. My left arm and leg have wasted
into pipe-stems, and I try always to keep them covered. When I
think about how my body must look to others, especially to
men, to whom I have been trained to display myself, I feel ludi-
crous, even loathsome.

23   At my age, however, I don't spend much time thinking about
my appearance. The burning egocentricity of adolescence, which
assures one that all the world is looking all the time, has passed,
thank God, and I'm generally too caught up in what I'm doing
to step back, as I used to, and watch myself as though upon a
stage. I'm also too old to believe in the accuracy of self-image. I
know that I'm not a hideous crone, that in fact, when I'm rested,
well dressed, and well made up, I look fine. The self-loathing I
feel is neither physically nor intellectually substantial. What I
hate is not me but a disease.

24   I am not a disease.

25   And a disease is not—at least not singlehandedly—going to
determine who I am, though at first it seemed to be going to.
Adjusting to a chronic incurable illness, I have moved through
a process similar to that outlined by Elizabeth Kübler-Ross in
Death and Dying. The major difference—and it is far more significant than most people recognize—is that I can't be sure of
the outcome, as the terminally ill cancer patient can. Research
studies indicate that, with proper medical care, I may achieve a
"normal" life span. And in our society, with its vision of death
as the ultimate evil, worse even than decrepitude, the response
to such news is, "Oh, well, at least you're not going to *die.*"

26   Are there worse things than dying? I think there may be.

27   I think of two women I know, both with MS, both enough
older than I to have served me as models. One took to her bed
several years ago and has been there ever since. Although she
can sit in a high-backed wheelchair, because she is incontinent
she refuses to go out at all, even though incontinence pants,

which are readily available at any pharmacy, could protect her from embarrassment. Instead, she stays at home and insists that her husband, a small quiet man, a retired civil servant, stay there with her except for a quick weekly foray to the supermarket. The other woman, whose illness was diagnosed when she was eighteen, a nursing student engaged to a young doctor, finished her training, married her doctor, accompanied him to Germany when he was in the service, bore three sons and a daughter, now grown and gone. When she can, she travels with her husband; she plays bridge, embroiders, swims regularly; she works, like me, as a symptomatic patient instructor of medical students in neurology.

Guess which woman I hope to be.   28

At the beginning, I thought about having MS almost inces-   29
santly. And because of the unpredictable course of the disease, my thoughts were always terrified. Each night I'd get into bed wondering whether I'd get out again the next morning, whether I'd be able to see, to speak, to hold a pen between my fingers. Knowing that the day might come when I'd be physically incapable of killing myself, I thought perhaps I ought to do so right away, while I still had the strength. Gradually I came to understand that the Nancy who might one day lie inert under a bedsheet, arms and legs paralyzed, unable to feed or bathe herself, unable to reach out for a gun, a bottle of pills, was not the Nancy I was at present, and that I could not presume to make decisions for that future Nancy, who might well not want in the least to die. Now the only provision I've made for the future Nancy is that when the time comes—and it is likely to come in the form of pneumonia, friend to the weak and the old—I am not to be treated with machines and medications. If she is unable to communicate by then, I hope she will be satisfied with these terms.

Thinking all the time about having MS grew tiresome and in-   30
trusive, especially in the large and tragic mode in which I was accustomed to considering my plight. Months and even years went by without catastrophe (at least without one related to MS), and really I was awfully busy, what with George and children and snakes and students and poems, and I hadn't the time, let alone the inclination, to devote myself to being a disease. Too, the richer my life became, the funnier it seemed, as though there were some connection between largesse and laughter, and so my

tragic stance began to waver until, even with the aid of a brace and a cane, I couldn't hold it for very long at a time.

31   After several years I was satisfied with my adjustment. I had suffered my grief and fury and terror, I thought, but now I was at ease with my lot. Then one summer day I set out with George and the children across the desert for a vacation in California. Part way to Yuma I became aware that my right leg felt funny. "I think I've had an exacerbation," I told George. "What shall we do?" he asked. "I think we'd better get the hell to California," I said, "because I don't know whether I'll ever make it again." So we went on to San Diego and then to Orange, up the Pacific Coast Highway to Santa Cruz, across to Yosemite, down to Sequoia and Joshua Tree, and so back over the desert to home. It was a fine two-week trip, filled with friends and fair weather, and I wouldn't have missed it for the world, though I did in fact make it back to California two years later. Nor would there have been any point in missing it, since in MS, once the symptoms have appeared, the neurological damage has been done, and there's no way to predict or prevent that damage.

32   The incident spoiled my self-satisfaction, however. I renewed my grief and fury and terror, and I learned that one never finishes adjusting to MS. I don't know now why I thought one would. One does not, after all, finish adjusting to life, and MS is simply a fact of my life—not my favorite fact, of course—but as ordinary as my nose and my tropical fish and my yellow Mazda station wagon. It may at any time get worse, but no amount of worry or anticipation can prepare me for a new loss. My life is a lesson in losses. I learn one at a time.

33   And I had best be patient in the learning, since I'll have to do it like it or not. As any rock fan knows, you can't always get what you want. Particularly when you have MS. You can't, for example, get cured. In recent years researchers and the organizations that fund research have started to pay MS some attention even though it isn't fatal; perhaps they have begun to see that life is something other than a quantitative phenomenon, that one may be very much alive for a very long time in a life that isn't worth living. The researchers have made some progress toward understanding the mechanism of the disease: It may well be an autoimmune reaction triggered by a slow-acting virus. But they are nowhere near its prevention, control, or cure. And most of us

want to be cured. Some, unable to accept incurability, grasp at one treatment after another, no matter how bizarre: megavitamin therapy, gluten-free diet, injections of cobra venom, hypothermal suits, lymphocytopharesis, hyperbaric chambers. Many treatments are probably harmless enough, but none are curative.

The absence of a cure often makes MS patients bitter toward their doctors. Doctors are, after all, the priests of modern society, the new shamans, whose business is to heal, and many MS patients rove from one to another, searching for the "good" doctor who will make them well. Doctors too think of themselves as healers, and for this reason many have trouble dealing with MS patients, whose disease in its intransigence defeats their aims and mocks their skills. Too few doctors, it is true, treat their patients as whole human beings, but the reverse is also true. I have always tried to be gentle with my doctors, who often have more at stake in terms of ego than I do. I may be frustrated, maddened, depressed by the incurability of my disease, but I am not diminished by it, and they are. When I push myself up from my seat in the waiting room and stumble toward them, I incarnate the limitation of their powers. The least I can do is refuse to press on their tenderest spots.

This gentleness is part of the reason that I'm not sorry to be a cripple. I didn't have it before. Perhaps I'd have developed it anyway—how could I know such a thing?—and I wish I had more of it, but I'm glad of what I have. It has opened and enriched my life enormously, this sense that my frailty and need must be mirrored in others, that in searching for and shaping a stable core in a life wrenched by change and loss, change and loss, I must recognize the same process, under individual conditions, in the lives around me. I do not deprecate such knowledge, however I've come by it.

All the same, if a cure were found, would I take it? In a minute. I may be crippled, but I'm only occasionally a loony and never a saint. Anyway, in my brand of theology God doesn't give bonus points for a limp. I'd take a cure; I just don't need one. A friend who also has MS startled me once by asking, "Do you ever say to yourself, 'Why me, Lord?' " "No, Michael, I don't," I told him, "because whenever I try, the only response I can think of is 'Why not?' " If I could make a cosmic deal, who would I put in my place? What in my life would I give up in

34

35

36

exchange for sound limbs and a thrilling rush of energy? No one. Nothing. I might as well do the job myself. Now that I'm getting the hang of it.

Response Questions

1. We probably can all relate to the embarrassment of falling or tripping. Why do we care?
2. Nancy Mairs writes, "As a cripple, I swagger." Substitute in that sentence a word or phrase that describes you.
3. Mairs discusses the widening "gap between word and reality." Describe what this means to you.
4. Respond to "I accept all gifts." She thought this when she realized she wasn't going to die. What might this statement mean in your life?
5. Mairs mentions two feelings she succumbs to: a sense of guilt when she cannot meet others' expectations and a fierce desire to please others. Why do you think she has these emotions?
6. What similar feelings do you react to?
7. Do you agree with Mairs's belief that self-image is not accurate? Why or why not?
8. The author writes that one never finishes adjusting to MS and one doesn't finish adjusting to life either. How does this apply to your life?
9. What in Mairs's essay is the most important to you?

WRITING ASSIGNMENT: DEFINING YOURSELF

Your assignment is to write a paper describing yourself. What are your hopes, dreams, values, expectations, talents, and strengths? You may want to focus on one area of your life or one time period. Consider what pattern of development is best suited to your specific topic and what you want to achieve in the paper. A combination of patterns may best suit your purpose.

Writing about yourself can be difficult, but you will find that making an outline before beginning is helpful. What are your main topics? What is your thesis? (What was Mairs's?) You must use examples, illustrations, sensory perceptions, and details to make your essay believable to readers. Your instructor will explain how long the piece should be and other qualifications. Use an entire writing process to produce a polished copy.

13

Making Decisions

We make choices all the time: when to get up in the morning, what to eat, what to wear, what tasks to do first. Many of our daily choices are trivial and fairly simple. We make decisions to get us through the day and to get the business of our life taken care of. We make longer-lasting decisions, too. We decide whom we will be friends with and how we will spend our time. You made an important decision in deciding to attend college. Other significant decisions are your choice of a major and ultimately your career choice. Writing plays an important part in wise decision making.

Making Choices through Values and Interests

The decisions we are happiest with are those that match our personal values, interests, and likes and dislikes. Even with everyday choices, we are more content and feel better about ourselves if the choices reflect our values and interests. An example is our choice of what food to eat. If you value a healthy body, then you will base your daily food choices on questions such as "Are there foods that are good for me that I haven't eaten for a while? What do I need to eat to keep in good health?" Other values that may affect your food choices may be the values of working on studies, earning money, and spending time with friends. That is, the time needed for these values may interfere with the time or social occasions you need in order to eat healthy food. A wide range of values and interests, then, may be involved in the seemingly simple choice of what to eat. We don't consciously go through all our values when we make everyday decisions, but we need to be aware of our priorities to some extent so that the compromises and balances among values give us a high level of satisfaction.

The next reading, "How to Make the Right Decision" by Donna Brown Hogarty, addresses the problems inherent in decision making. Hogarty wrote the article for a national women's magazine, and the introduction speaks to that audience; however, the steps Hogarty explains are helpful to women and men of all ages. Read the article and take notes to use in discussion.

How to Make the Right Decision

DONNA BROWN HOGARTY

1   For weeks now, you and your husband have been arguing about whether to buy that new house. On the plus side is a shorter commute to work for both of you, a lot more space and a safer neighborhood. But you have many good friends in your present neighborhood, and you've heard that the grade school your daughter would attend if you move is academically weak. You're feeling frustrated, and somewhat embarrassed, by your inability to make a final choice.

2   Unfortunately, this dilemma is quite common. "Many women, to some degree, have trouble making decisions," says Barbara Holstein, Ed.D., a psychologist in private practice in Long Beach, New Jersey. And that difficulty only intensifies when a woman needs to make a joint decision with her husband. "Women have the capacity to see both sides of an argument," says Holstein. Wives are masters of appreciating their spouse's point of view, and are often more focused on a peaceful compromise than on pushing for what they want.

3   When a woman does take the lead in making a choice, she may get nervous about whether her decision was the right one. "Some women fear the ramifications of a decision much more than the decision itself," says Holstein. So, if her choice turns out to be not as good as she'd hoped, she's often all too ready to assume the blame. As a result, the next time she's faced with a variety of options, she obsesses and vacillates, wasting precious time and energy and losing her decision-making confidence.

4   If all this sounds familiar, take heart. In just five simple steps, you can learn to make quicker, and better, decisions.

Identify Your Priorities

Before you can make a sound choice about any important   5
issue, you need to know what it is about the decision that matters most to you. J. Edward Russo, Ph.D., a professor of marketing and behavioral science at Cornell University, in Ithaca,
New York, likens this step to "framing" a photograph with a
camera. "You must focus on what's important, and cast into
shadow those elements that are unimportant," he explains.

Say that you've been offered a plum spot on a community   6
group in your town. You'd like to accept the position, but you
feel torn—becoming a member of the group will mean meetings and extra work on evenings and some weekends, and you
have two small children at home. You worry about spending
too much time away from them (even though your husband
has agreed to watch them), but you feel the issues facing your
community are extremely important—and affect your children's
future as well. In this case, you decide your top priority is to
join the community group and help make positive changes for
the families that live in your town.

Gather Information

Now that you've got a fix on your priorities, you need to find   7
out as much as possible about your options. For instance, you
and your husband decide you'd like to rent a house in the mountains for your vacation this year. But first, you need to figure out
exactly where you want to go, how much you want to spend
and what type of rental house you'd prefer (for instance, rustic
or modern).

Where should you begin? You can get a good start by look-   8
ing through travel magazines for vacation spots that appeal to
you. Then, call people you know who have also rented vacation
homes, and ask for any advice they have. Finally, call the visitors' bureau or the chamber of commerce in the towns you're
interested in and ask them to send you information about the
area, as well as the names of reputable house-rental agents. "It's
amazing how much information you can gather in a half hour
on the telephone," says Russo.

Doing your homework will also help you identify additional   9
options. Talking to experts and friends or brainstorming with

your spouse can point you in a new direction. Say that your new boss is unbearable, and you're thinking about resigning to save your sanity. By doing some research at the office—talking to co-workers in other departments, exploring opportunities with your personnel director—you might find a suitable slot to move into within your company, thus saving yourself a job search. The bottom line: You'll seldom regret a decision if it's a well-informed one.

Use Your Intuition

10 While you gather solid information on your decision, be sure to take your gut feelings into account. Although some decision-making experts discount the value of intuition, others believe that our "sixth sense" is a valuable tool, especially when balanced with logic and deduction.

11 To put your intuition to work for you, your first step must be to get in touch with it. According to New York psychotherapist Laurie Nadel, Ph.D., the author of *Sixth Sense* (Avon Books, 1992), everyone experiences intuition differently. Some people get a physical signal, such as a fluttering in the diaphragm or a warm sensation in the chest. Others have a visual flash or a dream. The key, says Nadel, is to learn to recognize your particular signal. Think about the times in your life when your intuition turned out to be right, and analyze how it worked. Did you experience intuition physically or emotionally?

12 If your sixth sense is difficult to pinpoint, try this method from psychologist Barbara Holstein: Discuss an upcoming decision with a trusted friend or family member. What are your secret fears about the decision? For instance, if you're considering a new job but fear that you won't fit in with your colleagues, you may have intuitively picked up signals during interviews that the office atmosphere is unpleasant.

13 Although intuition is extremely useful, you should avoid giving *absolute* credence to it. Sometimes gut feelings result from fear rather than intuition. "Intuitive people need to have their feet on the ground," cautions Nadel. For example, your concern about changing jobs might actually arise from the challenges and insecurity that any new job brings, rather than a true sixth sense that the office is uncomfortable.

How can you test your intuition? Behavioral scientist Russo 14
suggests that you try to find evidence that runs *counter* to your
hunch. Since most people subconsciously focus their information-gathering on confirming their initial conclusion, "this step
can enable you to be much more certain that you're making the
right choice," he says.

Weigh Your Options

Now that you've done your research and put your intuition to 15
work, it's time to compare potential choices. One tried-and-true
method: Simply list the pros and cons of each option, and cross
out counterbalancing characteristics. This method worked for
Sheovaun LaLonde, a thirty-nine-year-old mother of one in
New York City, when she was wrestling with whether to stay in
interior-design school. "For me, the pros were getting a degree
and launching a career that was potentially financially lucra-
tive," she explains. "Under cons, I listed that I found the program
stifling and that although my head was telling me to stay in
school, I knew in my heart that I wouldn't be happy in this profession." LaLonde decided to quit and is now content with her
career as a counselor and teacher.

If listing the pros and cons doesn't work for you, try a more 16
elaborate system. Say you're grappling with what sort of car to
buy. Money is tight, so you lean toward buying an inexpensive
model. Your husband believes, however, that if you spend more
on a quality car now, you'll save money in the long run. To decide, list all the important issues—cost, *Consumer Reports* ratings,
mileage, expected maintenance expenditures—and rank them
from one to four in importance. Your overall scores will help you
to make a final choice—and could prevent an argument, especially if you and your husband weigh the items together.

Test Yourself

After you've made a final decision, subject it to one last check, 17
says Russo. Imagine the worst consequence that could possibly
arise from your choice. For instance, say your best friend has
asked you for a loan. You want to help her out, but you know that
she's not very responsible when it comes to money. If you can

imagine yourself remaining on good terms with her—and not getting resentful or angry if she doesn't pay you back on time—then giving her the loan is probably the right thing to do.

18   Remember that no one can accurately predict the future—if a decision doesn't pan out because of unforeseeable events, realize that you still did your best. "No one should judge the quality of her decision-making solely on the outcome," says Russo.

19   Even the strongest decision-makers occasionally make the wrong decision—often for all the right reasons. If this happens to you, don't punish yourself for failing to take into account things that you couldn't possibly have known about. Instead, "give yourself a break, and view the decision as a choice that needs to be updated, rather than a mistake," says Barbara Holstein.

20   Ultimately, you'll be a top-notch decision-maker if you're comfortable with *how* you arrive at conclusions. "What really counts," says Holstein, "is the process of making the decision—of carefully pondering alternatives and reflecting on what's best for you." By confronting life's major choices in a rational, thoughtful way, you'll always make the best decisions possible.

Response Questions

Respond to each of the five points Donna Brown Hogarty describes.

1. Identify your priorities: In decision making, how does one go about deciding what is important? Consider the relationships between priorities and values.
2. Gather information: What sources could information come from? Check with others so that you have an expanded list of sources. The list will vary somewhat depending on the kind of decision you are making, but not as much as you might think. For example, knowledgeable people are often excellent sources. This step of gathering information is vitally important and should not be omitted.
3. Use your intuition: The article is addressed to women, who are often credited with possessing acute intuition. Do you think women have more powerful intuition than men? Use personal examples to illustrate your opinion.
4. Weigh your options: What kinds of choices does one have in a given situation? How could you know what your options are?
5. Test yourself: How can you do this?
6. The final advice Hogarty gives is that the way you arrive at a decision —the process itself—is of primary importance. What does this mean to you?

Writing Activity: Making a Group Decision

You will use some steps of the decision-making process Hogarty describes in this writing activity. Assume you are looking for an apartment to rent. Write a list of qualifications that you think the apartment should have. The list might include distance to school or work, living space, size of yard, garage—whatever is important to you. Think in practical terms; don't describe a dream apartment.

Now, assume that because of the cost you need to share the apartment with other people, people outside your immediate family. (Even if you are married and/or have children, assume for purposes of this assignment that you have to share the apartment with other people.) When you have completed your list of what you want your apartment to have, meet in groups of three or four. These are the people who will be sharing the apartment.

The second step in this process is to share your lists of needs. You have to determine what qualifications will be acceptable to all of you. For some, permission to have pets may be a high priority—or what floor the apartment is on, whether it is barrier free, what the neighborhood is like, how close the street is to an elementary school, how much the apartment costs, or other considerations that may not have occurred to you. Discuss until everyone agrees on one list of qualifications. Everyone will have to compromise, and each person has to listen to the others. This is not an exercise in holding out for your own point of view, but a time for compromising. For example, suppose one person insists on a single bedroom, but others are willing to double up. An acceptable compromise might be for one person to get the smallest bedroom or to pay more rent, or whatever the group comes up with. You may want to look at newspaper classified ads to see what you find that fits the group's needs.

Once you have your list of agreed-upon qualifications, make a chart that you can use when apartment hunting. The chart includes your list of qualifications and space to record information from several apartments. If this were an actual situation, one or all of you would take the chart along when looking at possible places to rent. You would collect data to use when everyone met to look at the chart.

The activity you just completed was designed to illustrate how a group of people can work together to reach a decision, an important career skill. This same method is also useful when you are making a personal decision, such as shopping for a car, deciding on a vacation, or any of the countless decisions you have to make. The benefits of this process are that it requires you to consciously think through what is important to you and to keep a record of information (data) you collect. These steps simplify decision making and help keep you clear on why you made the decision you did. Decision making plays an essential part in shaping your life in the way best suited to who you are.

Making Career Choices

One of the biggest decisions facing you right now, regardless of your age, is probably the question of your future career. How do you go about making such an important decision? Choosing a career is more complicated than thinking about what you want in an apartment, but the same process is useful. Knowing what you want and what is important, especially over a long time period, takes a high level of self-knowledge.

In Don Marquis's "The Lesson of the Moth," Archy, the typing cockroach, laments the death of a moth and compares it to wanting something with great determination.

The Lesson of the Moth

DON MARQUIS

i was talking to a moth
the other evening
he was trying to break into
an electric light bulb
and fry himself on the wires

why do you fellows
pull this stunt i asked him
because it is the conventional

5

thing for moths or why
if that had been an uncovered   10
candle instead of an electric
light bulb you would
now be a small unsightly cinder
have you no sense
plenty of it he answered   15
but at times we get tired
of using it
we get bored with the routine
and crave beauty
and excitement   20
fire is beautiful
and we know that if we get
too close it will kill us
but what does that matter
it is better to be happy   25
for a moment
and be burned up with beauty
than to live a long time
and be bored all the while
so we wad all our life up   30
into one little roll
and then we shoot the roll
that is what life is for
it is better to be a part of beauty
for one instant and then cease to   35
exist than to exist forever
and never be a part of beauty
our attitude toward life
is come easy go easy
we are like human beings   40
used to be before they became
too civilized to enjoy themselves

and before i could argue him
out of his philosophy
he went and immolated himself   45
on a patent cigar lighter
i do not agree with him

myself i would rather have
half the happiness and twice
50   the longevity

but at the same time i wish
there was something i wanted
as badly as he wanted to fry himself
                                          archy

The idea of wanting something needs to be considered when you are making decisions. Why is that desire so important? Does it fit with your other decisions and goals? More importantly, does it fit with your values?

A good way to begin making a career decision is to think again about your values. Unless your career (or any other important life choice) reflects your values or allows you to live according to your values, it will not bring you satisfaction. What do you value in a career? In the following poem, Marge Piercy describes the value of work.

To Be of Use

MARGE PIERCY

The people I love the best
jump into work head first
without dallying in the shallows
and swim with sure strokes almost out of sight.
5   They seem to become natives of that element,
the black sleek heads of seals
bouncing like half-submerged balls.

I love people who harness themselves, an ox to a heavy cart,
who pull like water buffalo, with massive patience,
10   who strain in the mud and the muck to move things forward,
who do what has to be done, again and again.

I want to be with people who submerge
in the task, who go into the fields to harvest
and work in a row and pass the bags along,
who stand in the line and haul in their places,   15
who are not parlor generals and field deserters
but move in a common rhythm
when the food must come in or the fire be put out.

The work of the world is common as mud.
Botched, it smears the hands, crumbles to dust.   20
But the thing worth doing well done
has a shape that satisfies, clean and evident.
Greek amphoras for wine or oil,
Hopi vases that held corn, are put in museums
but you know they were made to be used.   25
The pitcher cries for water to carry
and a person for work that is real.

Response Questions

Piercy values people who "jump into work" and "submerge themselves in the task." Who does this remind you of? Discuss the values in
the poem.

We need to be aware of what really matters to us rather than accepting values that may not fit our personalities. Knowing our values
is essential to choosing a career that brings satisfaction.

The Balance between Work and Play

At this time in your life you are making the important decision
of your life's work. Because of this focus people too often forget
that what we do besides work is vitally important. Ellen Goodman's essay "The Company Man" in Chapter 11 illustrated an
imbalance between working and learning to take time out for
other pursuits.

We have all heard much about the amount of stress in our
lives and its undesirable consequences. We have to make a conscious effort to reduce stress. The following poem, "Crows Play
in the Updraft" by Dennis Crowe, while not intended as a comment on stress, nevertheless has an appropriate message.

Crows Play in the Updraft

DENNIS CROWE

I remember
how the unspoken
can be stronger than expected,
can even provide lift;
5   birds know this.
I know from their whistle
along the crest of the
windwave
made by the broadside rank of trees
10   along the road;
                  crows in the rising air
relish the weightless dance, and they
dive glide pitch and roll and they
cannonball down to the tree edge,
15   pop open their wings and climb,
never once flapping a wing
or doing an ounce of work.

Wind, rising column,
the currency of play.

Response Questions

How does the poem relate to your life? A weightless dance seems the opposite of being overburdened with work. How might you avoid stress in your life and still work at your career and all your other commitments?

Guidelines for Decision Making

When we need to make big decisions, the prospect often overwhelms us. We can cut big decisions down to a manageable size, however, by considering one part or aspect at a time. The following guidelines can be helpful.

1. First, think through all the possible choices. Think in terms of options—"what else could I do?" For each option, ask yourself, "What are the possible outcomes?"
2. Write down the options and rank order them. This provides you with a concrete list to work from, even though the ranking may change later.
3. Talk with other people to gather information. The people you talk with could include both family members, who care about your best interests, and knowledgeable people outside the family, who can give you additional information about the possibilities inherent in your decision.
4. Stay open to new ideas. Don't jump to hasty decisions, but explore many possibilities.
5. Redefine and evaluate your course of action as the decision plays out in your life. Decision making is an ongoing process, and this is especially true in large decisions.

We are obliged to make our own decisions and to be responsible for our choices. What matters to us and how we live are based on choices we must make. We have a better chance of success if the choices are made thoughtfully and deliberately.

WRITING ASSIGNMENT: A SIGNIFICANT DECISION

The final paper for this chapter is an essay on a significant decision you need to make. You may write about a possible career choice, or you may discuss any other important decision you must make. Follow the guidelines given above: Begin with all the possible choices that you are seriously considering. Then rank order them and explain the reasons for the ranking. Such reasons may include your preferences, your talents, or any other factor that has a bearing on the decision. Talk to other people to gather information and opinions. Cite these sources in your paper. The conclusion will be your decision at this time. (If you write about a career choice, the decision may be a field of work rather than a specific job.) The reader needs to understand why you are making this particular choice. Your paper must reflect thoughtful consideration.

14

Writing Research Papers

The purpose of research papers is to find answers to questions. A writer collects information from a wide variety of sources and looks for connections that will yield answers to the question(s) under investigation. Documentation is an important part of research writing because of the fact that the information comes from many sources. Each source must be acknowledged. Not only is it important to give appropriate credit, but both the writer and the readers of the paper need to consider the source of each piece of information.

All research begins with questions; it does not begin with a topic to find information about. Questions are vital for focusing your research. You may have been encouraged to narrow your topic—good advice, but not specific enough. It is true that too broad a topic does not allow a paper to be as interesting, thoughtful, and informative as it could be. But to narrow a topic effectively, you need to think through what you want to know. Even though during college you are writing research papers in response to assignments, you write from your own perspective, prior knowledge, and interests. For example, you may be given an assignment to write on the issues surrounding the effectiveness of juries. One person might ask how historical developments have led to present-day juries; another might investigate how the legal system affects jury selection; a third might explore how jury members themselves view the system. All of these choices address the assignment. And all begin with the writer formulating questions that need answering.

Developing Questions

To help develop the questions that will focus your research, use freewriting (described in Chapter 1). In freewriting you reflect on the topic—for example, juries—and put down whatever you already know about it. Do not use any sources, but recall all you can—what you've read, heard, seen. Don't concern yourself with organization or even with accuracy, but keep thinking about the topic as you write. One idea leads to another in freewriting. You may want to come back to this, each time adding more information. Do not revise or edit. The freewrite is the basis for your research questions.

Writing Activity: Practicing Freewriting

Choose a topic you have an interest in. Your instructor may provide a list of options or let you choose your own. In either case, do a freewrite on the topic. Keep coming back to the freewrite over a period of a day or two so that you give yourself time to think about the topic.

Now read over your freewrite on your topic and organize the material in outline form. As you organize the material, write down the questions that occur. For example:

❑ What other information do I need?
❑ How do I know this is true?
❑ What would support this idea?
❑ What areas do I know little about?

As you organize and develop questions, the focus of your interest will sharpen and a specific direction will emerge. To continue the example of juries, perhaps one line of questioning would be, "What do people think of juries? What are their opinions based on? Does it matter where they live, or their age, or their employment?" Another might be, "What rights and powers do juries have?" Knowing the questions before researching for answers is vital. Without the focus that questions provide, you can waste a great deal of time reading material, hoping to find something about a topic. When you read looking for specific answers to questions, you can skim the material, take only pertinent notes, and know which quotes will enhance and support the information you are gathering.

Writing Activity: Refining Your Questions

For practice, choose an issue that has been in the news lately. It could be the site of road construction, the location of a shelter, the sale of liquor licenses, utility rates, peace in Northern Ireland, free trade—whatever interests you. Write the topic at the top of a page. Follow with a freewrite of what you know about the issue. Now write the questions you have about the issue. After completing the list, revise the questions by both combining and narrowing until you have a series of questions that are researchable and that will help you learn about what you are interested in. Share in groups and help one another refine the questions.

Using this process of developing and refining questions enables you to use your time to the best advantage; to write focused, organized research papers; and to locate information specific to your topic.

Gathering Information

The research questions are the structure for gathering information. You collect data and information for each specific question. The easiest and most logical way to accomplish this is to write each question at the top of separate sheets of paper. I do not recommend note cards, because the cards are too difficult to organize. The material on the cards is not organized according to your research questions. Later, when writing the paper, you must read all of the note cards—and you may have a large stack—searching for information on each of your questions. This could be a monumental task. Another problem lies with the sense of urgency of obtaining a certain number of cards, rather than searching for information that pertains to your topic. The emphasis on gathering information becomes displaced.

With one question to a sheet, begin reading an article on your subject and, as you discover answers to one question, write informational notes under that question. As you continue to read, you probably will discover information for another of your questions. What you are accomplishing is organization by topic as you take notes.

In addition to the organizational benefit, this method lets you easily see when you have found enough information to answer a given research question adequately. For example, if you are researching the question of job security in a particular profession, at a glance you know if you need to look further for additional information. As you gather information, you will need to add additional sheets; staple together all of the sheets devoted to one question. Use a folder for all of your notes.

On the sheets of notes, add source page numbers for both paraphrasing and quotes, with an abbreviated notation of the source (article, book, etc.). On a separate sheet of paper keep detailed documentation information for all of your sources. Even if you are not sure if you need volume numbers or dates of all of the editions of a work, write everything down. You will save yourself countless hours trying to relocate the source in order to discover a detail needed for the "works cited" page.

Paraphrasing, note taking, and summarizing are vital for accurate information gathering. You may want to review these skills from Chapter 2. To avoid plagiarizing, be sure to identify quoted material and give credit for summaries and paraphrases of others' work.

Authenticity of Sources

You will most likely choose sources because they seem to have some information that you are looking for. But you are responsible for verifying sources' authenticity and reliability. Who are these authors that you are assuming know what they are writing about? Check to see what their backgrounds are. Have they published on this topic before? Does the publication date affect the accuracy of the information? Depending on your topic, the date may be vital or may matter little.

Verifying the author's knowledge is especially difficult on the Internet. Many people give credence to almost anything they read on the Internet. The reputation of the Internet as the source for all information leads some to believe that this information is accurate. While much is, remember that anyone can put information out there for the world to read. No one edits it, checks for verification, or gives any feedback. We need to be responsible for what we accept as truth, and this requires critical thinking and evaluation.

We need to check the World Wide Web sites we find for copyright, source, date, and any other information we can gather. Many sites are published not to provide information in general but to give a slanted view reflecting a particular belief. Web pages, as a rule, are not reliable sources; academic sites usually are. Pay attention to the web address to check on the classification of the source. This doesn't tell you everything, but at least you have some idea of where the "information" is coming from.

We tend to limit the sources of information we utilize and, by doing so, limit the possibilities of finding a wealth of information. Besides the obvious choices of articles, books, and the Internet, we have many others available to us. For example, interviews, films, personal experiences, friends, teachers, television shows, newspapers, and pamphlets may provide interesting and accurate information, depending on the research topic. Library indexes are helpful, and librarians are an excellent source of guidance. Remember, though, that every source you use must be documented, even if it is not in written form.

Interviewing

Interviews with knowledgeable people offer insights not usually available in other ways and have the added advantage of being current. Preparation is essential for an informative interview. First, you need specific questions, whether the interview is face-to-face or by telephone. Ask yourself what research questions could perhaps be answered by this interview. Be sure to focus on questions whose answers will be useful to you. For example, asking how long a person worked in a particular career may not elicit an answer that addresses job satisfaction. Form your questions in a way that will help you gather the information you are looking for. Take a written copy of the questions to the interview.

Always call ahead to set up a time for the interview, even if the interview itself is to be conducted by phone. Identify yourself, if necessary, and explain the purpose of your research paper and the reason for the interview. Tell the person how long you expect the interview to take. If you need to tape the interview, you must ask permission beforehand, not when you show up for the interview with the recorder. As a general rule, however, it is better not to tape; many people are more comfortable and speak more naturally without a tape recorder running. After asking your questions and taking notes, ask the interviewee if there is anything he or she would like to add. Often a person will have additional information or an opinion not covered by your questions. Follow the interview with a written thank-you note, even though you have thanked the person at the conclusion of your time together.

Integrating Sources and Your Own Thoughts

To write a paper that flows well from topic to topic, you need to make connections between the sources and your own thoughts about what you are discovering. When you use a quote, always explain its significance, what it means to you, or how it connects to previous sources. In other words, why did you include the quote? It must fit into the flow of the paper, not stand on its own. The only exceptions to this guideline are quotes placed at the beginning or end of a paper to comment on the subject.

Your own opinions are valid in the paper. You are reading and writing to discover information and connections, so naturally what you think about your discoveries is appropriate to include. Research papers are formal in that they follow a structure, but that does not mean your views have to be excluded. Depending on the topic of the research, there are times when using the first person is acceptable. In the research assignment you will be doing for this chapter, you have to use the first person. For other classes and situations, ask your instructor.

Writing a Conclusion

A conclusion for a research paper is a thoughtful account of what you have learned. It is not a summary but a discussion of how the answers to your research questions relate to each other, what conclusions you (and the reader) can draw by considering those answers, and what further study would be appropriate. In a sense, it is a beginning: Now that I know all this, what else do I need to find out? The more one learns, the more one questions, and questions lead to further research.

Documentation

Whenever writing a research paper, ask your instructor what style of documentation you should use. You may wish to review the discussion of styles of documentation in Chapter 7. Generally English classes use MLA (Modern Language Association) style, but check anyway. One style is not better than another, but particular styles fit some subject material better than others. Knowing more than one style is especially helpful in college, when you are writing in different academic fields. Handbooks are indispensable for correct documentation practice.

WRITING ASSIGNMENT: RESEARCH PAPER

Your assignment for this chapter is to write a research paper on the topic of what career you are best suited for. The paper is a culminating result of all the reading and writings you have done throughout this book. You are to investigate a career and how you are suited to it by examining your personality, talents, values, and dreams. You will be able to draw upon much of the work you have already done in previous writings for this course; and you may use your own papers as sources, in addition to many outside sources.

To begin, follow the process explained throughout this book: Brainstorm, freewrite, and develop questions. The questions will be not only on a career as such but on how you fit the career requirements.

The paper is to consist of four main sections. To create a cohesive paper, pay special attention to the transitions between sections.

Section 1. Look back over your life in a reflective manner to discover connections between your past and your future. How do your past experiences inform your future? What are the connections between your younger life and the kind of person you are now? You may use the readings and writings you did in the first half of this book, although you may also wish to add more sources. Your family, friends, teachers, school records, diaries, and so on are all sources of information.

Section 2. In this section write about your present values, your personality, what is important to you, and your dreams for the future. Again use the readings and your writings from this class, adding other sources as well.

Section 3. Research a career or careers. Begin by enumerating the questions you are exploring and articulating why you chose these questions. You must have several references citing a variety of sources, including an interview. Use current information or it won't be of value to you.

Section 4: Conclusion. Tie all the sections together. How does the information from Section 1 relate to Section 2? How do both sections relate to Section 3? What have you learned that will be of help to you? Where do you go from here in the research process?

You should also include an introduction and a "Works Cited" page. And again, thoughtful transitions between sections will help tie the parts into a coherent whole.

A student, Amy Turk, wrote a research paper based on this assignment using several of her own writings as sources. Excerpts from her research paper follow.

STUDENT PAPER

THE RIGHT CHOICE
Amy N. Turk

Introduction

Looking into my future also means looking at my past and examining my present. To understand what career I am best suited for, I need to consider my family, friends, and personal experiences and relate them to my values, personality, and dreams. Then, I need to find information about a future career as a teacher. Discovering if a career in education will match who I am and hope to be is as important, if not more so, than finding information only about a teaching career. Is the right choice for me a career in education?

Section 1: My Background

As I look back on my life, I realize there were many people and experiences that made me into who I am today. When I was five years old, I started kindergarten and my mother went back to work. I would wake up early every morning and head off to one of my mom's friends. I would stay at one house one day a week; it was our way of child care. It was there that I began to see just how important it was to be flexible. I saw many different lifestyles and learned many different rules. This made it easier for me to adapt to any new changes I encountered.

My relationships with my parents have always been close, especially with my father. I remember the day I became a "daddy's girl." It was after supper one evening and both my brother, Scott, and I were hanging around our mother. She was getting irritated because she had things to finish, and she told us to go bother our father for a while. Scott said, "No." The look on my dad's face showed how disappointed and sad he was. I decided that I should give him all my attention, and Scott could do the same with Mom (Turk, "Memory" 1). From that moment on, it was Dad and me. I remember thinking he must be the smartest man in the whole world (Turk, "Dad" 1). In my eyes, there was nothing he could not do. He helped me with my homework with incredible patience. He could always make me smile, and I knew I could always count on him (Turk, "Memory" 2).

My relationship with my brother has been a lot like my relationship with my parents. When I was little I always wanted to hang out with my big brother. I admired him more than anybody. He could do many things that I could not, but that didn't stop me from trying. My family called me "Me, Too" because I was always right behind Scott (Turk, "Best" 5). If he did something new, I would be trying to do it, too. Although I'm sure I often bugged him, he did not act annoyed. He thought it was great that I wanted to push myself to my limits. As we grew older, we had our share of disagreements, but even these seemed to bring us closer together. Scott and I have been through a lot together, and where one of us has a weakness, the other would pull us through.

When Scott was about thirteen years old and I about ten, we took our first plane trip alone to visit our grandparents in Florida. On our flight home we had unexpected problems. Our plane was about to take off when the brakes slammed on, and we headed back to the terminal (Turk, "Easter" 1). Scott and I were alone in a huge airport not knowing what to do next. Scott started to panic, and I realized I had to take control (Turk, "Easter" 2). With a lot of patience and help from others, we worked our way into another flight home. That day we saw how well we really do complement each other. Now Scott goes to the same university as I do, and he has been a tremendous help to me. Not having any

of my friends here made it lonely for me. I do not
know what I would have done without him.

Friends have been an important part of my life.
I met my best friend, Gretchen, eight years ago.
She has given me more hope and optimism than anyone
else (Turk, "Friendship" 2). She was the kind of
person to never say a bad thing about anyone. I
always knew I could go to her with any problem I
had. The best part about her was she always told me
exactly what she thought, even if it was something I
did not want to hear (Turk, "Friendship" 1). Unfortunately, I do not see her often anymore, but I do
think of her often. My family and friends have not
only been a constant source of support for me, but
they have helped shape my values also.

Section 2: Values, Personality, and Dreams

Growing up I learned honesty from my parents.
Neither would tolerate a lie. Because my parents
stress honesty so much, it has become one of my
highest values. I find myself looking for the same
value in others. If someone has lied to me, or even
to someone else, I find it difficult to overlook.

A second strong value I hold is altruism.
Helping others brings me a strong sense of satis-
faction. I often give money to charities and am
involved in environmental clubs such as Greenpeace.
I belong to other clubs as well: the World Wildlife
Fund, the Earth Island Institute Whale Adoption

Club. I am open to new opportunities to help provide additional humanitarian needs. Helping others
has made me realize how much I have, and if I can
help someone less fortunate than myself, I will do
so. Each time I help someone I feel that I have
accomplished something important.

Love is another dominant value. I believe the
saying, "It is better to have loved and lost than
never to have loved at all." I have always received
loving care from my family. We have relieved
stressful situations by going for walks, rides, or
in some way removing ourselves from saying something we would regret later. I think this has made
a big difference in my life and has made our house
a more loving place to be.

My values are directly related to my personality. I am guided by my strong values, and I want my
future to follow along with these values. I took
the Myers-Briggs Type Test and the results made
it clear to me that I have an Introverted Feeling
with Sensing (ISFP) personality. When I look at
my personality, I see someone who is flexible,
patient, and easy-going. I do not have to have a
daily schedule to be satisfied, but if I do have
one, I will usually follow it. I learned patience
from my dad and I hope to follow his wonderful
example. I am not easily aggravated if things are
not going my way. Even if I disagree with someone,
I listen to them without arguing. I tend to avoid
disagreements whenever possible (Myers-Briggs, 19).

I love to help others and will do so as often as I can. My love for the outdoors and wildlife is prevalent. The Myers-Briggs test states that I have an affinity for nature and for beauty in all living things--people, plants, and animals. This clearly describes me.

Also, I see myself as someone who smiles easily and is not usually moody. I do not like to see people upset and I try to help them. However, I do need my quiet time to gather my thoughts, and if I do not have enough time by myself, I am short tempered.

As far as friendships go, I would rather have a few close friends than a whole group of friends. I agree with Judith Viorst in her article "Friends, Good Friends--and Such Good Friends" when she stated, "Women are friends when they totally love and support and trust each other, and bare to each other the secrets of their soul, and run to help each other, and tell harsh truths to each other when harsh truths must be told" (1). To me, what she is describing is one true friend. I could never share my problems with a lot of people. They are too personal to me. Overall, I think I am an easy person to meet. I am relaxed and enjoy a good time. I look forward to meeting new people and going on new journeys.

In the future, I hope to have a stable career in education and have started my own family. I would love to live on the west coast or in the Rocky Mountains area. I do not want to forget all the activities I am involved in now. I hope to continue to play tennis and be active in other sports as well, such as downhill and water skiing, biking, and Rollerblading. I would like to become involved in riskier hobbies such as rock climbing and sky diving. I truly love the outdoors. The kids in the story "Climbing the Daymarker" by Jim Tolley remind me of my brother and me because they, too, loved the outdoors.

I also look forward to traveling. I want to visit Europe, as well as travel throughout North America. I would learn much through traveling, in addition to having fun. All of my dreams, values, personality, family, and friends are linked closely to a future career in teaching.

In Section 3, Amy researched careers in teaching. She was unsure if she wanted to go into elementary education or early childhood education, so she explored both options by comparing and contrasting the two careers. Her research questions included what is required day by day; what are the job opportunities and where are they located; what personality traits are required; what disadvantages do teachers have; what are the sources of job satisfaction; what education is needed, now and for continuing education; what are the expected income levels; and what will future employers look for in hiring?

For information, Amy interviewed teachers, read professional articles, and explored the software program SIGI Plus 4.23. In her conclusion, Amy related all three sections, comparing her personality and lifestyle preferences to a teaching career.

In the works cited page, she included her own essays that she used as references, as well as published professional ones.

This research paper should reflect your best work, and consequently response groups are crucial. You need to meet often in order to benefit each other. The following response guide may be helpful.

Response Guide for Research Paper

1. What does the writer want you to focus on for content?
2. In the section on careers, what questions still need to be answered?
3. Where can information be condensed or expanded?
4. In the first section, the background, how does the information tie into the careers section? What else could the writer add?
5. In all sections, what examples help explain the main ideas?
6. What does the writer want you to focus on in terms of writing skills?
7. Where can sentences be expanded? Combined? Check carefully for run-on sentences.
8. Read the introduction and then the conclusion. How can they better reflect the major points in the paper?
9. Check for the introductions to references. Where could they be improved?
10. What is the strongest part of the paper?
11. What could you suggest as the area that needs the most work?
12. Where are strong examples used?

Writer's name _____

Names of people in response group _____

_____

_____

_____

Credits

Index